K.B

D0216659

WITHDRAWN

Shades of the
Sunbelt

SHADES OF THE SUNBELT

Essays on Ethnicity, Race, and the Urban South

EDITED BY RANDALL M. MILLER
AND
GEORGE E. POZZETTA

CONTRIBUTIONS IN AMERICAN HISTORY, NUMBER 128

Greenwood Press
NEW YORK • WESTPORT, CONNECTICUT • LONDON

Library of Congress Cataloging-in-Publication Data

Shades of the Sunbelt: essays on ethnicity, race, and the urban South
   edited by Randall M. Miller and George E. Pozzetta.
      p.   cm.—(Contributions in American history, ISSN 0084-9219
   no. 128)
   Bibliography: p.
   Includes index.
   Contents: The development of the modern urban South / Randall M.
Miller—The palmetto and the maple leaf / Robert F. Harney—
Jewish migration to the Sunbelt / Deborah Dash Moore—Ethnicity,
urbanization, and historical consciousness in Savannah / Gary W.
McDonogh—Race, ethnicity, and women's lives in the urban South /
Julia Kirk Blackwelder—The changing face of neighborhoods in
Memphis and Richmond, 1940–1985 / Christopher Silver—Race,
ethnicity, and political change in the urban Sunbelt South / Ronald
H. Bayor—Ethnic politics in Miami, 1960–1986 / Raymond A. Mohl /
From Dixie to Dreamland / Raymond Arsenault and Gary R. Mormino—
Migration to the urban South / George E. Pozzetta.
   ISBN 0-313-25690-X (lib. bdg. : alk. paper)
   1. Ethnicity—Sunbelt States. 2. Sunbelt States—Ethnic
relations. 3. Sunbelt States—Race relations. 4. Sunbelt States—
Social conditions. 5. Urbanization—Sunbelt States. I. Miller,
Randall M.   II. Pozzetta, George E.   III. Series.
F220.A1S43 1988
305.8′00975—dc19   87-18164

British Library Cataloguing in Publication Data is available.

Library of Congress Catalog Card Number: 87-18164
ISBN: 0-313-25690-X
ISSN: 0084-9219

First published in 1988

Greenwood Press, Inc.
88 Post Road West, Westport, Connecticut 06881

Printed in the United States of America

∞

The paper used in this book complies with the
Permanent Paper Standard issued by the National
Information Standards Organization (Z39.48-1984).

10 9 8 7 6 5 4 3 2 1

To our children—
Adrienne, James, and Nathaniel

Contents

Preface

The genesis of this book occurred in 1984, when several of the contributors met at the University of Florida to discuss ethnicity and migration in the Sunbelt, especially Florida. The following year several members of the group reconvened in Miami at a conference on the Sunbelt, and they were together again in Minneapolis in 1985 for a session on ethnicity in the urban Sunbelt South and in Charlotte in 1986 for sessions on the urban South. What the contributors discovered in these and other less formal gatherings was a general confusion about terms, especially *Sunbelt,* which seemed to defy any agreement among scholars or journalists as to its boundaries, meaning, or even origin. More important, they discovered a common interest in the phenomenon of ethnicity, broadly defined, as it has developed within the post-World War II southern urban context.

With the take off of the latest new South economy and the migration of jobs and people and values southward, the rapidly urbanizing (and even more so, suburbanizing) South was a subject of immediate public policy importance requiring historical perspective. A book collecting original essays from scholars drawing on diverse and developing methodologies in anthropology, demography, history, sociology, and urban planning promised to sketch the contours of a broad new inquiry into the dynamic of ethnic formation and adaptation in settings outside the much-studied northern cities; more than that, it also promised to suggest, among other subjects, how the immigration and migration of new and diverse people to southern metropolitan areas redefined the politics, society, and even physical arrangement of those places. By focusing on the urban South (only part of a larger Sunbelt phenomenon), the contributors also sought to identify those ways in which the nation's most intractable region, weighted by its history of racism and ruralism, has come of age since World War II.

The contributors were bound together by scholarly interest and also by personal experience. They were students of immigration and ethnicity in northern or midwestern settings (both Harney and Pozzetta with studies of Italians in various Canadian and American places, Moore with a book on Jews in New York, Bayor with a book on several ethnic groups in New York, Mohl with a book on Gary, Indiana, Mormino with a book on Italians in St. Louis, and so on). As such, they could not fail to notice the striking parallels (in politics, social organization, cultural adaptation, and so forth) between a modernizing urban South, basking in its self-proclaimed Sunbelt prosperity, and those once-burgeoning northern and midwestern cities which had attracted so many immigrants earlier in the century. They noticed such parallels because many of them were themselves living in those places associated in the popular mind with the Sunbelt South—Atlanta and Florida, especially. As transplanted Yankees they viewed the emerging new South through northern lenses and saw (as many native-born southerners have been unable or unwilling to see) in the new cityscapes, broker politics, and ethnic diversity of the urban South a world that bore resemblance to the northern places they had left behind. They also observed how the particular circumstances of environment and history kept those southern settings unique, never just mirroring images of northern ones or even of one another, however much they seemingly converged in experience and appearance. Appreciating the force of local environment and history, the contributors make no claim to comprehensiveness in their coverage or interest. They do invite readers to look closely at ethnicity and race in their relationship with an urbanizing Sunbelt South as one way to measure the interactive process whereby people define places and vice versa.

In that regard, the volume looks especially at Florida, where several contributors now live and work. Early in this century Florida was among the most rural, least ethnically diverse states in the South, but now it is among the most urban and heterogeneous in the nation. The pull of Florida's sun and surf reflects the force of leisure time interests in directing the southward flow of capital and human investment in America since the 1950s. Florida's experience of rapid urbanization, demographic change, and interethnic confrontation and adjustment etches in bold relief the changes, often less pronounced or discernable, under way elsewhere in the Sunbelt South. Its vestiges of a once-dominant rural culture in the state's northern counties now facing the economic and political emergence of multiethnic, urbanizing southern counties offer a microcosm of the South itself, transmuting from a society anchored in an agrarian past and mythology to one lurching toward modernism.

Such changes have sent native-born southerners to waving red flags (often with stars and bars) of warning. The rate of southern urbanization, which has exceeded that of the national average throughout the twentieth century, has only recently commanded significant attention from scholars, journalists, South watchers, and the home folk themselves. Once awakened to the phenomenon, many southerners recanted their calls for progress, for they saw in the urban sprawl, broker politics, and new people settling in cities the elements that threatened to make the South into the North. In his book, *The Americanization of Dixie: The Southernization of America* (1974), John Egerton signaled the demise of Dixie. In its embrace of northern industry and values, as embodied in southern cities, the South was recreating the "monster metropolis" of the North. Others have echoed Egerton's sentiments. Although southern cities were different in that they were smaller, less industrialized, and less dense than northern ones, the time southerners had to choose which way urbanization, and with that regional identity, would go was fast slipping by.

Cities were defining southern character in the post-World War II era, and, as Blaine Brownell concluded in 1974 (in his brief *The Urban South in the Twentieth Century,* p. 23), the peculiar moderating effects of southern interpersonal relations on urban culture notwithstanding, southern cities acquired their fundamental character "more from the fact that they are cities than from the fact that they are southern." In 1977, in a collaborative volume offering the first in a series of significant interpretations of the relationship between the city and the region (Blaine Brownell and David Goldfield, eds., *The City in Southern History: The Growth of Urban Civilization in the South* [1977], p. 150), Brownell extended his earlier observation by concluding that it was in the urban South where the regional culture met "the opportunities and demands of a modern era" and where "the largely static and homogeneous social life of the countryside broke into a welter of heterogeneity." The extent to which southern cities have yielded to modernity and divorced themselves from the region's rural culture remains a subject of intense scholarly and public debate. David Goldfield, more than anyone else, has wrestled with the issue by first arguing that, aside from the problems of racial segregation and overbuilding of downtowns, the low density of southern cities has promised to make them congenial, progressive places to live and work (Goldfield and Blaine Brownell, *Urban America: From Downtown to No Town* [1979], pp. 399-400), and more recently conceding that continued segregation, resistance to public services, and the inertia of regional culture have kept the southern cities hostages to the past (Goldfield, *Cotton Fields and Skyscrapers: Southern City and Region, 1607-1980* [1982], especially pp. 192-96; and Goldfield, *The Promised Land: The South Since 1945* [1987]).

In exploring the connections between urbanization and regional identity, most of the literature has remained preoccupied with economic development. Some scholars and others have assumed that Sunbelt prosperity is now a given, while others see it as the latest will-o'-the-wisp of "new South" boosterism. Writers do not agree on the sources of the southern Sunbelt boom or its durability (with the rapid rise and fall of the "oil patch" subregion from Louisiana through "Texarhoma" as a classic case in point). They list promotional efforts by local and state governments, abundant natural resources, attractive climate (now with air conditioning), cheap labor, federal money, and increasingly more leisure-oriented lifestyles as factors explaining the economic "take off" of the southern Sunbelt. Nor do scholars agree on the future agenda for research. In a special issue of the *Journal of Urban History* (February 1976) devoted to "Urban Themes in the American South," editor Brownell called on urban and southern historians alike to discover the southern city as a venue for studying any number of issues related to urbanization; but economic, rather than social, issues seem to have claimed the most interest. Such concern reveals itself anew in the latest survey of historiography on southern city and region, which in its title and content inextricably links "Sun Belt Prosperity and Urban Growth," while neglecting discussion of the human dimensions of urban growth in the Sunbelt South (Charles P. Roland in John B. Boles and Evelyn Thomas Nolen, eds., *Interpreting Southern History: Historiographical Essays in Honor of Sanford W. Higgenbotham* [1987], pp. 434-53).

The contributors to the present volume propose to enlarge the scope of inquiry concerning urbanization and ethnicity in the Sunbelt South by including discussions of the many diverse people whose very presence has reshaped the physical, political, economic, social, and cultural map wherever they have migrated. That one can buy bagels in Charlotte, cannolis in Memphis, tacos in Atlanta, and get eggrolls just about anywhere (including rural Mississippi); can have home delivery of the *New York Times* in Atlanta, Memphis, Richmond, and elsewhere in the "urban" South without fear of condemnation; can hear Finnish, French, Italian, Spanish, and any number of other languages spoken as the *lingua franca* in Florida communities—all point to some dissemination of ethnic diversity in a region traditionally associated only with barbecues and drawls. But the contributors ask for more than catalogs of dietary or linguistic preferences. They also seek to turn the equation around to ask not just how urban (or more properly, by some accounts, suburban and conurban) environments have been altered by their occupants and visitors, but also to learn how the peculiarities of specific southern Sunbelt metropolitan environments influenced the identity of the different groups who entered them. That dialectic of places and peoples forms the marrow of ethnicity anywhere. Understanding that process promises to reveal the ways in which black and white southerners, transplanted northerners, Canadian sojourners, Jewish retirees, and so many others, like the times, are "a-changin'."

The book consists of ten chapters. The first chapter serves as a general introduction to the setting. By focusing on urban growth in the South since World War II, it also reminds readers that the Sunbelt South represents a sharp break with the previous Souths. It is an urban (and suburban) and a post-World War II phenomenon of yet undefined proportions. Although several essays take the long view, examining pre- and postwar developments, all attend to the urbanizing Sunbelt South as a principal concern. Specific chapters treat the process of migration. Others examine the political, economic, or social dimensions of particular groups within southern urban confines or of the settings themselves. The concluding chapter discusses the essays as they relate to issues of ethnicity and suggests new lines of inquiry emerging from those issues.

In his contribution Robert Harney uses a comparative model of world labor migration to show how Canadians traveling to Florida moved in ways similar to those of European "sojourners" to the United States earlier in the century. Migration revealed the fragility of Canadian national identity, as Canadians clustered in Florida according to their ethnic identities—a pattern reinforced by brokers who profited from a commerce of migration. Thus, a Sunbelt was altered by an in-migration and investment of various Canadian peoples, but the migration and investment also changed the migrants themselves.

The dynamic, even syncretic, nature of migration also concerns Deborah Dash Moore, who argues in her essay that, for Jews at least, personal identity "is bound up with place of residence." Taking a wide-angle view of the Sunbelt that extends from Florida to California, Moore notes, among other findings, that Jewish migration to Sunbelt places occurred simultaneously with an upsurge in ethnic identity among Jews. The heightened ethnic identity, defined in part by particular place of residence, brought newcomers to Sunbelt cities into conflict with previously settled Jews in those settings. Like the Canadians Harney studies, who separate into ethnic enclaves in Florida based on their ethnic identities in Canada, the Jews Moore studies tend to divide among themselves according to places of origin, even as they retain and invigorate a common Jewish identity. For Jews, recent history still defines their sense of self.

In his anthropological study of white and black Catholics in Savannah, Gary McDonogh also shows how history, linked to a particular setting, shapes ethnic identities. For newcomers, access to that past is often closed, so that "participation in or interpretation of past events" separates the "native" from the "outsider" and provides the foundation for urban group identity. As the setting changes, however, the past must be reinterpreted, and, as in the case of Savannah which has promoted a "public history" as a means of attracting tourism and investment, that past actually invites outsiders into the process of remaking the city, interweaving "Old South" with "Sunbelt" or whatever to form a new urban social tapestry.

That new urban social tapestry included changed roles for women. As Julia Kirk Blackwelder argues in her survey of employment patterns of southern urban women since World War II, postwar economic change has been effecting a major transformation in the economic and social roles, even in the family structure, of southern women in urban settings. Comparing the employment experiences of native-born white and black southerners with those of Hispanic and European immigrant women in several cities, she concludes that the postindustrial economy opens new employment opportunities to women, freeing them from social constraints of the past, but that the service sector jobs are so organized and remunerated that they cannot sustain traditional family structures. The needs and interests of working women in southern cities demanded social and political redress; for many women, the civil rights movement was the way to do so.

Another manifestation of change in the urban South is the emerging power of local, or neighborhood, groups within particular cities. By using a comparative historical perspective, Christopher Silver shows how neighborhoods in Memphis and Richmond, despite common experiences with federal urban policies and planning models and ties to a common regional culture, developed distinct urban networks. Ethnic and racial lines drew social and political boundaries, but, as Silver reveals, class increasingly staked off neighborhood boundaries as ethnic groups were subsumed into the larger middle-class white population while blacks remained poor. The intersection of federal and local governmental policies, urban planning, and ethnic/racial neighborhood identities remade the cityscapes and redefined local political categories.

The altered political environment of the urban Sunbelt South is the subject of Ronald Bayor's essay. As Bayor observes, the entrance of new people into southern cities has redrawn the political landscape. Northern in-migrants carried their political outlooks with them, but, more than that argues Bayor, the increasingly pluralistic populations of selected Sunbelt cities and the heightened ethnic/racial/neighborhood consciousness within those cities demanded a new kind of politics. The civil rights movement legitimated black demands for sharing power with whites, and the process, once begun, became self-sustaining as new groups vied for power. Pluralistic intergroup relations bred pluralistic politics in several southern Sunbelt cities, much like the politics in northern cities.

The implications of pluralistic politics rooted in ethnic/racial/neighborhood identities are now apparent in Miami. In his essay Raymond Mohl tracks the development of ethnic politics in Miami by discovering how exile politics of Cubans, electoral politics, structural changes (city-county consolidation and the shift from the at-large to district system within Miami), administrative policies, and public policy generally all interacted to create a new political life in Miami. Miami's ethnic politics are no mere replica of northern urban politics, for the presence of a cohesive ethnic element (the Cubans) who practice, in part, a politics geared to the homeland and Miami's growing economic and cultural entanglement with the Caribbean sustain a politics of particular ethnic interest nowhere else practiced so fully in the United States. The peculiar demographic, administrative, and governmental configuration of the Miami-Dade metropolitan area also created a unique environment for south Florida's political development. Thrown together in "a struggle for jobs, residential space, and political power," Cubans and other ethnic and racial groups in Miami developed increasingly aggressive politics based on ethnic interest. Mohl concludes that rather than serving to hasten acculturation (and perhaps even assimilation) as politics had done in northern urban settings, Miami-style politics actually reinforce ethnic identities by providing an important means to achieve particular group goals.

The importance of Florida as a harbinger of the urban Sunbelt South as a whole becomes evident in Raymond Arsenault and Gary Mormino's portrait of the state's demographic and cultural profile. By comparing Florida in 1880, 1930, and 1980, they point to the recentness and rapidity of Florida's urbanization and social change. The ethnic politics Mohl describes in his chapter grew in a cultural and demographic hothouse of large, unregulated population and economic growth. South Florida especially has become so urban, so diverse in population, so oriented outward (toward Central and South American markets) in investment, and so indifferent to its physical environment that it has become almost a region unto itself. There are, conclude Arsenault and Mormino, many Floridas (as there are many Souths), but the seemingly inexorable advance of the Sunbelt mystique and reality threatens to overwhelm the older "cracker" Florida. Whether any "South" will remain in the Sunbelt is a question they leave readers to ponder.

A word about definitions: The unevenness of prosperity across the region and within metropolitan areas makes the Sunbelt tag difficult to affix with any certainty. Indeed, within the book no clearly delineated boundaries for the Sunbelt exist, though the authors do agree that service sector prosperity, in-migration, and leisure-oriented lifestyles are integral elements of any Sunbelt.

Florida stands clearly within anybody's conception of Sunbelt. As Arsenault and Mormino suggest in their demographic survey, Florida symbolizes the Sunbelt in the popular mind and, indeed, as early as the 1920s real estate boosters were strumming siren songs of profits and comfort that would lure capital and people southward to the sun. That association with Florida sun and Sunbelt also helped underwrite the commerce of migration, to use Harney's term, that sustained a regular traffic to particular Florida communities and, so, in advertising and investment alone, kept Florida's sun forever guiding Canadians and others southward.

Other contributors recognize that the growing metropolitan areas of Atlanta, Charlotte, Memphis, Houston, and San Antonio also wear the Sunbelt mantle (not quite yet the south Florida guayabera). Though more modest in scale, such cities as Savannah and Richmond fit comfortably into the generic Sunbelt mold. In the case of Savannah, as Gary McDonogh suggests in his essay, the rediscovery and exploitation of history provides a route to the Sunbelt without the high-rise office buildings and distain for old ways so often associated with the growth mentality of the Sunbelt boosters. And as Deborah Dash Moore demonstrates in her essay, in the minds of those persons seeking security, comfort, and/or opportunity in the postindustrial age, the Sunbelt spans the southern part of the nation, from Florida to Colorado to California. It exists in people's collective imagination, even if it is not precisely defined in census tables or scholarly discourse. Rather than imposing any artificial or arbitrary Sunbelt on the essays, the editors accepted the contributors' terms. It was possible to do so because the contributors shared the general interest in the urbanizing South and because so many used the Florida experience in some way as a touchstone for discussion.

R.M.M.

G.E.P.

Acknowledgments

This book grew out of friendly, if often spirited, discussions reflecting the short-sleeve collegiality of those scholars working the fields of ethnicity in the urban South. Several individuals not represented in the book offered their own good counsel and encouragement. The conception of the book benefited from suggestions by James C. Cobb and David Goldfield. The introduction profited from critical readings by Paula Benkart and members of the Chester Avenue Seminar in Philadelphia. At the University of Florida (the command center for the project) Mern Johnston-Loehner typed the manuscript, and David Colburn and Jeffrey Adler helped with critical readings of several parts. The leadership of the Department of History helped initiate the entire process by supplying the funds to support the Institute which first brought a critical core of the contributors together. To all these good people we say thanks and absolve them of any responsibility for errors in conceptualization, organization, or direction we editors may have committed.

1

The Development of the Modern Urban South: An Historical Overview

Randall M. Miller

In 1981 the Commission on the Future of the South concluded that the "future of the South cannot be separated from the future of Southern cities." Subsequent outpourings of journalistic and governmental reports seem to suggest such a prediction is almost self-fulfilling. Much of the metropolitan South (especially the suburbs) now dresses in "Sunbelt" motifs, giving the appearance of prosperous service sector economies, individual affluence and safety, and leisure-oriented lifestyles. And the people keep coming. Indeed, according to the latest estimates available from the United States Census Bureau (those for the period from March 1983 to March 1984), the number of Americans relocating has "increased significantly" since the 1970s, but of all the regions, the South alone has recorded a net in-migration from other regions, most of it to metropolitan areas.[1]

The growth has been uneven, to be sure. The Census Bureau's inclusion in the statistical South of south Florida, which has acquired its own special character since the 1960s, tends to exaggerate the extent of regional growth and to disguise the real poverty that still grips much of the region consisting of the eleven former Confederate states. Among the metropolitan areas of the urbanizing South as well, some have shown more growth and prosperity than others, while very few of the cities themselves and virtually none of their inner-city districts have soaked up much of the Sunbelt phenomenon, except for the hot air of boosterism. Instead, the real growth and development is going on in the suburbs to which southern cities are losing population and power. This latest "New South" also is vulnerable to cycles of boom and bust, as evident in the empty office buildings and foreclosed houses in the "oil patch" from Louisiana to Texas. But even if uneven growth and development and unpredictable economic fortunes do becloud the Sunbelt South's present and its future, that future will be cast in urban terms.[2]

In emphasizing how an urbanizing South foretells the region's future, however, it is possible to forget that the urbanizing South has a past. Over the last half century at least, the population shift from farm to town ranks among the most important demographic facts about the South. In 1920 only one in four southerners lived in urban areas, but by 1980 more than two out of three southerners resided in such places. During those six decades the urban growth rate of the South exceeded that of all other regions in the United States and fundamentally altered the South's social, political, and economic landscape. Also important is that southern cities have been and remain different in some critical ways, for they traditionally have been smaller, have had lower population densities, and have been less dependent on manufacturing than have northern ones. Moreover, having matured roughly two generations later than their counterparts in the North, southern cities are really suburban cities, wedded to the automobile. In short, the urban South attracted different kinds of people to different kinds of economic, social, and political settings than did cities in other regions. As a result, in order to make sense out of the peculiar development of southern metropolitan areas and to anticipate their likely prospects, it is also necessary to consider the great extent to which southern cities have remained tied to regional culture and history, even as modernity in architecture, lifestyles, and business threaten to erase their distinctive look and character.

Southerners have been abandoning the farm and moving to town throughout the twentieth century. Until recently, however, the trend has been for southerners to leave the South for the beckoning industrial and commerical promise of northeastern and midwestern cities and, during and after World War II, for western communities as well. Nevertheless, although the outmigrating majority was not replaced by newcomers from either the North or abroad, there remained enough farm-to-town movement of native-born southerners to sustain the region's urban population growth in the years before World War II. During the 1920s, for instance, the South's urban population increased by almost 7 percent over the previous decade.[3]

In the twenties expanding urban economies attracted southerners to their region's cities. Continuing trends begun in the late nineteenth century, northern companies relocated or opened branch plants in the small cities of the piedmont, and Birmingham, Alabama, prospered as the "Pittsburgh of the South." At the same time, hints of a new urban South to come appeared in those places where entrepreneurs and bankers not only lured northern capital and businesses southward but also developed the service sector. In Nashville, for example, aggressive bankers expanded local insurance companies throughout the mid-South to make Union Street the "Wall Street of the South." That fact, when combined with the city's growing importance as the state capital and a center for religious organizations, education, and health care (roles that especially marked the city's post–World War II identity, along with the music industry), enabled Nashville to sow the seeds of what later grew into a full-blown, postindustrial "Sunbelt" economy.[4]

The prosperity did not continue unbroken in Nashville or anywhere in the urban South during the 1930s. The depression era hit southern cities hard. Urbanization declined amid low agricultural prices and regional poverty, silencing even the most rabid town boosters for the moment, while the exodus to northern cities continued.

Later, New Deal farm policies hastened the migration of poor black and white farm workers to towns in and out of the South. Price supports and allotment programs especially encouraged landholders to reduce their cotton acreage and, so, their labor needs. To avoid sharing federal subsidy payments with sharecroppers, planters refused to renew cropping contracts. Farm tenants and sharecroppers then either hired on as laborers or, more generally, left the rural South altogether. In their own ways, the boll weevil and agricultural extension agents each persuaded planters to try new crops. As the introduction of farm machinery, chemical fertilizers, and pesticides completed the revolution in southern agriculture, poor and displaced southern farmers and farm laborers had little recourse but to try their luck in town.[5]

The transformations of southern agriculture affected southern urban growth and life in a number of ways, but most importantly by promoting regional modernization. Rising farm incomes and new crops and products have helped to underwrite regional and urban economic growth since World War II. New agricultural concerns have pushed the region further into the international financial and commodity markets, broadening the southerners' world view and requiring increasingly sophisticated technical services, which southern metropolitan areas have sought to supply. The changed labor needs of diversified agriculture drove off tenants, but they also forced growers to turn to migrant workers during harvest season, thereby bringing Caribbean and Mexican laborers to Carolina and Texas truck farms and Florida citrus groves. Some of the foreign-born migrants have stayed on, settling in southern urban areas while looking for work and contributing to the changing political and social dynamics of those cities, in some cases by needing social services southern municipalities have traditionally been reluctant to provide.

Despite the agricultural transformation, most southern farms have remained small and vulnerable, and their failure rates, which are among the highest in the nation, have contributed to the peculiar nature of southern urban growth since the 1930s. The new agricultural hard times of the 1970s and 1980s, caused by low staple prices and high interest rates, merely have sustained an ongoing flow of Dixie's farmers into southern towns and cities, where their country music and residential and occupational clustering preserve rural cultures in urban environments. To be sure, most southern-born migrants to southern cities since World War II have come from small towns rather than directly from farms, but regional agricultural needs and rural population migration still influence local urban growth and tie the cities of the South to the countryside. Meanwhile, suburban and exurban development relentlessly encroaches on adjacent farmland.

In addition to transforming southern agriculture, federal policies have significantly defined and directed the character and growth of southern cities. World War II, especially, signalled the federal government's increasing involvement in southern economic development. If nothing else, the war ended the economic depression gripping the regions' cities. Federal defense spending had slighted the South before the war, with the northeastern and midwestern industrial regions garnering the lion's share of military contracts and installations, but by the 1940s the South's economic ills worked to give it a competitive advantage in the federal government's allocation of contracts and location of military bases. Having identified the South as the nation's "number one economic problem," New Deal planners sought ways to build up the region. World War II provided the occasion for a dramatic expansion of regional revitalization programs begun during the New Deal and of efforts, already under way in the late 1930s, that favored the South in getting contracts for building ships and airplanes. The military planners' desire to decentralize defense work reinforced southern congressmen's appeals for more military training centers and defense plants in their home districts. During the war the federal government responded by spending roughly $8 billion on military facilities and defense contracts in the South.[6]

The South's cities hummed with new activity. Charleston, Mobile, Savannah, Tampa, and other warm-weather coastal ports boomed with naval operations and teemed with sailors, ship workers, contractors, and others called to work in the naval-related industries. Shipyards in Houston, Mobile, Norfolk, Pascagoula, Pensacola, and elsewhere in the South clamored for workers to fill the many jobs created by wartime contracts. Such interior metropolitan areas as Atlanta, Fort Worth, and Tulsa parlayed their open spaces into sites for aircraft production and testing. Attracted by the South's moderate climate and abundant undeveloped land, the armed forces established training bases whose large numbers of recruits and support facilities further stimulated the regional economy.

A nation in transit during the war discovered the South. Wartime prosperity and military duty brought tens of thousands of newcomers to Dixie. For the first time in many years, migration to the South exceeded out-migration from it. Southerners themselves continued on the move, increasingly lured from their farms to defense-related work in towns and cities. Southern metropolitan populations exploded. Indeed, in the early war years, southern metropolitan counties experienced the largest relative growth in the nation. At the height of the war boom in 1943, forty-three of the South's forty-nine metropolitan areas recorded population increases, in contrast to only twenty-five of seventy-four northeastern and midwestern metropolitan areas.

The wartime urban population buildup unleashed social problems—and possibilities—that would nag southern cities thereafter. Crowded with large numbers of unattached young men during the war, the cities suffered inevitable increases in crime and demands on public services. The influx of jobs, money, and people overwhelmed once-dormant towns and cities unaccustomed to the hurlyburly of rapid growth and the fast-paced lifestyles of so many young men with cash to spend. Women also flocked to the wartime industries, finding in good wages a brief liberation from the unremitting toil of the cotton fields and textile mills and from the demands of their men. If contemporary accounts of the breakdown of "traditional values" and even family structure during the war are to be believed, the men and women thrown together in boom towns seemed to have abandoned the most conservative social strictures of southern rural life—at least for the moment.

Mobile, the fastest-growing city in the nation with a population increase of over 60 percent between 1940 and 1943, was a case in point. John Dos Passos, in 1943, aptly described the once "mouldering old Gulf seaport with its ancient dusty elegance" as now "trampled and battered like a city that's been taken by storm," with sidewalks and streets jammed, gutters clogged, garbage cans overflowing, and frame houses and trailer camps bulging with people. The mayor complained that he could not enforce the laws or even provide clean water. A Washington, D.C. reporter observed that the invasion of Mobile by "primitive, illiterate backwoods people" uncomfortable with the regimen of industrial discipline and city life caused the newcomers to become "hostile, defiant, suspicious, and terrified." Competition for jobs, housing, and recreation burst forth into violence. Shootings, lynchings, and riots occurred in frightening numbers in Mobile, as elsewhere in the wartime urban South.[7]

As wartime conditions overburdened city services, they also weakened racial etiquette. Both whites and blacks understood that the war threatened to alter race relations fundamentally, especially in the social hothouse of booming urban economies. In response to pressure from national civil rights activists such as A. Philip Randolph, who insisted that the American "arsenal for democracy" should afford "democracy in Alabama," the federal government began to demand an end to discrimination in defense industries. Those efforts triggered two days of racial violence in Mobile in 1943, when white workers protested the Alabama Dry Dock and Shipbuilding Company's attempt to satisfy a Fair Employment Practices Commission order to end discrimination in the hiring and job placement of blacks.[8]

Wartime Mobile differed from other southern cities only in degree. Boom conditions, fed by federal government largess, exposed social fault lines across the urban South. Even though the pace of population growth slackened after the war, such fissures widened thereafter as metropolitan economies grew on federal subsidies and contracts and as new, larger and more heterogeneous urban populations wrestled for advantage.

Although sometimes temporary and unevenly distributed within the region, heavy federal spending continued to bolster southern urban economies in the postwar era. Few metropolitan areas experienced serious losses in the reconversion to peacetime activities during the late 1940s and the early 1950s. The robust defense budgets of the Cold War picked up the slack, especially in places with established defense facilities (for example, Mobile, San Antonio). Between 1952 and 1970 the South registered a steady increase in its per capita share of federal government expenditures, finally reaching parity with the other regions in the 1970s and, by some accounts (much disagreement continues on this score), surpassing them for a time, until blocs of northeastern representatives and the increasing power of westerners in Congress redressed the imbalances somewhat in the 1980s.[9]

Throughout the postwar period southern governors and state development agencies lobbied aggressively for their "fair share" of federal dollars. Even while railing against federal intrusion in such matters as civil rights, southern public officials, without any apparent sense of irony or shame, lined up at the federal trough. Flexing their legislative muscle, southern congressmen and senators, whose seniority allowed them to dominate most of the key defense-related and appropriations committees in Congress, sent millions of defense dollars south—so much so that pundits began to refer to the Pentagon as a five-sided building facing south. Whole cities were invigorated (for example, Charleston, South Carolina, thanks to L. Mendel Rivers) and even transformed (for example, Huntsville, Alabama) by massive infusions of federal money. Atlanta benefited from the location of federal regional offices there, and Miami, Tampa-St. Petersburg, indeed much of Florida grew as a result of Social Security and other government entitlement programs.[10]

The most significant aspect of the southerners' grasping for defense and other federal dollars, however, is not the economic development it has fostered, which has been spotty and not always sustained anyway; rather, it is how such money has opened the urban South to outside influence. Since World War II the most apparent change in the South's political economy has been the movement of southern state governments away from their preoccupation with maintaining white supremacy and social stability toward the promotion of business and industrial development. That shift invited investment and migration to the South, and it helped make possible the civil rights movement. Through such change, urbanizing areas of the South would wriggle out from the regional cocoon of social and political homogeneity to assume a new life as Sunbelt phenomena.[11]

Federal spending exercised its most profound effects on southern cities indirectly. Returning GIs, armed with educational and housing benefits, and consumers with maturing U.S. war bonds to cash in spurred the region's post-World War II growth in services, business, and construction. Mortgage insurance programs further encouraged the construction of single-family homes, and beginning with the 1949 Housing Act, the federal government provided a hefty subsidy to builders capable of developing large tracts of new homes, thus promoting suburban growth at the expense of urban neighborhood rehabilitation.

Even more than the housing programs, federal support for interstate highway construction during the 1950s and after redefined southern living patterns and cityscapes. Highway construction made the cities of the interior more accessible and, when in the next decade computerized telecommunications made decentralized manufacturing and service industries possible, southern urban growth patterns shifted from the coastal and river cities to such piedmont metropolitan areas as Atlanta and Charlotte. Highway transportation secured Atlanta's regional leadership when trucks replaced railroad freight cars and river barges as the principal means of moving goods. Networks of easy-access highways similarly allowed for the development of manufacturing plants and wholesaling facilities in the suburbs, where new one-story factories and warehouses more suitable to modern mechanized production and distribution sprang up in the large open areas outside city limits. The establishment of air freight facilities and passenger airline hubs in newly built or expanded airports, likewise located on the outskirts of cities and benefiting from federal subsidies, intensified the centrifugal force of the highway and road systems that drew jobs and population away from the city centers.[12]

The modern southern city was born in the age of the automobile and since the 1920s was always beholden to it. When the federal housing legislation and highway policies of the postwar decades gave southern cities the familiar appearance of low population densities and sprawling, uncontrolled development, with but few exceptions (for example, the old trolley system in New Orleans) mass transportation failed to develop. Indeed, in 1980 less than 5 percent of southern commuters used public transportation, and, indicative of how transportation affected and reflected segregated residential and occupational patterns, most of those riders were poor and black. Most commuting to jobs in southern metropolitan areas today is cross suburban rather than from the suburbs to the city core. Commercial activity has shifted away from the central business districts to suburban offices and shopping malls and to the fast-food and discount retail outlets strung along commercial strips. There, the neon lights and golden arches give southern metropolitan areas a plastic quality befitting the new urban South's worship of the culture of consumption.[13]

More directly, federal urban redevelopment funds underwrote urban renewal efforts, with sometimes contradictory and disastrous effects on the physical environment of southern cities. The bulldozer ruled the first phase of urban renewal in the 1950s and 1960s, when federal programs, in conjunction with the downtown business interests who controlled city administrations, sought to eliminate the physical problems of cities by tearing down old structures and building up central business districts. By making downtowns clean and attractive and by providing easy access for automobiles and abundant parking, business owners believed they could reclaim the patronage of customers who had abandoned the cities for the suburbs. Urban renewal programs razed low-income neighborhoods to provide parking and space for public-oriented institutions such as hospitals, universities, cultural and civic centers, sports and convention complexes, and high-rise offices and hotels—all intended to lure white-collar folks back to town to spend their money. Meanwhile, using the hub-spoke-rim model of freeway construction, as developed so fully in Atlanta, planners radiated roads out from the downtown hub to connect the central business district with the suburbs and constructed an outer ring intended to link the suburbs together and divert long-distance highway traffic around the city.[14]

Because land clearance and highway construction programs inevitably pitted downtown business interests against poor and run-down neighborhoods, during the 1950s and 1960s redevelopment too often meant displacing the poor and disfranchised to benefit the rich and powerful. In New Orleans, for example, Mayor DeLesseps S. Morrison's success during the 1950s in clearing slums to build a civic center complex and other downtown improvements earned praise from the business community and civic reformers but cost some poor people their homes.[15] Throughout the urban South, low-income residents saw their neighborhoods bulldozed to make way for new highways, office complexes, or civic centers. Habits of racial segregation worked especially against blacks in the postwar era to make their neighborhoods the likely targets for "urban renewal." Those driven from their homes crowded into other neighborhoods, making concentrations of the poor more segregated and dense and forcing middle-class blacks to seek relief by moving into white areas—if possible. Many whites, in turn, fled to the suburbs.

Despite strenuous efforts to capture suburbanites' interest and dollars, southern center cities lost ground since the 1960s. This was especially true for those cities unable to annex additional territory. In that regard, Atlanta's experience was revealing. In the midst of Atlanta's downtown building boom in the 1960s and 1970s, the city's population grew only slightly during the 1960s and suffered a net loss of approximately 70,000 residents during the 1970s. In the same period, Atlanta's suburban population doubled, and the malls in its northern suburbs alone reported higher sales volume than did Atlanta's downtown stores. The metropolitan employment base shifted to the suburbs as the automobile-centered economy became the arbiter of metropolitan economic and demographic growth. Between 1960 and 1980, for example, Atlanta's share of its metropolitan area's office space declined from 90 percent to approximately 42 percent. In sum, growth in the southern Sunbelt, like that in the Far West and elsewhere in urban America, remained suburban. Migrants from outside the region joined out-migrants from southern cities to fill up suburban tracts, and branch offices provided employment and services, making suburban dwellers increasingly independent of the cities and even of one another.[16]

In the 1970s federal money played a new role in helping to define southern cities. For a host of political and fiscal reasons federal policymakers (from the Nixon administration on) began to redirect funds away from large urban renewal projects toward rehabilitation and restoration projects, and they started to return to local governments and interest groups effective authority over housing, zoning, and urban renewal. Such policies coincided with a movement within cities to build on the uniqueness and diversity of historic business districts and neighborhoods as counterweights to the bland and plastic appearance of suburbia. In 1966 federal legislation provided financial incentives for preservation and, perhaps equally important, encouraged cities to protect blocks of buildings by allowing for zoning of historic districts.

Changes in urban renewal approaches were also responses to changes in American lifestyles. During the leisure-oriented 1970s and 1980s large numbers of Americans with disposable incomes, lengthened paid vacations, and desires for relaxation ventured southward via the interstate highways and airlines to play in the Florida sun or elsewhere in the Sunbelt. Sleepy towns, such as Orlando, metamorphosed into Sunbelt cities by inventing fantasy lands, while older cities (for example, Richmond, Charleston, Savannah, St. Augustine, New Orleans) tried to capture the tourist dollar by recovering their history.[17]

Historic preservation was not new to the urban South. Indeed, with little notice and only modest success, private efforts at historic preservation had been going on in Charleston and New Orleans for almost half a century. But the combination of federal policy shifts, downtown business needs and sympathetic local politicians, and a growing interest in popular history made historic preservation projects a national mania during the 1970s and 1980s. From Boston to Baltimore and on down the eastern seaboard, cities rescued waterfront areas from urban blight. The small size of southern cities and the regional respect for history made historic preservation projects more immediately effective in saving districts that had been scheduled for the wrecking ball or left to mildew and rot in drowsy indifference. Such cities as Charleston, Savannah, and New Orleans that, by inertia as much as planning, had retained much of their old building stock were in excellent position to join eagerly and successfully in the historic preservation cult. Politically and socially inbred Charleston and Savannah, where old families continued to exercise significant power well into the 1970s, relied on private initiative, but other southern cities, with less housing stock, no readily convertible waterfront, and more diverse and competing social, economic, and political interests took a different route to historic preservation. The different approaches revealed the continued diversity among southern cities and also the potential for social and political fragmentation as a consequence of southern urban development.[18]

Regardless of the redevelopment strategy employed, the white business leaders and their allies who dominated southern city governments for most of the century used a variety of devices to retain control over the character of their cities. Since early in the century southern cities had enacted zoning regulations to define and enforce the physical boundaries of race and class. During the 1910s, for example, Richmond had adopted a residential segregation ordinance, and in 1922 Atlanta passed a zoning ordinance establishing neighborhood categories ("White District," "Colored District," and "Undetermined"). Although the federal courts struck down both laws, southern cities continued to find ways to maintain segregation.[19] Indeed, until the modern civil rights movement, local governments not only had a free hand in enforcing racial or ethnic segregation but even found an ally in the federal government. During the 1950s, for example, the Federal Housing Administration (FHA) openly advocated homogeneous neigborhoods, advising new suburban communities to use racially restrictive covenants to keep the races apart and counseling builders to limit developments to a single race or ethnic group. Also, by excluding ("red lining") many black and minority sections of cities from FHA loans, the FHA's policies in effect invited private lenders and real estate agents to pursue discriminatory policies and hastened the deterioration of poor neighborhoods, unable to get credit or insurance to maintain and protect property. The combination of federal and local governmental policies kept blacks and other minorities in their place and subject to decisions made by powers outside the black and poor neighborhoods.[20]

After World War II, southern businessmen quietly endorsed improvements in the blacks' economic condition and, for the sake of both public image and fairness, were not overtly hostile to the civil rights movement. Defusing racial tensions was necessary to attract outside capital and to minimize outside interference in local matters, but it in no way implied a willingness to share political power or to spare black neighborhoods from demolition.[21]

By the 1970s, however, business leaders no longer held unchallenged sway in determining the shape and character of metropolitan development. At the same time that local developers were beginning to scale down their projects and to think in terms of improving already established neighborhoods and districts rather than paving them over into parking lots, federal housing policies had begun to dovetail with the historic preservation movement. Therefore, those policies now recognized the importance of maintaining and restoring existing housing stock and, more important, required that local governments incorporate recommendations from local citizens' groups into any development projects receiving federal funds.

Within the cities, too, a new urban political dynamic, increasingly defined by neighborhood and ethnic/racial interest politics, combined with the changes in federal housing policies to deflect power from downtown business blocs. For years in southern cities, the white business interests and their allies had kept control of local government by using at-large electoral systems to choose representatives for city councils, diminishing the power of black, Mexican American, and other poor voters who tended to be concentrated in a few neighborhoods. In the wake of the Voting Rights Act of 1965, however, federal courts ordered local governments to introduce district electoral systems that increased minority representation in local government and made the neighborhoods, which often conformed to the electoral districts, the new venue of politics. From Richmond (with blacks asserting their power) to San Antonio (with Mexican Americans asserting their power) during the 1970s and 1980s many of the old at-large systems gave way to district systems. The steady increase of black and minority populations further transformed the political base of southern cities. In cities such as Atlanta, Birmingham, and New Orleans, where more than half the population within the city limits was black by 1980, the old politics of racial exclusion proved increasingly irrelevant, if not downright anachronistic. Black majorities voted in black mayors in several southern cities during the 1980s, and across the South in the 1970s and 1980s black and brown faces began to appear in city government and to point the direction of southern urban development.[22]

During the 1970s as well, southern cities experienced a general shift of power downward to community-based organizations. Rickety coalitions built across class and even ethnic/racial lines rose in several southern cities to promote specific neighborhood or district concerns. Building on the interest in rehabilitating existing housing generally and the historic preservationists' insistence on restoring the "contextual environment" of whole districts, neighborhood groups successfully reclaimed the Fan District in Richmond and the predominantly black Victorian District in Savannah, among other places. Elsewhere, coalitions of neighborhood groups organized to block development. In New Orleans and especially in Atlanta the so-called freeway revolts reordered local politics. In the case of Atlanta, in 1973 the predominantly white, middle-class anti-freeway alliance and a set of young black community leaders eager to share in the city's power structure came together in opposition to Atlanta's development-oriented downtown business elite and paved the way for the election of Maynard Jackson, Atlanta's first black mayor. Significantly, Jackson had pledged during the campaign to increase neighborhood involvement in municipal decisionmaking.[23]

As northern migrants of diverse ethnic and religious backgrounds, black and white southerners, and immigrants have entered southern cities, a kind of pluralistic politics has been realized in the neighborhood movement. In several cases, southern urban politics has begun to function like northern urban politics, with various interest groups based on race/ethnicity and neighborhood competing for social space and political place. To be sure, race still looms large and defines political categories. The South cannot wholly escape its past. But in such cities as Atlanta, a broker politics has emerged in which Jewish, Asian, and Hispanic voters, among others, mix with black and white Protestant southerners to create shifting political alliances and configurations and on some issues, ethnic polarization.[24]

Ethnic-related politics, like urbanization itself, was not unprecedented in southern experience. During the nineteenth century Richmond, Charleston, Savannah, and Memphis practiced a primitive variety of ethnic politics in that the Democratic party courted German and Irish immigrant voters by placing several of their countrymen on local ballots. In Tampa for almost fifty years in this century Cuban, Italian, black, and "Anglo" groups vied for power. New Orleans, the most cosmopolitan and ethnically diverse southern city throughout the nineteenth and most of the twentieth centuries, had long been schooled in the politics of diversity. There, French and Irish Catholics carried their private internecine struggles into the public arena of politics, while also combining against the "Americans" (read white Protestant migrants). Irish and German immigrants also figured prominently in the Crescent City's political calculations during the mid-nineteenth century, and the "Italian issue" inflamed local politics in the 1890s. Defying all attempts to fit it into a southern mold, Louisiana's politics, a "festival of labyrinth," as it has been called, produced both Huey Long and, more recently, French-speaking Edwin W. Edwards, the first governor of Cajun descent elected in the twentieth century. Save perhaps for Florida, no southern state can pretend to match the cultural diversity found in Louisiana's parishes. Still, until the 1970s, in no twentieth-century southern city (other than Tampa with its Italian and Cuban population) did nonsoutherners or nonwhites write the political agenda or control local political councils. For over a century middle- and upper-class white southerners ruled the cities, and race and class overruled all other factors in allocating power.[25]

Nevertheless, in those southern cities with large black or other minority populations where neighborhood movements are under way ethnic factors seem destined to influence local political dynamics, as they already do in Miami, the most "northern" city in the federal census area of the Southeast. As late as the early 1950s Miami was a southern city, marked by its own history of Ku Klux Klan violence directed against blacks, Jews, and Catholics and its own variant on southern patterns of segregation and political exclusion.[26] But since the late 1950s northern in-migration and Caribbean immigration have transformed Miami into a Sunbelt city, or more accurately into the capital of a Caribbean-oriented subregion, where immigrant/ethnic factors govern local politics. Such currently volatile issues as bilingualism bespeak the force of ethnicity in defining the political agenda in the Miami metropolitan area, and the recent election of a Cuban mayor attests to the power of ethnic voting blocs in the city of Miami. In no other southern city do immigrant populations determine the city's social and political character as they do in Miami (though San Antonio has moved significantly in that direction), but several cities now wrestle with a new politics based on neighborhood and ethnic/racial identities and competition with downtown business interests.[27]

Rising crime rates, social fragmentation, and declining city services all are liable to make the South's new ethnic politics acrimonious. Glittering downtowns ringed by poor neighborhoods still characterize some southern cities, despite the best efforts of historic preservationists and others to improve and restore neighborhoods, and that disparity points up the segmented economic and social character of those cities and the political dissonance that resounds within them. In Houston, to cite one example, such contrasts were graphically summarized by one *New York Times* reporter in 1978, when he compared the "citadels of Exxon and Shell" in the downtown to the "one-story shacks with rusting tin roofs, peeling paint, and rickety porches on concrete blocks" only a five-minute walk away.[28]

Outside of south Florida, moreover, urban ethnic politics is not yet metropolitan politics. As whites continue to leave the cities for the suburbs and nonwhites arrive in the cities, the isolation of the nonwhite city from the white suburbs has become evident. Increasingly, the residents (both southern and northern born) of southern suburbs tend to be newly arrived, white, affluent, and Republican; the residents of southern cities tend to be nonwhite, poor, and Democrat. Suburban dwellers also have become disassociated from central cities as jobs have moved outward along the highways and interstates. The pillars of the service sector economy of the burgeoning Sunbelt South—corporate and government administration, banking, and insurance—are now being located in the suburbs, where the well-educated, middle-class workers they attract now choose (and can afford) to live. Healthy metropolitan economies, however, belie the fragmentation in employment and interest within metropolitan areas, for the prosperity of the suburbs has not been uniformly shared by the cities.

For much of the postwar era, urban-suburban fragmentation was slowed by the aggressive annexation policies of southern cities that captured the out-migrating whites and diluted minority political power within the urban core. Atlanta's "Plan of Improvement" in 1952 added approximately 100,000 residents to the city. In Texas lenient annexation laws allowed both Houston and San Antonio to grab hundreds of square miles of new territory between 1948 and 1970. Between 1940 and 1970 Charlotte and Memphis extended their boundaries dramatically. In 1967 Jacksonville, Florida, swallowed most of Duval County. And so on. Similarly, a pattern of city-county consolidation launched by Baton Rouge in 1947 was pursued by several tidewater Virginia communities in the 1950s and by Nashville and Davidson County in 1962.[29]

More recently, however, outlying areas have fought off annexation. Atlanta, for example, is now hemmed in. The southern urban tendency to grow horizontally, all the while begetting satellite towns, has bred what are called conurbations, such as the one that stretches along the Gulf Coast from Houston to Pensacola. As southern cities grew together, annexation became less possible. As city populations changed, suburbs began to incorporate to protect their peculiar social homogeneity and political autonomy. As suburbs grew in size and wealth, they were able to provide their own services and had less need of cities anyway.

Finally, the cities themselves began to question the wisdom of annexation as a policy. Houston provided a glaring example of the dangers of overannexation. Having gorged itself on its surrounding territory, Houston choked on perpetually jammed highways leading into the city, sank due to excessive pumping of underground aquifers, and cringed in fear while waiting for an undermanned police force to cover a vast territorial expanse.

As had annexation, efforts to consolidate city and county services have claimed attention—but not much success. Only in Miami, in 1957, did voters adopt a two-tiered metropolitan federation wherein city and county shared responsibilities and engaged in metropolitan-wide planning. In the Metro-Dade arrangement Dade County assumed responsibility for certain metropolitan functions (for example, mass transit, planning, and public health), while the metropolitan area's separate municipalities remained intact as political entities and retained control over other services. As in so many things, Miami was sui generis. Outside of south Florida, talk of metropolitan consolidation remained largely talk in the urban South, and cities and suburbs continued to tug in their separate directions.[30]

Miami's seeming uniqueness, however, points to changes under way in the recent urban South, for in many ways the extraordinarily rapid growth and development of south (and one might add central) Florida has given the South a chance to observe the consequences of unplanned urbanization. Florida exploded in population and development in the last half century. In 1940 Florida had as many people as South Carolina; by 1980 it counted three times as many. As late as the early 1970s, Florida maintained a "southern" look in politics and social policies; by the 1980s, to some observers, Miami was so "foreign" in capital investment, interest, and population that it seemed no part of the United States, much less the South. The Sunbelt brought wealth and power, but it also brought pollution and loss of ties to the region. Florida has become notorious for the environmental damage caused by rapid, unregulated growth. Miami's water is so heavily contaminated with chemicals that some wags contend that pollution is a conspiracy by grocery chains to sustain a thriving trade in bottled water, and even a serious report on Florida's water supply charged in 1982 that "in many locations, Floridians have, in essence, run a hose from their toilet to the kitchen faucet."[31]

Elsewhere in the developing Sunbelt South pollution of fragile ecosystems threatens to destroy the very environment that has made the Sunbelt so attractive for prospective vacationers and migrants. To survive at all, the new urban South must now resolve problems of sewage facilities, trash removal, water supply, traffic control, and many other concerns that southern cities historically have been lax in addressing. And it must do so in ways that respect the integrity of historic districts and neighborhood interests.

Some observers believe that urbanization in the South heralds a new kind of urban society—one marked by its reliance on the automobile, its dispersed population, its ties to the countryside, and its low-rise residential and commercial look. In the words of David Goldfield, it is an urban society that is "more private, less confrontational, and more relaxed" than that of the older urban areas of the nation.[32] In any event, the future of that new urban society hinges on how it understands its particular past and plans for its future.

The Sunbelt is not wholly southern, and it might not be southern at all. Whether the urbanizing South will remain southern is a question that now supports a cottage industry of journalists and scholars. If the South's soul is rural, can an urban South be southern? If the central theme of southern history is how to keep the South a white man's country, can cities experiencing in-migration and immigration and sharing power among competing racial, ethnic, and neighborhood groups be southern? And so on. Southerners traditionally have abhorred a mixture. They take their religion, politics, and whiskey straight. Black or white—no middle way, no blurring. The new urban South, by its diversity alone, challenges that simpler South. But as southerners adapt to the new urban worlds growing up in their midst, they likely will discover that in their very diversity of culture, interest, and power those cities have ample room for southern ways as well. To some extent, they always have.

NOTES

1. Pat Watters, ed., *The Future of the South: A Preliminary Report/1980 Commission on the Future of the South* (Research Triangle Park, N.C., 1981); and for the recent census estimates, see *Philadelphia Inquirer,* November 21, 1986, p. 10-A.

2. The literature on the Sunbelt and on southern urban development is abundant and growing. Excellent introductions to the issues and the literature, which guided my own writing considerably, are available in David R. Goldfield, *Cotton Fields and Skyscrapers: Southern City and Region, 1607-1980* (Baton Rouge, 1982), especially pp. 139-96; and Goldfield, *Promised Land: The South Since 1945* (Arlington Heights, 1987). The following also were useful in directing my work: Carl Abbott, *The New Urban America: Growth and Politics in Sunbelt Cities* (Chapel Hill, 1981); Abbott, *Urban America in the Modern Age: 1920 to the Present* (Arlington Heights, 1987); Richard M. Bernard and Bradley R. Rice, eds., *Sunbelt Cities: Politics and Growth Since World War II* (Austin, 1983); John B. Boles, ed., *Dixie Dateline: A Journalistic Portrait of the Contemporary South* (Houston, 1983); Blaine A. Brownell and David R. Goldfield, eds., *The City in Southern History* (Port Washington, N.Y., 1977), especially 123-91; James C. Cobb, *Industrialization & Southern Society, 1877-1984* (Lexington, Ky., 1984); David Perry and Alfred Watkins, eds., *The Rise of the Sunbelt Cities* (Beverly Hills, 1977); and the special issue, "Urban Themes in the American South,"

of the *Journal of Urban History* 2 (February 1976). Various publications of the Southern Growth Policies Board have been useful, especially Patricia J. Dusenbury, *Report of the Task Force on Southern Cities* (Research Triangle Park, N.C., 1981); *Current Issues on Immigration and Refugee Policy* (Research Triangle Park, N.C., 1980); *An Urban Economic Development Strategy for Southern States* (Research Triangle Park, N.C., 1980); and *Suburbs in the City: Municipal Boundary Changes in the Southern States* (Research Triangle Park, N.C., 1981). Also revealing is the White House report, *Growth and the Cities of the South: A Study in Diversity* (Washington, D.C., 1977), which reminds us of the variegated nature of southern urban growth. Two good recent surveys of the literature are James C. Cobb, "Urbanization and the Changing South: A Review of the Literature," *South Atlantic Urban Studies* 1 (1977), 253-66; and Charles P. Roland, "Sun Belt Prosperity and Urban Growth," in John B. Boles and Evelyn Thomas Nolen, eds., *Interpreting Southern History: Historiographical Essays in Honor of Sanford W. Higginbotham* (Baton Rouge, 1987), pp. 434-53. A readable and perceptive overview of the recent South is Pete Daniel, *Standing at the Crossroads: Southern Life since 1900* (New York, 1986). I have already attempted definitions of the Sunbelt and the character of southern metropolitan growth in my "Migrations and Economic Growth in the Metropolitan Southern Sunbelt," *Perspectives on the American South* 4 (1986), 163-86. Throughout my chapter, statistical data derive from published U.S. census tables.

3. A good summary of out-migration is Jack Temple Kirby, "The Southern Exodus, 1910-1960: A Primer for Historians," *Journal of Southern History* 49 (1983), 585-600.

4. On Nashville's growth, see Don H. Doyle, *Nashville Since the 1920s* (Knoxville, 1985).

5. On the agricultural transformation in the South and its effects on southern life and population movement, see Pete Daniel, *Breaking the Land: The Transformation of Cotton, Tobacco, and Rice Culture Since 1880* (Urbana, 1985); Daniel, "The New Deal, Southern Agriculture, and Economic Change," in James C. Cobb and Michael V. Namorato, eds., *The New Deal and the South* (Jackson, Miss., 1984), pp. 37-61; and Gilbert C. Fite, *Cotton Fields No More: Southern Agriculture, 1865-1980* (Lexington, Ky., 1984). On the effects on blacks and poor farmers, see also David E. Conrad, *The Forgotten Farmers: The Story of Sharecroppers in the New Deal* (Urbana, 1965); Paul Good, *The American Serfs* (New York, 1968); Everett S. Lee, "The Disappearance of the Black Farmer," *Phylon* 35 (1974), 276-83; Paul E. Mertz, *New Deal Policy and Southern Rural Poverty* (Baton Rouge, 1978); Charles R. Sayre, "Cotton Mechanization Since World War II," *Agricultural History* 53 (1979), 105-24. That black farmers headed to town is shown in John D. Reid, "Black Urbanization of the South," *Phylon* 35 (1974), 259-67. My comments on economic transformation and social change draw heavily on Gavin Wright, *Old South, New South: Revolutions in the Southern Economy Since the Civil War* (New York, 1986).

6. The effects of World War II on the South are often mentioned but little studied. The best brief accounts are George Tindall, *The Emergence of the New South, 1913-1945* (Baton Rouge, 1967), pp. 687-713 (especially pp. 694-703 on economic and social changes); Daniel, *Standing at the Crossroads,* pp. 135-49; and Goldfield, *Promised Land,* pp. 1-20. On the need for study, see Morton Sosna, "More Important Than the Civil War: The Impact of World War II on the South," *Perspectives on the American South* 4 (1986), 145-61.

7. John Dos Passos, *State of the Nation* (Boston, 1944), p. 92 (quote); and Agnes E. Meyer, *Journey Through Chaos* (New York, 1944), pp. 202-12 (p. 210 quote). See also Selden C. Menefee, *Assignment: U.S.A.* (London, 1944), pp. 51-56. For comparably bad conditions in another southern wartime boom town, see Marvin W. Schlegel, *Conscripted City: Norfolk in World War II* (Norfolk, 1951).

8. Tindall, *Emergence of the New South,* pp. 701-703; Merl E. Reed, "The FEPC, the Black Worker, and the Southern Shipyards," *South Atlantic Quarterly* 74 (1975), 447-67 (pp. 454-57 on the Mobile riot). On wartime stresses on racial issues, see also James A. Burran, "Racial Violence in the South During World War II" (Ph.D. dissertation, University of Tennessee, 1977); Richard M. Dalfiume, "The 'Forgotten Years' of the Negro Revolution," *Journal of American History* 55 (1968), 90-106; and Merl E. Reed, "The FEPC and the Federal Agencies in the South," *Journal of Negro History* 65 (1980), 43-56.

9. The broadest survey of postwar southern development, which includes much attention to nongovernmental factors, is Cobb, *Industrialization & Southern Society,* pp. 51-67. On federal spending and southern economic growth, see, for example, James Clotfelter, "The South and the Military Dollar," *New South* 25 (Spring 1970), 52-56; "The Second War Between the States: Special Report," *Business Week* (May 17, 1976), 92-114; Joel Haveman et al., "Federal Spending: The North's Loss Is the Sunbelt's Gain," *National Journal* 8 (June 26, 1986), 878-91; Robert J. Dilger, *The Sunbelt/Snowbelt Controversy: The War Over Federal Funds* (New York, 1982); E. Blaine Liner and Lawrence K. Lynch, eds., *The Economics of Southern Growth* (Durham, 1977), who argue that federal money played only a small role; Roger W. Lotchin, *The Martial Metropolis: U.S. Cities in War and Peace* (New York, 1984); Peter Mieszkowski and Mahlon Straszheim, eds., *Current Issues in Urban Economics* (Baltimore, 1979); Bernard Weinstein and Robert E. Firestone, *Regional Growth and Decline in the United States: The Rise of the Sunbelt and the Decline of the Northeast* (New York, 1978); and the charts and tables in *Southern Exposure* 1 (1973), 60-99. A revealing comparative study of recent developments is Thomas M. Stanback, Jr., and Thierry J. Noyelle, *Cities in Transition: Changing Job Structures in Atlanta, Denver, Buffalo, Phoenix, Columbus (Ohio), Nashville, and Charlotte* (Totowa, N.J., 1982). Also of interest is Truman Hartshorn, *Metropolis in Georgia: Atlanta's Rise as a Transaction Center* (Cambridge, Mass., 1976). Sharply critical assessments of the social costs of recent economic development are in the special issue, "Everybody's Business: A People's Guide to Economic Development," *Southern Exposure* 14 (September/October and November/December 1986). The changing employment picture for women is discussed in Julia Kirk Blackwelder's chapter in this book.

10. On postwar developments, see especially James Cobb, *The Selling of the South: The Southern Crusade for Industrial Development, 1936-1980* (Baton Rouge, 1982).

11. Florida was especially affected by such "outside" influences in the form of newcomers following the development strategies. On the rapid transformation of Florida, see the chapter by Ray Arsenault and Gary Mormino in this book. In her chapter (in this book) on Jewish migration patterns, Deborah Dash Moore also connects decisions to migrate to the governmental benefits (retirement programs) and a receptive south Florida region.

12. The centrifugal effects of federal programs and spending on cities are conveniently summarized in Kenneth T. Jackson, *Crabgrass Frontier: The Suburbanization of the United States* (New York, 1985), pp. 231-45 and *passim;* Abbott, *Urban America*

in the Modern Age, pp. 82-87 and *passim;* and Jon C. Teaford, *The Twentieth-Century American City: Problems, Promises, and Reality* (Baltimore, 1986), pp. 98-100 and *passim.*

13. The role of the automobile in shaping the urban landscape is discussed in Jackson, *Crabgrass Frontier,* pp. 246-71 and *passim.* On the early effects of the automobile on a southern city, see Howard L. Preston, *Automobile Age Atlanta: The Making of a Southern Metropolis, 1900-1935* (Athens, Ga., 1979); and more generally, Blaine A. Brownell, "A Symbol of Modernity: Attitudes Toward the Automobile in Southern Cities in the 1920s," *American Quarterly* 24 (1972), 20-44. For the modern city, see Dana F. White and Timothy J. Crimmins, "Urban Structure, Atlanta," *Journal of Urban History* 2 (1976), 231-56; and the "Urban Structure, Atlanta" special issue of *Atlanta Historical Journal* 26 (Summer-Fall 1982). Recent southern metropolitan commuting trends are summarized in Goldfield, *Promised Land,* pp. 208-9.

14. The efficacy of 1950s-1960s urban renewal policies is debated in James Q. Wilson, ed., *Urban Renewal: The Record and the Controversy* (Cambridge, Mass., 1966); and Jewel Bellush and Murray Hausknecht, eds., *Urban Renewal: People, Politics, and Planning* (Garden City, N.Y., 1967). On urban renewal experiences, see the useful summaries in Abbott, *Urban America in the Modern Age,* pp. 117-31; and Goldfield, *Promised Land,* pp. 157-59.

15. On Morrison, who did much good work in ending corruption in New Orleans, see Edward F. Haas, *DeLesseps S. Morrison and the Image of Reform: New Orleans Politics, 1946-1961* (Baton Rouge, 1974). For an excellent discussion of development policies in New Orleans, see Arnold Hirsch, "New Orleans: Sunbelt in the Swamp," in Bernard and Rice, eds., *Sunbelt Cities,* pp. 100-37.

16. Bordon Dent, "The Challenge to Downtown Shopping," *Atlanta Economic Review* 28 (January/February 1978), 29-33; Truman Hartshorn, "Getting Around Atlanta: New Approaches," *Atlanta Economic Review* 28 (January/February 1978), 43-51; Neil Peirce, "The Southern City Today," in Boles, ed., *Dixie Dateline,* pp. 104-5; Bradley R. Rice, "Atlanta: If Dixie Were Atlanta," in Bernard and Rice, eds., *Sunbelt Cities,* pp. 38-42; Alexander S. Wright, III, "The Office Market: Central City vs. Suburbs," *Atlanta Economic Review* 28 (January/February 1978), 34-36; Abbott, *Urban America in the Modern Age,* p. 114.

17. On the different uses of history by urban residents based on race and class, see Gary McDonogh's chapter in this book.

18. Peirce, "The Southern City Today," 108-12; Philip Morris, "Five Southern Towns Change and Stay the Same," *Southern Living* 13 (January 1978), 3-12; and Goldfield, *Promised Land,* 209-11.

19. On early zoning and planning in southern cities, see especially Blaine A. Brownell, "The Commerical-Civic Elite and City Planning in Atlanta, Memphis, and New Orleans in the 1920s," *Journal of Southern History* 41 (1975), 339-68. On residential patterns, see, for example, Ronald H. Bayor, "Ethnic Residential Patterns in Atlanta, 1880-1940," *Georgia Historical Quarterly* 63 (1979), 435-47; Robin Flowerdew, "Spatial Patterns of Residential Segregation in a Southern City," *Journal of American Studies* 13 (1979), 93-107 (on Memphis); Barry J. Kaplan, "Race, Income, and Ethnicity: Residential Change in a Houston Community, 1920-1970," *Houston Review* 3 (1981), 178-202. For the most probing treatment of planning in a southern city, see Christopher Silver, *Twentieth-Century Richmond: Planning, Politics,*

and Race (Knoxville, 1984). For a comparative view of Memphis and Richmond, see Silver's chapter in this volume.

20. On FHA policies, see Mark I. Gelfand, *A Nation of Cities: The Federal Government and Urban America, 1933-1965* (New York, 1975), pp. 216-22; and Jackson, *Crabgrass Frontier,* pp. 203-18.

21. On southern businessmen's practical (and also self-serving) approach to civil rights, see Elizabeth Jacoway and David R. Colburn, eds., *Southern Businessmen and Desegregation* (Baton Rouge, 1982). For a less generous view, see Virginia H. Hein, "The Image of 'A City Too Busy to Hate': Atlanta in the 1960's," *Phylon* 33 (1972), 205-21.

22. While black political activity in southern cities from the 1950s on has attracted attention, little work has been done on the foundations of that activity or even on black life in southern cities, particularly for the pre-"Brown" period. On this concern, see Dan T. Carter, "Southern Political Style," in Robert Haws, ed., *The Age of Segregation: Race Relations in the South, 1890-1954* (Jackson, Miss., 1978), pp. 57-66. Good essays surveying one city's recent experiences are in David R. Johnson, John A. Booth, and Richard J. Harris, eds., *The Politics of San Antonio* (Lincoln, Nebr., 1983). Also interesting is F. Arturo Rosales, "Mexicans in Houston: The Struggle to Survive, 1908-1975," *Houston Review* 3 (1981), 24-48. For Atlanta, see note 23.

23. In this book neighborhood-based political coalitions are discussed in chapters by Ronald Bayor (on Atlanta, Houston, and San Antonio) and Christopher Silver (on Richmond and Memphis). On Atlanta, specifically, see also Rice, "Atlanta: If Dixie Were Atlanta," pp. 44-53; F. Glenn Abney and John D. Hutchinson, Jr., "Race, Representation, and Trust: Changes in Attitudes after the Election of a Black Mayor," *Public Opinion Quarterly* 45 (1981), 91-101; Peter K. Eisinger, *The Politics of Displacement: Racial and Ethnic Transition in Three American Cities* (New York, 1980); Floyd Hunter, *Community Power Succession: Atlanta's Policy Makers* (Chapel Hill, 1980); Charles Little, "Atlanta Renewal Gives Power to the Communities," *Smithsonian* 7 (July 1976), 100-108; John D. Hutchinson, Jr., and Elizabeth T. Beer, "In-Migration and Atlanta's Neighborhoods," *Atlanta Economic Review* 28 (March/April 1978), 7-14; Bill Schemmel, "Atlanta's 'Power Structure' Faces Life," *New South* 27 (1972), 62-68; Clarence N. Stone, *Economic Growth and Neighborhood Discontent: System Bias in the Urban Renewal Program in Atlanta* (Chapel Hill, 1976); and Peirce, "The Southern City Today," pp. 107-108.

24. On the ethnic face of recent southern urban politics, see Ronald Bayor's chapter in this book.

25. On immigrants in southern cities before World War II, see, for example, Kathleen C. Berkeley, " 'Like a Plague of Locust': Immigration and Social Change in Memphis, Tennessee, 1850-1880" (Ph.D. dissertation, University of California, Los Angeles, 1980); Randall M. Miller, "The Enemy Within: Some Effects of Foreign Immigrants on Antebellum Southern Cities," *Southern Studies* 24 (1985), 30-53 (especially pp. 47-52); Miller, "Becoming New Orleanians: A Variant View of Immigrants and Acculturation in the Crescent City," in M. Mark Stolarik, ed., *Forgotten Doors: The Other Ports of Entry to the United States* (Philadelphia, forthcoming); Herbert Weaver, "Foreigners in Ante-Bellum Towns of the Lower South," *Journal of Southern History* 13 (1947), 62-73; Lawrence H. Larsen, *The Rise of the Urban South* (Lexington, Ky., 1985), pp. 41-50; Richard Gambino, *Vendetta* (Garden City, N.Y., 1977); Gary R. Mormino and George E. Pozzetta, *The Immigrant World of Ybor City:*

Italians and Their Latin Neighbors in Tampa, 1885-1985 (Urbana, 1987), especially chapters 4-6.

26. Wyn Craig Wade, *The Fiery Cross: The Ku Klux Klan in America* (New York, 1987), p. 292.

27. See Raymond A. Mohl's chapter in this book. On Miami's unique character, see also Raymond A. Mohl, "Miami: The Ethnic Cauldron," in Bernard and Rice, eds., *Sunbelt Cities,* pp. 58-99. Also of interest for contemporary Miami is T. D. Allman, *Miami: City of the Future* (Boston, 1987). The strongest statement on the fragmentation of Sunbelt city politics is Abbott's *Sunbelt Cities.* Important in appreciating the ethnic dimension are the essays on Miami (by Raymond Mohl), Tampa (by Gary Mormino), Houston (by Barry J. Kaplan), and San Antonio (by David R. Johnson) in Bernard and Rice, eds., *Sunbelt Cities.*

28. Quoted in Goldfield, *Cotton Fields and Skyscrapers,* p. 151.

29. Aspects of annexation are discussed in William Black, "Empire of Consensus: City Planning, Zoning, and Annexation in Dallas, 1900-1960" (Ph.D. dissertation, Columbia University, 1982); Brett W. Hawkins, *Nashville Metro: The Politics of City-County Consolidation* (Nashville, 1966); Barry J. Kaplan, "Houston: The Golden Buckle of the Sunbelt," in Bernard and Rice, eds., *Sunbelt Cities,* pp. 200-202; Rice, "Atlanta: If Dixie Were Atlanta," pp. 34-36; David Temple, *Merger Politics: Local Government Consolidation in Tidewater Virginia* (Charlottesville, 1972); and generally in Jon C. Teaford, *City and Suburb: The Political Fragmentation of Metropolitan America, 1850-1970* (Baltimore, 1979).

30. Edward Sofen, *The Miami Metropolitan Experiment* (Bloomington, Ind., 1963).

31. On environmental issues, see the excellent brief discussion in Goldfield, *Promised Land,* pp. 196-205 (p. 198 quote); and Albert E. Cowdrey, *This Land, This South: An Environmental History* (Lexington, Ky., 1983), pp. 169-93 (pp. 190-91 on south Florida). See also Nelson M. Blake, *Land into Water—Water into Land: A History of Water Management in Florida* (Tallahassee, 1980). The effects of rapid population growth on the quality of life in south Florida are briefly discussed in the Arsenault/Mormino chapter in this book.

32. Goldfield, *Promised Land,* p. 155.

2

The Palmetto and the Maple Leaf: Patterns of Canadian Migration to Florida

Robert F. Harney

This study began as a light-hearted assent to a request to prepare a research paper about Canadian ethnicity in the Sunbelt. Canadian ethnicity is an elusive quality in terms of both content and boundaries. So too is the concept of the Sunbelt. Perhaps because things are not as simple as the standard labels make them seem, studying the Canadian migrants in Florida has emerged as a less tongue-in-cheek exercise than it began. The story of Canadian migration—seasonal, polyseasonal, and permanent—for recreational sojourning offers rich situations and materials for study of migration processes, of the nature of the commerce of migration, and of the relative fragility of a Canadian national identity among Canadians abroad.

The convenor of the 1984 conference on ethnicity in the Sunbelt lured me to the event by including a remark in his letter of invitation, which was uncharacteristically immoderate and even hinted of a vexed, if mild, form of nativism. He wrote "to drive the roads of Florida in winter is to think that half of all Canada is down here!" A little research proved his statistics wrong but his sense of invasion appropriate. During each year of the early 1980s, almost a million and a half Canadians visited Florida. A statistical extrapolation, made by a public relations firm hired by the Florida Chamber of Commerce (Tourism Division), an agency at the very heart of the commerce of migration that has arisen between Canada and Florida, demonstrates that Canadians spend about 24,000,000 "person nights" in Florida each year.[1] That figure of 24,000,000 is approximate to the total population of Canada. So, if it is not true that "half of all Canada" is on the roads of Florida in the winter, it is true that each and every Canadian, or his fellow national surrogate with more leisure time and means, can be said to enjoy at least a "one night stand" in Florida annually.

21

Since only about 250,000 Canadians are permanent residents of Florida, and since only about 20,000 Canadians arrive annually to take up legal residence in the entire United States, it follows that this mass migration to the South is characterized by impermanence, transience, shifting migration targets, a high level of initially brokered rather than chain or serial migration, and a high proportion of time spent traveling to the migration target in relation to actual duration of sojourn. In fact, during the 1980s, the average Canadian sojourn in Florida was approximately sixteen "person nights." Length of stay and type of accommodation clearly changed with the life cycle, as it does for all migrations. Fifty-two percent of the sojourners stayed in hotels or motels, 20 percent in apartments, and 17 percent with friends. The missing 11 percent, one must assume, lived restlessly in caravans and recreation vehicles at unincorporated sites just as the poorest and most exotic guest workers do in western Europe.

There is a saying among Finnish immigrants that once you have crossed the Atlantic you are never on the right side again. Canadians who taste Florida are like workers from the periphery who encounter the standards of living of industrialized western Europe and then find themselves spoiled and unable to adjust to the more rigorous quality of life, or limits of horizon, of their homelands when they repatriate. Such migrants usually undergo a slow process of "marginalization" fueled by their rising levels of expectation.[2] Just as a Turkish or south Italian guest worker in Germany or Sweden may imperceptibly lose his or her ability to cope with the ways and conditions of the home village after a period of seasonal or polyseasonal migration, so too Canadians, as they increase their Florida holiday experience and prosper, lose the moral fiber and Anglo-Canadian pride in austerity that once enabled them to survive winters in their homeland. (New Canadians, especially those of Mediterranean origin, may never have been possessed of such stoic northern virtue, and so Florida has a special appeal for them, once the annual trips to an Italian, Portuguese, Maltese, or Greek home village, typical of the migrant's first years in North America, lose urgency.) The pattern then is one in which sojourns grow longer and housing more elaborate as the Canadian migrant to Florida advances in the life cycle. The immigration legislation of the sending and receiving countries, the terms of pensions and medical coverage, and so forth cause a situation in which much sojourning is in fact covert settlement.

A knowledgeable Florida realtor, the agent of the commerce of migration who supplants the travel agent once sojourning turns to settlement, has observed the typical Canadian transition from guest rester to permanent resident alien. As the migrant, usually young and unmarried, reconnoiters the leisure target, he stays in Florida during his first season or seasons for a period of about three weeks in a rental accommodation. Later sojourns grow longer to include at least three winter months. Housing changes at that point, often to time-share apartments. The final stage, which comes with retirement or financial independence, involves the buying of a condominium and annual Florida stays of six months or more. The early stages of the migration also typically involve varied and unpredictable problems of encounter and insertion into the local culture, society, and economy with consequent high levels of "ghettoization."

The "guest rester" system that has evolved between Canadian leisure seekers and Florida's chief industry, tourism, has, as befits a phenomenon occurring in a "land of counterpane" worthy of Lewis Carroll, many characteristics that mirror the "guest worker" systems that prevailed in much of western Europe in the 1960s and, in a less acknowledged way among southern and east European laborers, in the United States in the 1900s. Most strikingly similar is the fact that neither the "guest rester" nor the host society seems, at least at first, to see the utility or propriety of permanent settlement. As the advanced industrial states of western Europe welcomed guest workers because of the way they could serve the host economy, so Florida welcomes Canadian guest resters because of the almost $600 million dollars they contribute to the state by their annual spending in Florida. In neither case would permanent settlement improve the symbiosis from the host society's point of view. Short-term tourists spend at a higher rate per diem than settlers and lack interest or influence in local affairs; sojourning guest workers work harder, demand less in services, and can be moved about more readily than native and settled workers.[3]

In many of the towns of southern Italy, returned immigrants see the world in terms of a hierarchy of migration targets in which cities such as Saarbrucken and Stuttgart in Germany are viewed with *odiosamato* (love/hate), as places where one can make money but at a high price in terms of civility and the maintenance of proper values.[4] In the sending towns and cities of Ontario and Quebec, a similar attitude prevails about Florida as a migration target. Clearwater, Fort Lauderdale, and other Florida resort cities are thought of as places to find sun and rejuvenation quickly but also as cesspools of American commercialism, southern redneck politics, and racial unease.

Seasonal and short-term migration usually produces sojourners with little or no interest in the circumambient society. Such a pattern is typical of both labor migrants and the guest resters. It encourages the growth of enclaves, fosters mutual misunderstanding, and offers opportunity to the sort of agents, go-betweens, and brokers who prosper from a commerce of migration.[5] It is in such a context that one can look at the world of the Canadian guest resters in Florida as if it were, as it may well be, a part of the general pattern of modern labor migration across national boundaries and of sojourning in foreign lands for greater or lesser stretches of time, a pattern that characterizes much of the industrial world today.

A second theme of the paper has to do with the impact leaving home and polity has upon the migrant's national feeling and ethnic sense of self.

Since Canada is, like so many of the great lands of emigration, more a polity than a nation state, it is natural that centrifugal subnational patterns emerge in the migration. Some U.S. census figures of the early 1900s showed the presence of five million *Austrian* immigrants in New York City. Those immigrants were, of course, Jews, Hungarians, Croats, Czechs, Poles, Slovenes, Germans, and others from the Hapsburg monarchy. Similarly, the Canadian migration cohort that travels to Florida each year is insufficiently described by the adjective *Canadian.* Rather it is composed of English and French Canadians—Canada's so-called charter groups—along with large contingents of Jews, Italians, Finns, Hungarians, and Slavs (especially Poles, Ukrainians, and Slovaks) who may hold Canadian citizenship, but who have very often been resident in Canada for only a single generation. Studying the patterns of sojourning, enclaving, and ethnocultural activities of all these migrants from the Canadian polity raises questions about the fissiparous nature of Canadian national identity, the persistence of subethnic and ethnic networks and their salience in the daily lives of the migrants, and the ways in which either hyphenated Canadian identities emerge or Canadian culture proves itself to be a "veneer less than a generation thick." Many of the Canadians of non-English and non-French background who migrate to Florida annually have a profound sense of being part of the dispersal of their own kind throughout the world, a sense summed up in words and phrases such as diaspora, Polonia, "the Finnish upper Great Lakes," landsmann, paesani, and nation in exile.[6] If migrants from Canada find it natural, they have not acquired some of the anti-, or at least, non-American values that are part of traditional English-Canadian culture, to gather in fellow feeling with people of their own ethnic group, whether American or Canadian citizens. In fact, oral testimony (especially from Finns, Italians, Jews, and Hungarians) suggests that the annual winter sojourn in Florida has the quality of an ethnocultural rendezvous, a planned "gathering of the clan" of countrymen and women, friends and kinsmen who spend the rest of the year widely dispersed throughout North America. Charter flights from Finland to Lake Worth on Florida's east coast and to other Finnish North American enclaves indicate that modern transport and communications make possible a "globalizing" of the ethnic group, and encourage the maintenance of what W.E.B. Du Bois called "double consciousness," that is, concern for and awareness of both sending homeland and adopted nation. This process is now so familiar in Italy that it has a nomenclature of its own, including words such as *apaeseamento* and *mondializzare,* which roughly mean bringing the hometown up to date or "globalizing" it by reforging links with emigrants and their descendants.

In effect, what happens in Florida is that the alliance of interest among anglophones of many ethnic origins that exists in Canada loses some of its relevance. As a consequence, "English Canadians"—in the majority of Anglo-Celtic background—appear almost to undergo a regressive ethnogenesis of their own, which gives the adjective *English* in their hyphenated identity more than linguistic freight. The emblematics and networks of this ethnicized English-Canadianness can be seen most graphically in places like Dunedin, Clearwater, and Ft. Myers on the Florida west coast. Those rather overt Anglo-Celtic enclaves are matched by francophone and Quebecois settlements around Fort Lauderdale and by Maritimer encampments in the St. Augustine area. The pattern of settling and sojourning is ethnic, not regional. English-speaking Quebeckers tend to join the Ontarians on the west coast. Migrants from resource towns with quite similar socioeconomic structures near one another in northwestern Quebec and northern Ontario divide along linguistic lines, following different routes to different destinations. English-Canadians (not all, but enough, wearing tam o'shanters, driving big cars with the British royal crown at the center of their license plates, and using their unique pronunciation of the dipthong, *ou* [say out like hoot]), or Quebecois (speaking Joual French, watching Stanley Cup hockey playoffs in bars that cater to francophones, and behaving with a boisterous lack of inhibition on the beaches) are easy enough to spot, especially in those areas of Florida where their concentrations have led to the sort of nativism that makes "foreign traits" more salient. Abetted by local stereotyping, their characteristics become what ornithologists studying migratory birds call diagnostic marks. It is, however, more difficult to discern the clustering of Canadian Jews, Italians, and Poles in the various resorts and vacation towns precisely because they tend to spend their vacation or retirement time in areas where many American internal migrants of the same ethnic groups also have chosen to visit or settle.

Ironically, placing the Canadian guest rester system squarely within the context of modern labor migration studies and describing the migration, as well as the commerce and some of the political and moral discourse that surround it, in the same terms as one would the great westward migrations of the late nineteenth and early twentieth centuries, or of labor and leisure migration in Europe today, provides that sort of oblique angle that social anthropologists of the Clifford Geertz school believe can be used to discover what is extraordinary in what we take to be ordinary.[7] All over the industrialized world, systems of leisure migration to break the monotony of the work year have emerged. The parallels of experience among retired midwestern factory workers settling in Florida, Ontario businessmen basking in the sun for months at a time, and Italians, Yugoslavs, and Turks retiring to their hometowns after living as *gastarbeiter* in industrial northern Europe should be clear enough. When such migrations are thought of as part of a single, continuing global phenomenon, even the social class and ideological patterns of leisure sojourning acquire more nuance.[8]

Florida is not the only possible winter migration target for Canadians. Some working-class francophones have lately gone instead to Haiti. Although unstable politics and images of disease may make it a less attractive target than Florida to some, cheaper prices and accommodation costs as well as respect for and use of the French language make Haiti an alternative target on the mental maps of global opportunity of others.[9] By the same token, there are English-Canadians who find American (or perhaps southern) ways so jarring that they limit their choice of winter vacation targets to former British possessions in the West Indies.

In fact, there is in Canada a recurring debate about the propriety and wisdom of seeking a latter-day colony in the Turks and Caicos Islands.[10] The chief reason for harboring this colonialist fantasy is probably the thought that the annual $600 million that Canadians spend in Florida might more easily be recouped or kept Canadian. As with all imperial schemes, however, there is also a strong sense that migration is a hemorrhage not just of money or manpower but of national values, a sign of national weakness. The parliamentary advocates of West Indian island annexation schemes believe that in the Turks and Caicos islands a Canadian sojourner would be able to have the sun without having his Canadian culture assaulted and possibly breached by the wild and wooly ways of the "dollar republic." The same sort of political and cultural sensibilities converge with target choice in the annual winter migration southward of Scandinavian workers, a migration made easier by SAS and Finnair, the national carriers who are subsidized by the various governments of the region on the assumption that cheap access to leisure time in Tenerife, Majorca, or a Greek island is a necessary safety valve in keeping the Nordic labor market free of upheaval. Each winter while some French and English Canadians choose a West Indian island over Florida because the latter is "too American" even for a sojourn, leftist Finns make a similar choice and take their holidays at Black Sea resorts in the Soviet Union rather than face the ideological ambiguities and the many demeaning or uncomfortable petty capitalist moments that tourism in the Mediterranean always provides. Swedish sojourners, imbued with the political morality that characterized their national discourse whether they are social democrats or not, find it much more to their liking to vacation in Spain now that it is free of Franco and in Greece now that it is rid of rule by colonels. The slow but steady development of a stream of west European tourists to Cuban resorts has depended partly on elements of political sympathy and anti-Americanism in that clientele. It might be added, without trying to put too fine a point on the role of class politics in the leisure migration of Canadians, that almost 80 percent of them arrive in Florida by air, and that a study commissioned by the Florida Chamber of Commerce suggests that only about 10 percent of all tourists who arrive by air belong to the working classes. (The study, in keeping with American political idiom, refers to that 10 percent, not as working-class, but as blue-collar workers.)[11]

If we turn from the contemporaneous global context in order to look at Florida migration patterns through the simulacrum formed by historical texts about turn-of-the-century transatlantic migrations, the ways in which aspects of Florida leisure migration can be compared to the great labor migrations of the past become more obvious. Some general postulates about such migrations, all of which offer new directions for study of Canadian guest rester migration to Florida, follow:[12]

1. Each great migration has included both migrants who intended to sojourn and those who wished to settle.

2. Government legislation and regulations, as well as changing realities in the sending and the receiving countries, shape and reshape the individual's migration project in terms of the reason for going, the preselected target, and the planned duration of sojourn.

3. The migrant is forced to try to *arrangiarsi*,[13] as Italian immigrants in North American and *gastarbeiter* in Europe put it. That is, he or she must find humane and rational ways to carry out a migration project, do one's duty to family and friends, and maintain an acceptable lifestyle in the face of recalcitrant bureaucracies, legal obstructions, and sometimes hostile environments.

4. In this "arranging" of the migration process, the individual turns to two sources for help. He can look to family, friends, and ethnic fellows for ways to make easier the migration path and settlement or sojourn. The individual can alternatively turn to the commerce of migration, to those who (from travel agents, customs brokers, and immigration counsellors to real estate agents and land promoters) mediate and broker the process. Since some of those who make their living from the commerce of migration are ethnic chameleons or those who specialize in serving or exploiting a particular ethnic clientele, the two support systems that the migrant turns to are distinct but sometimes treacherously intertwined.

5. In most migration movements, there is a prehistory in which a few pioneers reconnoiter a new target of opportunity and then, informally and often unintentionally, report on it to the sending towns or country. If the target proves attractive and the right push factors are present, the trickle of migrants probing opportunity turns to a mass phenomenon, often described as a pathological condition, a "fever."

6. Once such a "fever" takes hold, analyzing the preselection of migrants resembles the efforts of an epidemiologist trying to identify who, in a given population, will prove susceptible to a disease after it is already pandemic. As favorable news about a target grows, as competition brings down transportation and accommodation costs, a migration tradition is born. As with the increasing vulnerability of a population to a disease, so too the spread of a migration tradition tends to reduce the significance of social, economic, and age characteristics in the preselection of migrants and to involve everyone.

7. Economic competition among those who profit from the commerce of migration, especially the transport sector, realtors, and those small businessmen who cater to the migrant's needs, leads to attempts to develop and control new opportunities for profit along the vector of migration or at the points of settlement. In this way, migration targets change and proliferate.[14]

8. Something which, for purposes of argument, can be called a discourse grows up around and within the specific migration tradition. Speakers in the discourse can

range from those returned migrants who describe their adventures in conversation with family, friends, and neighbors to those who produce the texts, sympathetic or hostile, about migration. Businesses that have a major stake in the commerce of migration create an "organic intelligentsia" to produce texts to counter the case against migration, which is often presented by more traditional speakers in the discourse.

9. Finally, the sojourner's or the settler's duration of stay and the place he or she is domiciled reflect a complex interplay of individual migration projects, the collective migration tradition, the migrant's processual sense of identity, the mediation of agents of the commerce of migration, economic conditions, and government attitudes.[15] Thus, the frequent emergence of class, ethnic, and subethnic clustering in the target country has to do with more than economy, for it also includes both the manner in which the host society views the particular migrants and how they view themselves.

It is the application of the last two general axioms mentioned about the migrations—that a discourse is created within the migration tradition that is accessible to content analysis and other tools of modern literary criticism, and that a reassertion of ethnic and subethnic loyalties occurs among migrants abroad—that are most intriguing in the case of the Canada-Florida flow.

The receiving society (seen as the United States, Florida, or the local target community) has always welcomed the migrants as tourists, people who spend money and create work opportunities for the local population, but generally Canadians have not been welcomed as competition in the work force. In that sense, the traditional niching of Canadians in Florida has been as precise, if oppositive in nature, as that of Turks in a German industrial town now, or Croats in a Pennsylvania mining town at the turn of the century. In Florida, Canadian guest resters encounter a native population and government agencies that encourage them "to sleep in our motels and lie on our beaches" but do not allow them to work while sojourning lest they take away jobs from the natives.

Originally most Canadian migrants had only leisure in mind, and so the lack of work opportunity meant little. In the same way, guest workers in western Europe came initially to sojourn, to work hard, maximize savings, and return to their homelands. Being told that they could "earn good wages digging our ditches and working in our heavy industries" but could not expect to become citizens, achieve upward mobility, or higher education for their children in the host country meant little to them at first as well. For many migrants, however, sojourning has a way of turning to quasi-settlement or the desire to stay indefinitely.[16] Just as Italian, Yugoslav, Portuguese, Arab, and Turkish migrants in industrial Europe try to escape the factories and a sense of transience by moving into petty capitalism, so many Canadians in Florida wish to work either because they hope to turn their seasonal migration into an act of immigration, hope to extend their sojourn, or simply hope to improve their quality of life while there. For the most part, they cannot do so legally because of American federal laws and Immigration and Naturalization Service regulations.

Remarkably, Florida's legislation against foreign workers dates back to the 1870s, and Canadians were the offending aliens even then. In 1874, Florida's politicians, under pressure from the Workingmen's Association passed laws requiring all stevedores to have lived in the state for at least six months before they could be hired. Two years earlier, there had been nativist violence, with black and white Floridians joining in the common cause against Canadian migrants in the Pensacola area. The Canadians had come to Florida during the winter to work in the lumber industry and on the docks.[17] The trouble occurred then because of differences between the rhythm of the American and Canadian, or more properly between the sub-Arctic and semitropical work years.

A similar disjuncture exists now. For although most well-established Canadian sojourners wish only to vacation, certain migrant cohorts, probably differing significantly in average age by ethnic origin, and certain occupational groups wish to work in Florida and to extend their time and investment there. For example, many Italian Canadians who sojourn in Florida in the winter do so mainly because winter is the slack season for building and development in Canada. Such sojourners are neither of retirement age nor culturally prepared to lie about on a beach all day. With the construction trade skills so many of them have, and their entrepreneurial attitudes toward "keeping busy," maximizing opportunity, and owning land anywhere, Italian Canadians in Florida either join the underground economy or try to circumvent the laws that keep them from working.[18] No laws keep them from investing. One well-known Italian Canadian businessman is credited in the local Toronto folk wisdom with having made a fortune by knocking on farmhouse doors along the road from the Dade County airport to Miami and offering the locals—viewed as witless in the narrative—cash on the barrel head for their land on each of his annual trips (starting in the early 1950s). More typically, a Florida situation emerges for the migrants in which the Italian Canadian, most often an Italian-born immigrant to Canada, invests his *gruzzolo* (nest egg) in a Florida motel or small business but finds himself legally barred from working in his own establishment. Similar situations occur, of course, for other Canadian investors, and this may be one of the forces that draws Canadians of a given ethnic background together with Americans of the same group. For as David Potter has noted, nationalism is based on community of interest as well as community of culture.[19] The same principle obviously holds for ethnicity or ethnicism. A Calabrese or Fruilano businessman from Canada may well find through regionalist or ethnic "fellow feeling" a reliable American partner or front man. It is at this point that the migrant has reached the confused nexus where individual migration project, ethnoversion, and the commerce of migration meet.

A typical account from the oral testimony about Italian Canadian business in-migration follows:

One of the first persons that I know that went to Florida was a gentleman named Camillo. He was a real estate broker in Toronto; he moved to Florida and bought some little hotel and got into some kind of work with my uncle. His business wasn't to run a motel; his business was hustling, making a commission. So he got in with some kind of local real estate board, some local agents, and he went back and forth to Canada bringing clients. This was in Clearwater. My uncle is now involved there in a little motel, a bakery, and he bought a restaurant.[20]

Currently in Toronto at least ten travel agencies, dealing mainly with Italian Canadians, list Florida ahead of Italy as the chief migration target of their clientele.

The commerce of migration, as it goes on within the migrant's own subculture, is tied to the larger competition within the transport sector and among various land development schemes, many of which possess resonances of the earlier efforts of railway and state land agents to recruit immigrants from Europe. The role of the major carriers, charter airline companies, travel agents, and land developers in creating the Florida fever in Canada deserves the same sort of study as that devoted to the steamship cartels, *padroni*, and recruiters of nineteenth- and early twentieth-century Europe.[21] As in the earlier migrations, native carriers (in this case, Air Canada and Wardair) seek a monopoly in the moving of migrants; they encounter stiff competition from foreign carriers trying to break into the lucrative trade.

It is from this competition that some of the texts of the discourse within the migration tradition are born. The carriers seek to influence government regulations, and their subagents seek to influence public opinion. Discussions in the Canadian press about Amtrak plans to ship automobiles to Florida or about the fact that Scandinavian World Cruise Lines "will transport cars from Canada via New York every Saturday to Freeport in the Bahamas and from there to Miami" are countered by alluring flight, accommodation, and rental car "packages" offered by the airlines. At the turn of the century, the great Italian navigation companies lobbied the Italian government to stop the flow of migrants through Chiasso in northern Italy, across the Swiss border, and on to Le Havre or Liverpool to embark for America on the ships of Cunard, Allan, or Compagnie Générale Transatlantique (CGT).[22]

The monopolists based their argument on Italian national interests: the benefit to the economy that would come from controlling the migration trade and the importance of protecting one's emigrants from scoundrels and exploiters, presumably more often foreigners than one's own. In our time, the airports just across the U.S.-Canadian border at Buffalo and Detroit play much the same role as Chiasso did, and a glance at Sunday travel sections and supplements in Canadian newspapers shows how the foreign carriers and their subagents penetrate and influence the Canadian discourse. The struggle to draw guest resters to alternative targets within Florida, or elsewhere, leads to a proliferation of articles about the advantages to the less affluent of migrating to Myrtle Beach in South Carolina. Cancun, Acapulco, Hawaii, and a host of Caribbean islands such as St. Lucia and Jamaica are proposed as new and better targets than Florida. In the face of this barrage of information, the prospective migrants, like the millions of Europeans who made the choice to leave home before them, must use all of their cunning, their networks of trust, and the agents of the commerce of migration, in whom they wisely or wrongly place faith, to shape their migration project and choose their target. Whether it is because of the mores of our time or the inevitable impact of nonprint media, one is bound to observe that juxtaposing the advertising techniques of the carriers at the turn of the century and now stretches the comparative framework to the limits. The image of a prospective migrant of 1900 from a south Italian or east European village being confronted with the salacious and suggestive advertisements, ripe with beckoning stewardesses and half-clad women on beaches, which are the stock in trade of the new commerce of migration, boggles the mind. Perhaps it should not, perhaps images of New York in the rambling conversation of returned migrants, or the picture of the freedom of the American frontier drawn from a penny dreadful in the 1890s, served exactly the same purpose then as "come fly me" and smiling Air Jamaica stewardesses do now. The "organic intelligentsia" who serve the transport sector and the flim-flam men who call swamps future retirement villages use the same methods as agents always have to penetrate the prospective migrant's networks of trust.[23]

Chief among those methods is the use of one migrant's testimony to give "authentic voice" to advertising claims. (Critics might say it is the use of a Judas goat to lead the sheep peacefully to slaughter.) One way of using this technique is to offer well-known public figures a free trip and tour in return for sympathetic endorsements or press coverage. However, with the increasing sophistication about demographics and motivation that characterizes modern advertising, the planted story or advertising copy most often now includes the testimony of an individual who represents the ethnic, class, or age cohort one is trying to attract. Thus a planned community on the Florida west coast uses the testimony of a French Canadian woman to alter its once exclusively English-Canadian market. "It's gorgeous; the security is excellent, and the people were exceptionally courteous."[24] In one sentence from one of their own, prospective French Canadian migrants have been disabused of what the Market Facts of Canada survey for Florida's Tourism Department in 1982 had described as the chief negative stereotypes held about the target. Florida is, according to the lady from Quebec, neither a dull and unattractive landscape nor a dangerous place; more important, perhaps, its population, even in those areas with many English Canadians about, is not unpleasant to French Canadians.

Discussion of the details of the commerce of migration, as the last paragraphs testify, inevitably moves into an uncertain and disconcerting world. It is a world in which understanding the reality behind the written word of texts is even more a game of wits between reader and authorial intent than it is normally in our culture of "hype" (it is worth recalling that "hype" is short for hyperbole) and language as an amoral medium of capitalism. It is not just that an "organic intelligentsia," paid to be the speakers for the industry and committed to confusing reality with perceptions of reality, arises. In the face of the legions of travel columnists, flacks, and advertising copywriters who arise to see specific modes of transport, migration targets, land, and accommodations, counter texts appear.

This phenomenon has been studied for earlier migrations. Fernando Manzotti, in his *La Polemica sull'Emigrazione nell'Italia Unita,* for example, has shown how forces against Italian emigration (nationalists, those concerned with maintaining a cheap labor force, and those involved with the *patronato*—that is, interested in protecting their emigrants from exploitation by the agents of the commerce of migration or the receiving host society) tried to combat the promigration texts with their own texts.[25]

In less virulent form, the same antimigration forces exist in Canada. Just as emigration was viewed as a national shame and a mark of failure by many intellectuals in the newly unified German and Italian states at the end of the last century, so now does the Florida exodus afflict Canada. It occurs at a time when Canada is struggling to move beyond British colonialism and French-English dualism to nationhood. Even if the migration is, for the most part, temporary, it is a disturbing phenomenon to those involved in nation building since it affects the economy and weakens national sentiment. If the greatest threat to Canadian sovereignty and cultural uniqueness is the American Babylon to the south, then annual dosages of Americanism administered in a beguiling vacation atmosphere must rank with the invasion of American television as one of the chief impediments to the emergence of a Canadian people. (It would take a more elaborate and subtly Marxian argument than the one made here to demonstrate that the Canadian ski resort industry as well as Canadian developers and investors in West Indian vacation spots abet the discourse of the economic and cultural nationalists.)

Arguments against the crass commercialism of the United States, even the culturally extreme Floridian portion, carry little weight in a sending country that shares most of the same laissez-faire values as the target. Preliminary content analysis of English Canadian press coverage about Florida seems to suggest that the antimigration nationalists have found a theme for the discourse that they believe dampens enthusiasm, even if it does not significantly stem the flow.[26] That theme is an amalgam of varieties of criminality said to be rife in Florida. From accounts of land swindles to gangland violence, Florida is constantly and consistently portrayed in the news pages of the daily press and in magazines as a migration target that is potentially and almost randomly unsafe for Canadian migrants. In describing Florida as a perilous place, issues of race are scrupulously avoided, since it is one of the smug canons of the Canadian sense of superiority over the United States that white Americans are racist but white Canadians are not. On the other hand, Canadian media have been accused, with much justification, of trading in the stereotypes of the "mafia mystique" and of encouraging the association of Italians and French Canadians with organized crime and violence in the minds of its readers.[27]

Florida, as "Canada's eleventh province," is used to epitomize the *furia americana* generally and the far edge of capitalism that is the pathological world of organized crime's investments in "legitimate" business, the unbridled "free trade" in drugs, and dishonest land dealers in "cahoots" with corrupt public officials. Although it is clear that Florida has special problems in terms of crime, the insistence on exploiting them in the Canadian media always seems to contain the subliminal texts that these problems are the result of the "American way" and that such madness would not exist in the Canadian-administered Turks and Caicos Islands!

A glance at newspaper accounts about Florida in Toronto newspapers gives the reader a sense of the antimigration temper and the uses of the theme of criminality. Over a two year period, the following headlines appeared: "Mob War Threat in Florida," "Hard Sell for the Soft Life," "Weeks of Threat—Then Murder," "Miami Police Probing Slaying of Former Toronto Girl, 10," "Son of Slain Officer Charged with Murder," "Man Murdered in Miami Key Witness in Violi Trial," "Hail of Bullets in Miami Home Followed Threats." All of those headlines appeared in bold face, not in Toronto's tabloids, but in its more staid dailies; no headline items on Florida dealt with subjects other than crime or violence, except news of hurricanes. *The Fifth Estate*, a weekly news show broadcast on the CBC, Canada's national television network, kept pace with the print media. In fact a pattern of broadcasting unpleasant or frightening stories about Florida during the prime months of the migration—January, February, March—seems to emerge. Trailers for *The Fifth Estate* stories in 1982-1983 included the following:

Canadians make 2 million trips a year to Florida and some of them encounter the unpleasant reality of America's urban disease—crime in the streets. Of America's ten most crime-ridden cities, six are in Florida.

Hana Gartner investigates the murder of a young Canadian near a Florida racetrack and questions the justice system which allowed his accused killer to go free.

Many Canadians have bought time-sharing vacation homes in Florida and other southern climes. Some have found it to be a business of high-pressure salesmanship and broken promise. A few have found that when their condo goes bankrupt, they don't really own anything at all.

A final subtheme that appears in the texts about crime in Florida replicates some of the Italian discourse about emigration at the turn of the century.

The target is not only dangerous in itself; it is also the national refuge or playground for criminal elements from the sending country. Thus, the Italian press made much of *mafiosi* who had settled in New Orleans or *camorristi*, fugitives from justice in Naples who fled to New York to ply their black-hand extortionist trades. In the same manner, *The Fifth Estate* has quoted Florida law enforcement officers to the effect that there are three or four hundred Canadian criminals in the state, at least a hundred of them connected with organized crime. Other accounts imply the prevalence of Canadians of Italian, Jewish, and French descent among those criminals.

In a sense, the two faces of the discourse about migration in Canada predict and provide mortar for the "two sides of the ghetto walls," which are available to Canadians sojourning or settling in Florida. The risk of contamination or injury from too much fraternizing with the native "crackers" or the Yankee guest resters certainly is one reason for the in-gathering of anglophones (especially those of British descent) on the west coast and in long-established enclaves around Palm Beach as well as of francophones on the east coast. Much of the "stuff," to borrow Frederick Barth's infelicitous phrase, of Canadian ethnicity, its ethnocultural content and emblems, is present to characterize English Canadian enclaves on the west coast. Such "stuff" includes everything from Labatt's and Molson's beer, golf (somehow the Scottish antecedents of the game become more salient among Canadian Anglo-Celts in Florida, as witness the swank St. Andrew's Society at Delray) and lawn bowling, OHIP (Ontario's remarkably reasonable "socialized" delivery of medical services so important to older Canadian sojourners in the land of catastrophic medical costs) information, folksy radio shows like "Canada Calling," and copies of the *Toronto Star* and *Montreal Gazette* in corner stores.

Equivalent sets of francophone symbols and institutions exist around Fort Lauderdale. A recent headline in the *International Herald Tribune,* "Even in the Florida Sun, 2 'Canadas' Remain Apart," describes the self-contained world of the francophones.[28] They have their own newspaper, *Le Soleil de la Floride;* the old-timers are depicted as playing *petanque* (their variation of lawn bowling) and watching French Canadian soaps on satellite television from Montreal, while the younger generations root on the Montreal Canadian hockey club. Each of Canada's charter groups, then, has created its physical or psychic ghetto in the land to which they have migrated. Of course, over time individual migrants may increase their levels of acculturation and their social and cultural intercourse with non-Canadians. Citing the case of Maple Leaf Estates (a planned community near Port Charlotte, where the streets have names like Beaver Lane, Victoria, and Trillium Place and where sing-alongs of Canadian and British tunes are common, where men are asked to wear a top if they are not within ten feet of the pool) merely reminds us that the creation of enclaves through reflective ethnicization is but a weak plagiarism of the ethnocultures left behind.[29]

The question of Canadian national identity is in fact far more complex than the simple question of whether one culture or two (French and English) sustain Canadian migrants in Florida. More than a third of Canada's population is neither French nor British in origin. As noted earlier in this study, most of that one third of the population and their children do not have family or cultural roots that were implanted in Canada before World War II. Often they came as labor migrants to Canada in the 1950s and 1960s; many have been successful and now sojourn annually in Florida. The ambiance of Maple Leaf Estates would be as alien to them as it is to Floridians and French Canadians. It is equally unlikely that many of them would be at home as members of organizations such as the Canadian Society of St. Petersburg, Clearwater Canadian Fellowship, Canadian Club of the Palm Beaches, and the Newfoundland Society of Florida. So although the reassertion of national identity among migrants (a phenomenon that Karl Deutsch has described as an effort "to erase again and again the eroding effects of the new environment" on their culture) does go on among Canadians in Florida, the symbols of that assertion generally fail to attract any but the old stock.[30] Listening to the distinctly Anglo-Celtic content of syndicated Canadian radio shows such as Finlay MacDonald's "Canada Calling" is not apt to bring modern Canada's vibrant polyethnicity to mind.

In the Florida sun, there seems to be a shrivelling up of that post-colonial national identity that has had a slender growth in Canada, carefully nurtured by government and nationalist intellectuals since World War II. The key to that identity in Canada has been state encouragement of bilingualism and of multiculturalism (a limited species of cultural pluralism). Both those aspects of Canadianness lose meaning once the individual Canadian migrant leaves the polity for Florida. However, even if the idea of Canada as a cultural entity is generally a concept alien to the French and other non-British Canadian sojourners, that idea, stripped of concern with bilingualism or multiculturalism, becomes more important than ever for the true English Canadians. It is they who, because of their linguistic and cultural affinity to Americans, run the risk of the apocalypse, of losing their cultural distinctiveness. As a consequence, English Canadian culture and society becomes more specific, more ethnically Anglo-Celtic in Florida, and, in turn, less likely to attract or welcome those Canadians of other origins. There is scattered evidence that many Canadian ethnic groups (especially Italians, Jews, and Poles) fluctuate between patterns of settlement and networks of acquaintanceship that reflect their emergence as separate Canadian elements in the Florida guest rester mosaic or join concentrations of Americans in Florida from their own ethnic groups. Only detailed field work could give clear answers to questions about individual and group "negotiation of identity" among Canadian migrants, but those questions themselves suggest the validity of the Canadian nationalist intelligentsia's fear of the impact of mass vacationing in Florida on efforts to create a common Canadian national sentiment.

A final axiom, borrowed from the literature of migration studies, deals with the relationship of labor migration to capital investment from the migrant-sending country in the target country. Italian apologists for emigration always predicted that the presence of large numbers of Italians overseas would create markets of scale for the home country, would trigger investments, and would serve the general health of the mother country. Their critics saw such a potential diversion of investment money from the home economy as yet one more tragedy following on the drain of population, or they simply did not believe it could happen.[31] In 1974, Canadians owned $112 million in Florida land and businesses. The figure has risen rapidly since then. Canadians are the largest group of nonnationals in Florida. Canadian companies outnumber all other foreign corporations doing business in the state. Lately, some of Canada's major land developers and investors, such as Hudson's Bay Company, Royal Trust, and Crown Life Insurance have invested heavily in planned communities in south Florida.[32]

The sense of invasion that prompted this chapter was prescient; there will be more Canadian presence in Florida and that will, as all great migrations do, have major consequences for both the sending and receiving countries. A recent Toronto television production, called "The Great Canadian Conspiracy," featured a skit in which Ann Murray's popular musical hit, "Snowbirds," was played backwards. Between the grooves was the subliminal message, "the Canadians are coming, the Canadians are coming, surrender peacefully, you will not be harmed."[33] The Canadians are coming; they are not sure who they are, and neither are the Floridians, but the impact of their migration—seasonal, polyseasonal, and permanent—on the Sunbelt and on Canada is and will be a fruitful topic of study.

NOTES

This chapter is dedicated with understanding and forgiveness to those Canadian academic and governmental agencies that did not realize the topic's significance or assumed that my application for travel funds was simply a clumsy ploy to enable me to join other members of the Ontario middle classes basking in the Florida sun. It has become clear in the preparation of this chapter that only a global perspective on leisure sojourning makes sense. Research trips and participant observation among Scandinavians in Tenerife, Germans in Taormina, Britons in the Greek islands, as well as return trips to Florida, will be necessary if the study is to be carried on properly.

1. This statistic and others in this chapter, unless otherwise cited, are taken from *Florida: Canadian Travel Patterns and Attitudes Toward Vacations in Florida,* a 1982 report prepared by Market Facts of Canada for the Florida Department of Commerce, Division of Tourism (Tallahassee), or from, *1982 Florida Visitor Study: An Executive Summary* also Division of Tourism.

2. John Baxevanis, *Economy and Population Movements in the Peloponnesus of Greece* (Athens, Greece, 1972).

3. Stephen Castles, *Here for Good: Western Europe's New Ethnic Minorities* (London, 1984).

4. Ann Cornelisen, *Strangers and Pilgrims: The Last Italian Migration* (New York, 1980); and Jane Kramer, *Unsettling Europe* (New York, 1980), especially Chapter 2, "The Invandrare."

5. See Michael Piore, *Birds of Passage: Migrant Labour and Industrial Societies* (London, 1979); Paul Siu, "The Sojourner," *American Journal of Sociology* 58 (July 1952), 34-44; and Robert F. Harney, "The Commerce of Migration," *Canadian Ethnic Studies* 9 (1977), 42-53.

6. I wish to thank Palmacchio DiIulio of the Italian Canadian Benevolent Corporation and Gianni Grohovaz of the Multicultural History Society of Ontario for arranging interviews with migrants to Florida.

7. Clifford Geertz, *The Interpretation of Culture* (New York, 1973), especially Chapter 1 on "thick description." Many aspects of Canadian life in Florida would seem to provide the sort of cultural artifacts into which one can read a narrative.

8. See Brinley Thomas, *Migration and Urban Development* (London, 1972); and Frank Thistlethwaite, "Migration from Overseas in the Nineteenth and Twentieth Centuries," in Herbert Moller, ed., *Population Movements in Modern European History* (New York, 1964), 73-91.

9. *The Globe and Mail* (Toronto, May 14, 1987), 1, 18. An article titled "Sex and Sun: Risk of Aids" seemingly has not deterred determined visitors to Haiti. The article describes tourist hotels there owned by Quebecois.

10. The most recent manifestation of an idea that has been around for over a decade can be seen in *The Toronto Star* (January 16, 1987), p. A-17: "Canada Could Have Its Own Place in the Sun: Annexation of the Turks and Caicos."

11. Photocopied Canadian supplement to *1982 Florida Visitor Study* based on *Canadian Travel to the U.S.—1982* (report of the U.S. Travel and Tourism Administration).

12. For overviews on the historical study of the great migrations and some current methodologies, see Juliana Puskas, "Some Recent Results of Historic Researches on International Migration," *Notes Critiques: Acta Historica Academiae Scientiarum Hungaricae* 23 (Budapest, 1977), 151-69; Süne Akerman, "From Stockholm to San Francisco: The Development of the Historical Study of External Migration," *Annales: Academiae Regie Scientiarum Upsaliensis* (Uppsala, 1975), 5-46; and William Peterson, "A General Typology of Migration," *American Sociological Review* 23 (1958), 256-66.

13. For the concept of *"arrangiarsi,"* see Roberto Perin and Franco Sturino, eds., *Arrangiarsi: The Italian Immigrant Experience in Canada* (Montreal, 1987).

14. Berit Brattne, "The Importance of the Transport Sector for Mass Migration" in Harald Runblom and Hans Norman, eds., *From Sweden to America: A History of the Migration* (Minneapolis and Uppsala, 1976), pp. 176-200. Also see Chapters 6-8 of Philip Taylor, *The Distant Magnet* (New York, 1971).

15. Robert F. Harney, "Imagining America: Prospective Immigrants Confront the Migration Tradition" (paper presented at "A Century of European Migrations, 1830-1930: Comparative Perspectives" symposium, Immigration History Research

Center, University of Minnesota, November 1986). The paper is based on interviews carried out in Calabria with returned migrants and other townspeople.

16. Hermann Korte, "Guest Workers, Question or Immigration Issue: Social Sciences and Public Debate in the Federal Republic of Germany," in Klaus Bade, ed., *Population, Labor and Migration in 19th- and 20th-Century Germany* (New York, 1987), pp. 163-89.

17. Lucius and Linda Ellsworth, *The Deep Water City: A Pictorial and Entertaining Commentary on the Growth and Development of Pensacola, Florida* (Tulsa, Oklahoma, 1982), pp. 60-61.

18. *Weekend Magazine, The Globe and Mail* (Toronto, March 11, 1978), 22. "It's a mistake to think of Florida as a retirement community; one quarter of the Canadian visitors are under 30. Many others decide in their late 30s or early 40s that Canadian politics and economics have cheated them in some way." The remark suggests that analysis of a preselection of those who migrate with the intention to settle rather than sojourn/vacation might be possible.

19. David Potter, "The Historian's Use of Nationalism and Vice-Versa," *The American Historical Review* 67 (1961-1962), 937.

20. The quote is from an interview with the director of Columbus Centre, the major Italian cultural center in Toronto. From the interview, it seemed likely that research would actually turn up patterns of Italian regional migration to Florida, much like those of a few decades before from Italy. Certainly Canadian Friulani, Calabresi, and Molisani sustain different chains of migration to Florida.

21. See, for example, the various land and immigration agents discussed in Merle Curti and Kendall Birr, "The Immigrant and the American Image in Europe, 1860-1914," *Mississippi Valley Historical Review* 37 (1950-1951), 203-30.

22. See Robert F. Harney, "The Padrone and the Immigrant," *Canadian Review of American Studies* 5 (1974), 101-18; and Harney, "Montreal's King of Italian Labour: A Case Study of Padronism," *Labour/Le Travailleur* 4 (1979), 57-84. See also Johann Chmelar, "The Austrian Emigration, 1900-1914," *Perspectives in American History* 7 (1973), 275-380.

23. See Robert F. Harney, "Emigrants, the Written Word and Trust," *Polyphony: The Bulletin of the Multicultural History Society of Ontario* 3 (Winter 1981), 3-8.

24. Quoted in the *Tampa Bay Business Weekly* (July 1-7, 1984), 1-2.

25. Fernando Manzotti, *La Polemica sull'Emigrazione nell'Italia Unita* (Rome, 1969).

26. Toronto's three major newspapers, the *Star,* the *Globe and Mail,* and the *Sun,* were studied in terms of the language used to describe Florida. An interesting recent use of content analysis by a historian that offers special insights into this sort of study is Dale Knobel, *Paddy and the Republic: Ethnicity and Nationality in Antebellum America* (Middletown, Conn., 1986); see especially Appendix A.

27. On the Canadian media and the Mafia, see Robert F. Harney, "Italophobia: An English-Speaking Malady," *Studi Emigrazione* 12 (Rome, 1985), 6-44.

28. *International Herald Tribune* (April 11, 1987), 5.

29. David Macfarlane, "The Sunset Years on Florida's Gulf Coast: The Canadian Residents of Maple Leaf Estates Have Created a Retirement Colony Natural as Disney Land," *Saturday Night* (December 1983), 28-42.

30. Karl Deutsch, *Nationalism and Social Communication: An Inquiry into the Foundations of Nationality* (Cambridge, 1966), 121.

31. See Alberto Aquarone, "The Impact of Emigration on Italian Public Opinion and Politics," in Humbert Nelli, ed., *The United States and Italy: The First Two Hundred Years* (Washington, D.C., 1976), 133-46.

32. Barbara Yaffe, "Canadians Leading Investment in Florida," *The Globe and Mail* (Toronto, February 15, 1978), 7.

33. "Down Home," *Weekend Magazine, The Globe and Mail* (March 11, 1978), 22.

3

Jewish Migration to the Sunbelt

Deborah Dash Moore ———————————————

This chapter explores the intersection of migration, ethnicity, life cycle, and community through the study of Jewish migration to the Sunbelt cities of the United States. In 1987 this process has neither ceased nor apparently reached its peak. It continues to upset established verities predicting Jewish political behavior, religious activity, communal consciousness, and family life. Frequent migration at critical times in the life cycle has emerged in the years following World War II as the key element constantly creating and reshaping Jewish communal life. Since migration is a process of change within which individual and collective identity find expression, the essay begins with some basic observations on migration before turning to Jewish migration patterns in the aggregate. Here the distinctiveness of Jewish migration appears. In its concluding section the chapter suggests how these movements relate to the elaboration of ethnic identity for the individual at different points in the life cycle and for the community that receives the migrants.

Migration can be defined as a permanent or semi-permanent change of residence. Each act of migration involves origin and destination and overcoming intervening obstacles. Students of migration recognize that factors at the point of origin—termed "the push"—as well as those at the destination—or "the pull"—influence migration, but these stimulants or deterrents are filtered through individual perceptions. Thus, migration is always selective, drawing those who are predisposed to move, who resemble the people at the point of destination, and/or who are at certain transitional stages of the life cycle, usually without the encumbrances of children. Theorists of internal migration—as compared to immigration—argue that the volume of migration varies directly with the degree of diversity of areas and peoples. Occupational opportunities can also pull individuals and scatter them around the country.[1] In the nineteenth century, Jewish peddlers, and in the early twentieth century Jewish merchants, spread throughout much of the United States because of the lure of their work. During the past two decades, Jewish professionals—especially salaried ones, engineers, scientists, and academics—have followed similar migration paths dictated by their occupations.[2] Migration also produces a snowball effect, increasing in size and rate over time unless stopped by adverse economic conditions. Migration travels along well-defined streams that usually produce a counterstream.[3] Thus, there should be a counterstream of Jewish migration away from the Sunbelt cities back to the Northeast and Midwest. Indeed, recent studies suggest this to be so, although the gross figures available for Jews are still incomplete and reveal a rather small counterstream.[4]

Finally, theorists of migration argue that if migrants are responding primarily to the pull of place of destination they tend to be of high quality—or positively selected. Those who are leaving because of push at point of origin are negatively selected.[5] This aspect of migration theory does not adequately describe the situation of American Jews. The selective factors are complex and relate directly to ethnic identity. Those who stay behind do not necessarily succumb to inertia but instead maintain different ethnic values, reflected in their choice of residence, from those who choose to move.[6] For Jews, not only of the immigrant and second generation but also of the third and fourth generation, where you live says a lot about who you are. Personal identity is bound up with place of residence. In fact, this partially explains certain "reservations" held by some Jews who move to the Sunbelt, especially the elderly, regarding the location of their "home."[7]

Prior to World War II, Jewish migration to the Sunbelt hardly followed the laws of migration outlined above. Jews came south reluctantly. Often only the direct stimuli of two programs, one designed to relocate Jews from New York City and another created to channel immigration from overseas to the Southwest, induced Jews to leave the industrial port cities of the Northeast. Jewish philanthropists and social workers initiated the relocation program by establishing the Industrial Removal Office (IRO) at the turn of the century in response to a sudden increase of Jewish immigration from Rumania. The volunteer effort of B'nai B'rith lodges throughout the nation placed qualified Jewish immigrants in cities in the Midwest, South, and West. It quickly grew into a philanthropic social service that operated until the outbreak of World War I. The IRO sent male immigrants with industrial skills to cities where jobs ostensibly awaited them. IRO policy assumed that the breadwinner would subsequently bring his family so that the organizational cost of relocation would be minimal. Many Jewish communities in the Midwest, South, and West did receive significant numbers of east European Jews as a result of the IRO.[8]

The second program of planned migration, the Galveston plan, recruited qualified immigrants and their families in Europe and persuaded them to sail directly for Galveston, Texas, as a point of entry, rather than New York or other eastern seaboard cities. Once disembarked in Galveston, the immigrants were scattered through the Southwest. Only a handful remained in Galveston, though many settled in Texas. Like the IRO, the Galveston project, which was supported by the wealthy banker and prominent philanthropist Jacob Schiff, aimed to relieve the congestion of Jewish immigrants in New York City and thus deflect mounting anti-immigration sentiment. The beginning of World War I in Europe put an end to the project, although a handful of immigrants came west after the war to rejoin their families.[9] Both of these efforts at controlled migration, considered successful by recent historians, bear scant relationship to the current Jewish migration to the Sunbelt whose roots lie in the post-World War II socioeconomic changes affecting the United States and the Jews in the Northeast and Midwest.[10]

These socioeconomic changes produced what demographers and geographers call "regional convergence." This means that the outlying regions of the South and West grew more rapidly than the developed section of the country, bringing their economies, social patterns, and cultural styles closer to national norms.[11] But the term "Sunbelt" implies more than regional convergence. It is a category designed to link fundamentally different parts of the United States to help explain rapid social change. Nicholas Lemann, the executive editor of *Texas Monthly,* argues persuasively that journalists invented the Sunbelt concept in order to speak about new political and economic trends. In the mid-1970s he wrote, "millions of people were living in the Sunbelt without one of them realizing it. They thought of themselves as Southerners or Texans or Los Angelenos. . . . "[12] Though he is displeased, even Lemann admits the concept's utility and staying power; indeed, its loose definition that links a wide variety of locales helps to explain its popularity. To speak of Jewish migration to the Sunbelt involves writing an ethnic variation on the theme of regional convergence and rapid social change. Jews favored certain Sunbelt cities over others, and in these cities the rate of Jewish population growth often exceeded that of the general white population.[13]

Prior to widespread Jewish migration to the Sunbelt, the distinctive distribution of the Jewish population in the United States could be easily characterized.[14] In the 1950s Jews were concentrated in large cities in the Northeast and Midwest and were in fact the most highly urbanized ethnic or religious group in the United States. Ninety-six percent of American Jews lived in urban places in 1957, compared to 64 percent of the total U.S. population, and 87 percent of American Jews lived in cities of 250,000 or more inhabitants. In other words, Jews not only lived in cities, they lived in big cities. Although Jews were only 3.5 percent of the American population, they comprised 8 percent of the nation's urban residents. The high concentration in the New York City area, which held approximately 40 percent of American Jewry and had in the prewar era accounted for half of the

Jewish population of the United States, contributed to the distinctive Jewish demographic profile.[15]

This substantial concentration of close to two million Jews overshadowed all of the other cities, although Chicago, Philadelphia, Boston, and Los Angeles each had populations of over 100,000 Jews. In 1957, of the Sunbelt cities, only Los Angeles and Miami had the number to suggest a sizable, dynamic, and diverse Jewish community. By contrast, Atlanta had a mere 12,000 Jews; Phoenix and Tucson counted 6,000 and 5,000, respectively; Dallas and Houston contained 15,000 each (and Fort Worth just 3,000); while Denver held 18,000. In California, Los Angeles had already reached enormous proportions with 400,000, but San Diego held a mere 7,000, Oakland 12,000, and San Francisco 51,000. These small numbers suggest the relative insignificance of the Sunbelt cities for Jews, although the two important exceptions of Los Angeles and Miami portended future growth.

Yet by looking at the percentage of Jews in the urban populations, rather than at absolute numbers, it becomes clear that after New York City, where Jews made up close to one third of the population, comes Miami, where Jews constituted 29 percent of the population, followed by Los Angeles with 18 percent and Atlantic City (of all places) with 17 percent. Chicago, Cleveland, Boston, Philadelphia, cities known for their substantial, vibrant Jewish communities, actually ranked lower among the top ten cities with approximately 10 percent of their populations being Jewish.[16]

Scholars of American religious geography have concluded from Jewish spatial distribution that Jews prefer culturally pluralist environments, finding safety in diversity, although these environments also promote interethnic conflict and competition. The recent movement to those culturally more homogeneous Sunbelt cities—to which Jews bring a measure of pluralism and ethnic diversity—may reflect a lessening of the saliency of pluralism as a criterion for Jews' choice of residential location.[17] It can also be, to quote Wilbur Zelinsky, that "the amenities would appear to play a greater role in Jewish internal migration than is observed among gentile groups in view of the unusually strong Jewish representation in the Catskill counties, Atlantic City, and the larger Florida communities, and such western centers as Denver, Tucson, and Phoenix."[18] While provocative, such monocausal explanations of Jewish migration patterns explain less than a multicausal analysis that recognizes that what draws Jews to Denver may not be the same as what draws them to Tucson, that different types of Jews will settle in Miami from those who choose to retire to San Diego, that migration to cities like Charleston or New Orleans—which have also received Jewish migrants from the North—will mean something qualitatively as well as quantitatively different from migration to Atlanta or Houston.

In order to unravel the different threads, it is best to start with some general trends, shifts in the proportion of Jews residing in different parts of the country. To go back to the prewar era in 1937, 69 percent of America's Jews lived in the Northeast (most of these in New York City) and 19 percent in the Midwest, compared to 27 percent and 30 percent, respectively, of the general American population. By contrast, only 7 percent of America's Jews lived in the South and 5 percent in the West. To get a sense of the rate of change between 1956 and 1984: Phoenix grew from 6,000 to 35,000, Tucson from 5,000 to 18,000, Denver from 18,000 to 43,000, San Diego from 7,000 to 34,000, Hollywood from 2,500 to 60,000, Atlanta from 12,000 to 60,000, Houston from 15,000 to 28,000 (but Dallas from 15,000 to only 22,000), Las Vegas from 2,000 to 17,000, Albuquerque from 1,000 to 4,000, and Miami from 100,000 to 253,000. Other cities have had their suburban areas grow, as is the case of both Los Angeles and San Francisco.[19] As a result, Jews have an utterly new geographic perspective on the United States, one that could no longer be captured by Steinberg's famous *New Yorker* cover. Indeed, the Jerusalem *Post* has offered an updated version that accentuates the importance of Miami as well as several Texas towns. In the *Post*'s version, a map of the United States, consisting of a dominant New York and Washington along with several prominent Sunbelt cities separated by empty desert, replaces Steinberg's view from Manhattan where the territory west of the Hudson River contains only a few place names and cities.

What draws Jews to the South and Southwest causing them to revise their geography? On the most basic level some Jews are motivated primarily by occupational requirements. If second-generation Jews sought financial success and a residence to reflect their achievements, third-generation Jews who move to the Sunbelt cities seek status and a residence to accommodate it. The sociologist Sidney Goldstein argues that migration of these young, ambitious Jewish professionals and managers measures the strength of economic motives over the salience of kinship ties. It points to the predominance of the nuclear family among American Jews. It suggests that the residential clustering so characteristic of northern cities no longer appeals to these Jewish migrants and that they are discarding an earlier preference for areas of high Jewish concentration. It reveals the extent to which Jews have come to resemble other Americans in social and cultural behavior, even as their distinctive occupational concentration propels them across the continent in search of jobs.[20] The decision to migrate, usually made when a person is aged twenty to thirty-five, also coincides with that point in the life cycle after the completion of education, when the individual is ready to break family bonds and eager to establish an independent life and career. Migration becomes one of the rites of passage, much as Bar Mitzvah initiates the child into adolescence.[21]

But the dramatic growth of Jewish population in Sunbelt cities cannot just be accounted for by an analysis of the migration of young Jewish adults. First, this pattern of migration affects older Snowbelt cities as well as Sunbelt cities. For example, in Toledo, Ohio, the expansion of Toledo University and the centering of several large national retail chains in the city enticed aspiring Jewish academics and managers to Toledo. But Toledo experienced no growth in Jewish population because 45 to 60 percent of the young Jews raised in Toledo abandoned the city after college, seeking opportunity elsewhere.[22] Similarly, Kansas City has had a relatively static Jewish population since the 1950s, but this has disguised both a substantial in-migration of Jewish professionals and managers—approximately 37 percent of household heads in 1976—and a sizable out-migration of adult children of Kansas City household heads. In the 1970s fully half of those sons and daughters who grew up in Kansas City no longer lived there.[23] The data on Omaha reveal a similar pattern.[24] If we were speaking just of the migration of young Jews, then, we would have a less dramatic picture, one of stream and counterstream flowing across the continent. Second, the growth rates of some cities vary considerably and prompts the researcher to ask why Jews seem to prefer Houston to Dallas, Phoenix to Tucson, Denver and Atlanta but not Austin and Memphis. The occupational distribution net should scatter Jewish professionals and managers somewhat more randomly than it actually does. Finally, we know that we are not speaking only of young Jews in discussing Jewish migration to the Sunbelt because it is obvious that enormous Jewish communities of the elderly have been established throughout Florida and southern California and in the Southwest. The migration of these elderly Jews—at a different point in their life cycle, when they retire from work—has added the drama to Jewish migration to the Sunbelt. In fact, the large numbers of Jews moving to Florida accounts for most of the growth of Jewish population in the South.

Jewish migration to Miami represents perhaps the only mass migration of the elderly in modern times. Prior to the recent study by Ira Sheskin of the greater Miami Jewish community, population figures for Miami were skewed in the 1950s and early 1960s. Because of Miami's poor showing in fund raising, Jewish communal leaders consistently underestimated the number of Jews in Miami to justify the meager monies contributed. Only in 1967 in the wake of the Six Day War did Miami's contributions jump from $1.5 million to $5 million. By 1974 this had leaped to a new high of $19 million, at which point the Jewish Federation was no longer embarrassed to admit to a Jewish population of 200,000.[25] But the true record is more remarkable. Now we know that Miami's Jewish population doubled, steadily, every five years: from approximately 8,000 Jews in 1940, doubling to 16,000 by the end of the war, more than tripling to 55,000 by 1950, and then doubling again to 100,000 by 1955, until it reached 140,000 in 1960. Thereafter the rate of growth slowed, although by 1970 there were 230,000 Jews in the Miami area.[26] The 1970 National Jewish Population Survey confirmed what all knowledgeable observers saw: that Miami has a lot of elderly Jews. One third of all area household heads are over aged sixty-five compared with 21 percent nationally. In the Beaches section of Miami, where Jews make up around 70 percent of the total population, over half of all household heads were over aged sixty-five. In fact, the most recent study of Miami confirmed that the median age of the Beaches was sixty-seven. Together with a relative absence of household heads in their fifties, the concentration of elderly and widows stands out.[27]

The impact of migration on an ethnic community appears in the distinctiveness of Miami Jews. Only 4 percent of the current residents were born in Miami, an extraordinarily low figure even for a Sunbelt city. Los Angeles, another magnet city for migrants, contains 16 percent local-born Jews.[28] Many of the Miami Jews have low educational levels, and thus a different occupational profile from other Jewish communities. In Miami, three quarters of the working household heads—only 41 percent of householders fit that category—are proprietors of businesses or managers. Professional employment is quite low, as are income levels. In the Beaches and North Miami where many retired people lived, 40 to 50 percent of the Jews earned less than $6,000 annually in 1970, while only 3 percent had incomes over $40,000. Reluctant to acknowledge poverty in their midst, Jewish leaders have disputed these figures.

Other interesting aspects of migration to Miami have yet to be documented. For example, we know very little about the character of seasonal migration and the role of a leisure community. (In this regard, comparison with Atlantic City and Brighton Beach would be worthwhile.) Do the large numbers who have visited Israel—more than half of those aged sixty-five and over—reflect a penchant for travel or is there an ideological element involved? While Jews claim most often that climate prompts them to move to the Sunbelt, it is legitimate to ask whether the dream of the golden land—the immigrant's *goldene medina*—doesn't spur a search for a new home. Since previous migration influences subsequent migration, there may be a pattern of solving problems at critical points in the life cycle through migration. Additionally, there is little study of how peer group societies are created, and scant analysis of the generational separation of immigrant from second and second from third that is so characteristic of the Miami community.

There is evidence of different migration relationships between selected northern and southern cities. The data on Denver, among the best of the contemporary community surveys, illustrate the point. The information on Jewish migration to Denver gathered in 1981 revealed that the northerners made up 10 percent of the recent migrants of the past five years, and of these only 4 percent came from New York. Considering that New York Jews constitute a third of the American Jewish population, this is a rather small percentage. (It is much higher for Houston, for example.) This handful of New York Jews do not randomly distribute themselves in Denver but tend to cluster in different parts of the city from the midwesterners, who disperse over larger sections of town. Migrants from the West and South to Denver present an altogether different pattern. The distinctive New York distribution (now to Aurora, previously to Boulder) correlates with a unique group of New York Jews who choose to come to Denver. Denver appears to attract single individuals, single-parent families, and mixed households (a euphemism for unusual "families") disproportionately from New York, while it disproportionately attracts married couples with children from the South, West, and Midwest.[29] Although we can only speculate what single parents or unconventional families see in Denver, clearly New York Jews perceive a different Denver from Chicago or Cleveland or Los Angeles Jews.

Unfortunately, the Denver survey does not indicate the impact these migrants have made upon the city, but the data from Houston suggests certain changes that correlate with a rapidly growing Jewish population. In 1955 there were a mere 12,000 Jews in Houston of whom over 50 percent were natives of the city. By 1970, as a result of migration, of the 20,000 Jews in Houston only a third were native, although 52 percent were southern born. A full 15 percent came from New York. Nevertheless, irrespective of their length of residence in Houston, these people often remained "newcomers," the word used to describe anyone not socialized in the Houston milieu. The arrival of these migrants corresponded with shifts in the location of the Jewish community from the southeast to the southwest of the city. Characteristic of the new neighborhood were garden apartments, often built by such Jewish builders and developers as Harold Far, Jenard Gross, and Allen Field. Thus, Houston in the 1970s came to duplicate some aspects of New York suburban life, with Jews living in apartment buildings—indeed, some buildings occasionally housed only Jews—while the non-Jewish majority resided in single-family dwellings. In fact, one third of the Jews in Houston lived in apartments, the remainder in single-family homes. Although apartment living correlated with income—the more money, the more likely to own a house—this was not true for the upper-middle-income bracket of those earning annually between $20,000 and $30,000. Nonetheless, a suburban lifestyle was accessible to many Jews, and veritable newcomers often assumed that all Jews in Houston were rich. The moderate-income people (those earning between $7,000 and $15,000 annually in 1970, or two thirds of the Jews) conformed to middle-class living patterns and were not particularly visible or isolated from the rest of the Houston community. Northeasterners also did not earn as much as native Texans: Their median annual income was $23,000 in 1976, compared to the Texans' $27,000 (but midwesterners earned the least, only $19,000). Perhaps to compensate, the northeasterners had smaller families than the natives.[30]

What has been the impact of Jewish migration to the Sunbelt cities? Here we enter the realm of impressionistic data where it is difficult to separate the influence of the migrants from other changes transforming the Sunbelt cities. The migration has coincided with an upsurge of Jewish ethnic assertiveness—for example, challenging the performance of Christmas plays in the public schools. Jews have become more identifiable as a group even as there are perhaps fewer differences separating them from the rest of society. The natives are not necessarily pleased with this revival of an ethnic identity. One rabbi of the prestigious Wilshire Boulevard Temple in Los Angeles, a monument of wealthy, assimilated Reform Jews, complained bitterly that "this is a different ballgame today—you've got another Brooklyn here. When I came here, it was Los Angeles. Now it's a Brooklyn." Perhaps the Dodgers' move foreshadowed the future more than anyone wanted to admit. Rabbi Edgar Magnin went on to explain:

I have no reason to go into the ghetto. One of my grandparents came out of it. I don't want to go back into it. I see these guys with their yarmulkes eating bacon on their salads at the club. They want to become more Jewish, whatever that means. It's not religious, it's an ethnic thing. What virtue is there in ethnic emphasis? Black isn't more beautiful than white, and white isn't more beautiful than black and we have beautiful Jews and we have stinkers, and so does everybody else. . . . You know, it's insecurity, the whole thing is insecurity. Roots, roots, roots—baloney![31]

Others point out that the new migrants have brought a heavier Jewish baggage—religious as well as ethnic—than previous settlers and that this has enriched the community as well as making it stick out. One rabbi in Atlanta argued that moving was a way of reconstituting ties. Jews from New York especially found a need to affiliate with a synagogue, he averred, a need for a "self-image" that they never felt before in the densely populated Jewish neighborhoods.[32] Although the numbers of Orthodox Jews grew very little during the 1970s, membership in Conservative and Reform synagogues in Atlanta increased 50 percent from 1970-1984.[33] Along with Jewish religious culture, Jewish gastronomic culture has spread. As one observer of the Dallas Jewish community notes, the natives can now recognize a bagel when it is shown to them. But the same observer also pointed out, with less sympathy, that there was a kosher deli within walking distance of Neiman Marcus, as if the two did not mix comfortably. Obviously, for this observer, kashrut is not yet fashionable.[34]

But studies of Denver and Los Angeles tend to throw doubt on these perceptions. Both reveal an amazingly low level of affiliation, high rates of intermarriage, and a strong identification with Israel. Jews increasingly appear to live in a psychological enclave, not an ecological one, that is supported by strong in-group Jewish occupational patterns. In Los Angeles 60 percent of the Jews work for a firm in which the owner-managers and the fellow workers are mostly or somewhat Jewish. Although Jews have moved away from religious and secular institutions and abandoned Jewish neighborhoods that provided a framework for socialization, they continue to define themselves as Jews, as members of an ethnic group. Israel is the most powerful indicator of Jewish identity though most Jews neither are Zionists nor have they visited Israel.[35] These contradictory tendencies are hard to correlate with migration patterns. More obviously related to migration are the new cultural communities that sustain memory and generate nostalgia as they forge a relationship between city of origin and place of migration. As early as the 1950s in Los Angeles, there appeared Jewish *landsmanshaftn* based on city of origin in the United States. Several dozen of these modern *landsmanshaftn* nourished the identity of Jews from such cities as Omaha, Milwaukee, Minneapolis, and Chicago.[36]

Such innovations suggest that Jews who choose to transplant themselves in Sunbelt cities may share more in common with their immigrant predecessors than with their acculturated peers who choose not to migrate. American Jewish historians have recognized that the distinctiveness of American Jewish culture and community rests as much upon renewal from without as upon regeneration from within.[37] The dramatic changes of the postwar decades may, in fact, disguise even more remarkable continuities. Despite all of the internal migration, Jews remain a clustered segment of the American population, distinctive in their geographical distribution (and still heavily concentrated in the Northeast, at least compared to the general white population).[38] The search for the golden land—the Jewish vision of the American dream—still may propel Jews across the United States and shape the contours of their collective and individual identity more than they would like to admit.

NOTES

1. Everett S. Lee, "A Theory of Migration," in George Demko, Harold Rose, and George Schnell, eds., *Population Geography: A Reader* (New York, 1970), pp. 290-98; Donald J. Bogue, "Internal Migration," in Philip M. Hauser and Otis Dudley Duncan, eds., *The Study of Population: An Inventory and Appraisal* (Chicago, 1959), pp. 297-99.

2. Arthur Goren, *American Jews* (Cambridge, Mass., 1982), 56-61.

3. Lee, "A Theory of Migration," p. 295.

4. See, for example, the *Philadelphia Inquirer* (April 15, 1984), 1, 12A; the *New York Times*, (April 2, 1984), C12.

5. Lee, "A Theory of Migration," pp. 296-97.

6. See Jack Kugelmass, *The Miracle of Intervale Avenue* (New York, 1986), for reasons given by Jews who choose not to move. Calvin Goldscheider, in "Residential Concentration, Migration, and Jewish Continuity" (paper presented at Conference on Jewish Settlement and Community in the Modern Western World, March 21-23, 1983), disputes this contention, arguing that economic factors override any ethnic values.

7. For a more extended discussion of this concept, see my article, "The Construction of Community: Jewish Migration and Ethnicity in the United States," in Moses Rischin and Robert Harney, eds., *The Jews of North America* (forthcoming).

8. Peter Romanofsky, " . . . To Rid Ourselves of the Burden. . . . ': New York Jewish Charities and the Origins of the Industrial Removal Office, 1890-1901," *American Jewish Historical Quarterly* 64 (June 1975), 331-43.

9. Bernard Marenbach, *Galveston: Ellis Island of the West* (Albany, N.Y., 1983), 181-95.

10. Gerald D. Nash, *The American West Transformed: The Impact of the Second World War* (Bloomington, Ind. 1985), pp. 56-74, 82-87.

11. Otis L. Graham, Jr., "From Snowbelt to Sunbelt: The Impact of Migration," *Dialogue* 59 (1983), 11-14.

12. Nicholas Lemann, "Covering the Sunbelt," *Harper's Magazine* (February 1982), reprinted in *Dialogue* 59 (1983), 24.

13. Ira M. Sheskin, "The Migration of Jews to Sunbelt Cities" (paper in possession of author), 26-27.

14. Before turning to examine the dramatic shifts in Jewish population in the last thirty years, I must pause to indicate the major problems afflicting Jewish demography in the United States where interpretation of the first amendment has mandated that there be no official census of religious identification. Statistics on Jewish population depend largely upon Jewish communal estimates—and these vary greatly in their accuracy as well as being subject to bias (as in the case of the Miami community, as we shall see). In the 1940s and 1950s Jewish organizations used the Yom Kippur method, which involved counting the number of children absent from public school on the high holidays and then estimating based upon a ratio of children to adults. Recently, this method has yielded to the distinctive Jewish names approach, which uses telephone surveys. Analysis of census data on Yiddish as a mother tongue also produces relatively reliable figures. The standard source of these figures is the *American Jewish Yearbook*, which will be used unless another source is indicated.

15. Sidney Goldstein, "American Jewry, 1970: A Demographic Profile," *American Jewish Year Book* 72 (1971), 37-38.

16. Wilbur Zelinsky, "An Approach to the Religious Geography of the United States: Patterns of Church Membership in 1952," in Demko et al., eds., *Population Geography: A Reader*, p. 355.

17. William M. Newman and Peter L. Halvorson, "American Jews: Patterns of Geographic Distribution and Change, 1952-1971," *Journal for the Scientific Study of Religion* 18 (June 1979), 190-92.

18. Zelinsky, "Religious Geography," 358.

19. Sheskin, "The Migration of Jews to Sunbelt Cities," 21, 25.

20. Goldstein, "American Jewry, 1970," 37, 44, 51.

21. Lee, "A Theory of Migration," 292-97.

22. Goldstein, "American Jewry, 1970," 50.

23. Avron C. Heligman, "The Demographic Perspective," in Joseph P. Schultz, ed., *Mid-America's Promise: A Profile of Kansas City Jewry,* (Kansas City, 1982), pp. 389-91.

24. Murray Frost, "Analysis of a Jewish Community's Outmigration," *Jewish Social Studies* 44 (1982), 231-38.

25. See Gladys Rosen's concluding chapter of her history of Miami Jews, "The Jewish Community of Miami: Response and Epilogue" (unpublished ms. in possession of author), 8, 20.

26. Ira M. Sheskin, "Demographic Study of the Greater Miami Jewish Community: Summary Report" (Report, The Greater Miami Federation, 1984), 4.

27. Sheskin, "Demographic Study," 8.

28. Sheskin, "The Migration of Jews to Sunbelt Cities," 28.

29. Eleanor P. Judd and Bruce A. Phillips, *Denver Jewish Population Study* (Denver, 1981), pp. 38, 41, 75.

30. Elaine S. Maas, "The Jews of Houston: An Ethnographic Study" (Ph.D. dissertation, Rice University, 1973), 66, 82, 86, 100-5.

31. "The Jews of Los Angeles: Pursuing the American Dream," *Los Angeles Times* (January 29, 1978).

32. Robert Lindsey, "Jews in the Thousands Join Migration to Sun Belt," *New York Times* (March 29, 1984), A16.

33. *Metropolitan Atlanta Jewish Population Study: Summary of Major Findings* (Atlanta, 1985), p. 9.

34. Irving L. Goldberg, "The Changing Jewish Community of Dallas," in Jacob R. Marcus, ed., *Critical Studies in American Jewish History,* (Cincinnati, 1971), p. 344.

35. Neil C. Sandberg and Gene N. Levine, "The Changing Character of the Los Angeles Jewish Community" (Los Angeles: Center for the Study of Contemporary Jewish Life of the University of Judaism, 1981), 2-3, 9.

36. Lloyd P. Gartner, "The History of North American Jewish Communities: A Field for the Jewish Historian," *The Jewish Journal of Sociology* 7 (June 1965), 26.

37. Henry L. Feingold, "Introduction," *American Jewish History* 71 (December 1981), 182.

38. Sheskin, "The Migration of Jews to Sunbelt Cities," 26.

4

Ethnicity, Urbanization, and Historical Consciousness in Savannah

Gary W. McDonogh

Post-World War II patterns of migration and urbanization in the Sunbelt South have brought new intensity and variety to ethnic consciousness. Nonetheless, ethnicity in southern cities also has been shaped by prior experiences of immigration, urbanism, and conflict. Indeed, "older" southern urbanites often anchor their group identity in a consciousness of the past, as well as its representation in religious or social institutions and political and economic action. This means that new immigrants must define themselves not only in relation to shared social labels—whether ethnic, religious, or racial—but also with regard to categories that appear closed to them because of their lack of participation in or interpretation of past events.

The interactions of social categories, history, and the changing population of southern cities may be suggested by a single anthropological case study: the Roman Catholic population of Savannah, Georgia. The Catholics of the Savannah metropolitan area form a limited religious group that is at the same time divided on the basis of race, class, ethnic origin, family, and work experience; the Catholic population also has been undergoing change as a result of new migration. Based on field work conducted since 1982, which includes collections of written documents, life narratives, and reflections on the formation of religious and civic identity, it is possible to observe the interaction of historical consciousness and ethnic identity. Work with several hundred Catholics of diverse backgrounds reveals that their historical consciousnesses, at least, form an important constitutive element of social groups and also provide bases for interpretation of the present and the future.[1]

To analyze the construction of urban group identity and its relationship to both historical consciousness and historical change, this chapter begins with an overview of Savannah and the Catholic experience there. Discussion concentrates on the perception of two key clusters of events for Catholics in twentieth-century Savannah: a "time of troubles" in the 1920s and "a time of changes" in the 1960s. The chapter suggests how structure has implied reproduction—that is, how a pattern of historical consciousness shapes perception of present and future events and defines the range of potential reactions and changes to be introduced by newly arriving immigrants. Finally, the conclusions set forth some programmatic hypotheses for future consideration in dealing with race, class, and ethnicity in a changing urban South.

Savannah today has 144,000 inhabitants, making it the third largest city in Georgia. It also serves as a port and regional center for Atlantic coastal development in the region's so-called coastal empire. Savannah combines the cultural and social values of the Old South with characteristics of the emergent Sunbelt. Its population grew by nearly 20 percent between 1970 and 1980, but this barely reversed urban flight after 1960 when the city's inhabitants had neared 150,000.[2] Savannah's urban plan focuses on a carefully restored historic center rather than the skyscrapers of Atlanta, Tampa, or Houston, but its suburbs include leisure-oriented developments and resorts. The city's economy has long depended on the port, the military, and key industries like the Savannah Sugar Refinery, Union Camp, and American Cyanimid.[3] Nonetheless, Savannah has also expanded into the high technology, real estate, and tourism markets associated with Sunbelt capitals. Gulfstream Aerospace, for example, is an international leader in the production of customized corporate jets.[4] These developments in turn have led to new immigration to the city and its metropolitan region. These immigrants, however, find themselves in a world whose politics, economics, and social interaction long have been defined by complex interactions of race, religion, and ethnicity. In order to be accepted into the public life of the city and to shape urban life to their own needs and goals, they must learn to deal with the histories and heritages of Savannah as they form and reform through time.

History, indeed, permeates many aspects of urban life. In addition to Savannah's renowned architectural preservation, the Georgia Historical Society, and a wealth of ethnic or genealogical heritage societies, museums, pageants, and publications also keep the past alive in Savannah. Urban renewal and the profits of tourism have enhanced further the appreciation of Savannah's inheritance in architecture and ambience. Both generic southern historical souvenirs and specific Savannah history have entered a thriving marketplace; promotional literature, guidebooks, inns, and a commercial historical exposition sell the presence of the past to those who visit the city.[5]

This public history is still only a part of the total historical consciousness of the community. Beyond such formal "texts," the interpretation of the past events is part of the conscious differentiation of many competing groups within the city. These versions of history are ambiguous, embedded in complex urban communities with fluid boundaries, as well as in struggles over who may speak for history. To talk of the meaning of ethnicity and group differentiation in contemporary Savannah, the anthropologist must ask what its histor*ies* have been, how they diverge, who feels that they have legitimacy to present or to celebrate them, and what such histories mean within the ongoing formation of urban life.

Rights to public history are clearly demarcated by urban power relations, especially as the latter are stratified with regard to race. As in other parts of the South, development has not always helped those in the lower classes, whose status has been maintained by racial prejudice and economic disadvantage. Savannah today is roughly 49 percent black; the county as a whole is 38 percent black. Although blacks have made strides in local politics, business, and culture since the civil rights movements of the 1960s, generations of powerlessness and poverty imprison many in run-down neighborhoods and inferior educations.[6]

Religion, too, plays an important role in Savannah life, social categorizations, and power. Over 250 congregations compete for the affiliations of its citizens. Baptists represent the largest single domination; Presbyterians, Methodists, Lutherans, Episcopalians, Catholics, Jews, and smaller Christian sects also play diverse but influential roles. The Roman Catholic population represents slightly over 10 percent of the total urban population, scattered among ten parishes.

Religious divisions are also an idiom for the ethnic, class, and racial divisions of secular society. The urban elite, for example, has traditionally been Episcopalian, although divided into black and white congregations. In both cases their heritage can be traced to the founding English families of the colony. Lutherans from Salzburg settled in nearby Ebenezer in 1734, and a German Lutheran church was also present in the city by the 1750s. Presbyterians have old and imposing presences in the black and white community as well. Baptists and Methodists are also associated with a Scotch-Irish or "Cracker" heritage, while other Europeans are represented among the Roman Catholics, the Greek Orthodox church, and the three synagogues formed in successive waves of migration since the eighteenth century. Congregationalists, the oldest Baptist churches, African Methodists, Episcopalians, Presbyterians, and Catholics tend to define the black middle-class. Charismatic and storefront congregations appeal to the poor and oppressed, black and white, of the city.[7]

Catholicism emerged in a context of power and social division set by earlier settlers in Georgia. Catholics were, for example, unwelcome in the colonial period. That fact denies Catholics participation in historical reconstruction and even genealogical appropriation of the colonial period, and it has overshadowed their history in relation to other older congregations. At the same time, it sets Catholics apart historically as a "marginal group" that has since become established. Competition over history also stimulates Catholic reference to the precedent of Spanish missionaries prior to the establishment of Georgia. As one writer observed in 1967:

To say that the Diocese of Savannah has a Catholic history older than any other area in the United States except north Florida seems incredible. To realize that three hundred years ago there were almost as many Catholics in the area as there are today seems unbelievable. Yet, these are the facts of history.[8]

The first Catholic masters and slaves from Saint-Dominque arrived in Savannah in the late 1700s. White French families remained the local Catholic elite for decades. By today, most have been absorbed through intermarriage with later immigrant families so that they no longer constitute a coherent and self-identifying French group. The recently formed French Heritage Society, for example, includes Jews, Huguenots, and Cajuns as well as descendants of early Catholic settlers.

Blacks outnumbered whites in early baptismal records, but were eventually eclipsed by new immigrants and different demands on the Catholic church. Irishmen arrived in the early nineteenth century to work in ports and on railroads. By the 1840s the Savannah Catholic community was able to support both a church and a school and was able, thereby, to function as a socially distinctive community. In 1850 Savannah had a large enough Catholic presence to separate from Charleston as a diocese. Its territory included all of Georgia and Florida. It also formed a cemetery distinct from public institutions, again emphasizing a demarcated Catholic identity.[9]

Irish immigration to the city grew through the nineteenth century. In 1865 the Catholic population on the west side of the city was sufficient to justify a second church, St. Patrick's. By the end of the century, a class division between "lace curtain" and "shanty" Irish was part of urban Catholic life. Meanwhile, the Catholic population became more diverse. Germans arrived by the last decades of the century, although they did not form a separate national parish, as was common in the North. German-speaking Benedictines, however, did handle a somewhat integrated urban parish, and briefly produced a German magazine. Italians arrived between 1870 and the early 1900s, often lured by the fishing trade. After 1917, furthermore, 400 Cajuns came from Louisiana to work at the sugar refinery constructed in nearby Port Wentworth.[10]

Black Catholicism in Savannah grew primarily through conversion rather than immigration. Educational missions were encouraged by the bishops after the Civil War.[11] Interest in the blacks remained sporadic, however, until the arrival of the Franciscan Missionary Sisters of the Immaculate Conception in the late nineteenth century and the Society of African Missions of Lyon between 1905 and 1907.[12] Both orders of white, foreign-born religious fostered schools and parishes for blacks; a black order of nuns was

also founded in Savannah. Black parishes recruited from Protestant families through the promise of quality neighborhood schools. Children would
convert, often leading their siblings and parents to Catholicism thereafter.
Hence, education and the school became the core of parish and community
life.

Immigrant Catholic acceptance by a wider southern society was slow
through the end of the nineteenth century. In 1895, for example, an anti-
Catholic group invited the notorious ex-priest Joseph Slattery to speak on
the hidden secrets of the church. A riot ensued.[13] Anti-Catholicism flared
into the open again in the 1910s with the Georgia demagogue Tom Watson,
at one time a classic agrarian populist who rebuilt his career on hatred for
Jews, blacks, and Catholics. His rhetoric vilified Catholicism by reference
to the same stereotypes used to denigrate blacks: "The African belief in the
conjure bag, is a progressive state of mind, compared to this Roman Catholic
belief in saints that secure tenants for vacant houses."[14] The Ku Klux Klan
also focused its venom on the same groups; torchlight parades of Klansmen
lit the Irish and black ghettos of the city. Nonetheless, anti-Catholic incidents
in Savannah were much less frequent and violent than in rural Georgia. The
Savannah Morning News, for example, opposed Tom Watson and celebrated
his repeated defeats in Chatham County in the 1920 senatorial race.

By the early 1920s, Catholics organized a statewide educational and pro-
pagandistic group, the Catholic Laymen's Association of Georgia, to fight
Georgia nativism. Confrontation continued through the decade, however,
especially in outlying rural areas, and anti-Catholicism was present in state
politics even if not so localized in the city.[15] The bishop and Savannah
Catholics were active in this struggle. In 1928 the Catholic Democratic
candidate for president, Al Smith, did poorly in the state but made a strong
showing in Chatham County, an indication of the sociopolitical divisions
between countryside and city and also a measure of the effectiveness of an
Irish-American Catholic political machine in Savannah. Public manifesta-
tions of sectarian hatreds declined during the Depression and World War II,
although they continued to crop up in sports rivalries and other minor social
forms for years.

Other urban changes indicate the increasing solidarity of Catholics in the
city. Benedictine Military Academy, founded early in the twentieth century,
became the forge for new coalitions of Catholic and non-Catholic leaders
in opposition to the public Savannah High School. Education, however, was
only one aspect of the increasing cohesion and influence of Irish Roman
Catholics. The Irish-American community grew to become a powerful presence in urban machine politics and still generally retains an alderman on
the city board. Socially, the history of Savannah's Hibernian Society reca-
pitulates the transformation of the Irish from poor immigrants to a major
Catholic bloc. It was established in 1812 as a beneficient society through
which wealthy Irish and sympathizers, including Protestants and a leading

Jew, could aid their indigent immigrant compatriots. Bishop John England was a frequent banquet speaker by the 1820s and 1830s, although the first Catholic president of the society was not elected until 1856, and Protestants and Catholics alternated thereafter for sixty years. Today, this association has become the consummate symbol of the social and economic triumph of the Irish Catholic—an elite, primarily Catholic club so exclusive applicants wait decades for acceptance. This organization thus maintains the structure of an existing ethnic group into its third and fourth generation rather than embracing new immigrants. Yet St. Patrick's Day celebrations have grown from an ethnic into a communitywide celebration, including serving "green grits," and a variety of shops and bars also offer a more commercial manifestation of "Irishness."[16]

Racial barriers separating Savannah Catholics remained intact. As the Catholic population increased in numbers and wealth, it also moved within the city. Five new predominantly white and suburban parishes were founded between 1940 and 1980, while a downtown church, St. Patrick's, was torn down in 1941. A new Catholic high school, St. Pius X, was built for blacks in the 1950s.[17]

Some Savannah Catholics, especially clergy, became involved in the struggle for civil rights by the 1930s, but serious reforms within the diocese were only gained by the black community in the 1960s. Parochial schools integrated, followed slowly and acrimoniously by such organizations as the Knights of Columbus; some women's associations remained all white.

The 1960s also witnessed major internal reforms in worldwide Roman Catholicism that deeply affected Savannah. In the Second Vatican Council, Pope John XXIII fostered a new era of discussion and reform that led to far-reaching changes in ritual, governance, and individual participation. These changes, in turn, spurred further attempts at innovation and counter reactions in the 1970s. In the midst of this, Savannah received a new bishop, who attempted physical reforms in the cathedral, which had served for many years as a symbol of the endurance of the local community. The reforms followed hierarchical guidelines to turn the altar toward the people and modernize the sanctuary space, but heated debate ensued, primarily over rights to control the cathedral, in which ecclesiastical politics were interpreted at times according to categories of resident versus outsider.[18]

This debate has by now faded into the past, while other changes continue in Catholic and Savannah life. One leader estimates that as many as 25 percent of all new immigrants are Catholics. Older downtown parishes are dwindling, while suburban parishes explode. Some of the suburban parishes, however, have continuous turnover, unlike the generations of faithful who used to constitute the parish family. In others, struggles between old populations and new suburbanites may divide the congregation. New groups also have arrived, exemplified in the formation of a Vietnamese Catholic community and parish.

The above brief historical survey of Savannah Catholicism, drawn from oral and documentary sources, identifies some of the movements and events that form part of the consciousness of individuals or groups and the building blocks of their historical narratives. While the church leadership might champion erudite memories, such as the recognition of Spanish martyrs in the precolonial friar's missions to the Guale Indians of the sea islands, which establish a historical "priority" for Catholics in the region, such obscure events dredged up from a distant past inspire little interest among today's lay Catholics. Tom Watson, Al Smith, or Vatican II are within the life experience and life narratives of more ordinary Catholics. Here, the selection and interpretation of such events becomes striking in understanding ethnic, race, and class consciousness. (Unfortunately, a lack of early texts from this same group does not permit us to analyze the formation of historical consciousness at earlier stages of Catholic adaptation.) The experiences of Catholics during the 1920s and 1960s represent major landmarks in historical narrative, but they are subject to widely variable interpretations. The first, denied to recent migrants, reinforces many of the social differences that define Savannah Catholicism. The latter is a continuing process that links old and new, while perhaps suggesting new divisions.

The 1920s remain vivid in the recollections of the Irish-American families who formed the bulk of the older white Catholic population in the Savannah sample. Most of these households were working class in the 1920s and located in Irish ghettos that had formed in industrial or port sectors of the city. An exodus to newer and more desirable sections of town began around World War I, although old neighborhoods like Yamacraw or the Old Fort continued to act as social referents for many families. These families attended Cathedral parish or St. Patrick's Church and School.[19]

The memories of elderly informants as well as the tales handed down from parents and grandparents to those in their thirties and forties recall job discrimination and friendships broken by sectarian bitterness. Some Irish Americans found Protestant children in the neighborhood forbidden to play with them. Many recalled Klan marches and other displays of bigotry.

Most older informants used key figures like Tom Watson to frame and explain the events. Watson could still inspire a vivid hatred sixty years after his death. A man in his eighties, for example, still spoke with venom in 1982:

Tom Watson, he'll burn in Hell. If he isn't in Hell, I'll never go. He had them pass the act to inspect the convents because he said there was a tunnel so nuns could go and sleep with priests. And yet he sent his granddaughters to Catholic schools!

The endpoint of the time of troubles was given variously as 1928 or the Depression. The former date was a definite landmark of triumph in the political arena. With the Depression, people were perceived as "getting more used to each other." Shared poverty became shared experience in historical recollection. Other families perceived more gradual changes, reflecting their social mobility and incorporation in the workforce of the city and the break-up of the Irish ghettos. This produced a fading away rather than a demarcation of the period as life settled into a truce. One Irish Catholic politician was praised because he moderated fairly among groups in his machine: "If a job was for Jews, a Jew got it; if it was Irish, an Irishman got it; if it was Cracker. . . . " Meanwhile, Savannah Catholics formed an Irish-American identity built around Benedictine football, the parish, the old neighborhood, and the parade that has also been transmitted from generation to generation.

Ironically, however, Irish-American identity has often been inconsistent with a strong Irish national identity within the clergy and sisterhood of the Catholic church. While Irish-American families sent daughters to the Sisters of Mercy or the Sisters of St. Joseph, Irish Franciscan Missionary sisters and the Irish branch of the Society of African Missions long took over the church's ministry to blacks. Those who served in black parishes recalled antagonism and epithets of "nigger sisters" thrown at them by their ostensible compatriots. A new recruitment of Irish priests for the diocese in the 1960s often continued the division of experience between national and ethnic labels and cultures, especially within the "Irish."

Irish-American Catholics use the 1920s in the construction of a narrative that is both ethnic and sectarian. For Protestants with whom I spoke, the 1920s did not carry the same associations. Many remembered no particular prejudice against Catholics. Insofar as they admitted that such bias ever had existed, it was cast back into a "mythic time" beyond their own life histories: "Maybe in the nineteenth century people acted that way, but I never heard anything about it." They used no particular periodization. Neither Watson nor Smith was significant as a historical figure or a chronological marker. Instead, history was structured around their own family, religious, and social experience. Jewish history, however, was focused by Watson's intervention in the Leo Frank case and the difficulties of their coreligionists in Atlanta, as it had been shaped by previous incidents of anti-Semitism. The entire German community also faced anti-German prejudice during World War I.[20]

In interviews, non-Catholics focused on the apparent success of Irish Americans, which was epitomized in the rise of a political machine that dominated Savannah from World War I until the 1940s. As anti-Catholicism crystallized a sense of Irish group identity that could be translated into political strength, Irish-American political and economic success fueled counteractions. The connection of bloc politics and prejudice, however, rarely figured in the narratives of either Catholics or non-Catholics. Sectarian ideologies still preclude such a holistic analysis for most Savannahians.

The strong historical consciousness of Irish Americans has been reinforced by its public representation in religious settings, schools, parades, and political organizations. However, this interpretation does not encompass all

Roman Catholics. In other interviews, the Germans of Savannah, Catholic and non-Catholic alike, felt that World War I was much more traumatic as a historical experience than the anti-Catholicism of the succeeding years. As in other American cities, pressure from their surrounding society forced them into rapid Americanization lest they be reviled as enemies.

German-American Catholics subsequently have tended to merge into the Irish-American community: "Irish" and "Catholic" are often used interchangeably in everyday Savannah conversation. A Methodist with a clearly Irish surname is therefore a "Cracker," while a family with a name like Schultz or Appelheim labels its bearer as "Irish," if Catholic. This coalescence of ethnic and religious identity is balanced by the identification of German and Lutheran. Catholics, including descendants of German immigrants, went so far as to discount any large population of German Catholics in the nineteenth century—deconstituting history on the basis of posterior experience. Incorporation into the large community was clearly a more important organizing theme for them than the trauma of ethnic and linguistic separation. The German Heritage Society has subsequently worked on the development of a fuller and more inclusive identity in Savannah, although there are no direct challenges to Irish-American hegemony within the religious life of the city.

The fifty or more Italian-Catholic families established in Savannah had a different experience during the 1920s. In the early decades of this century, these families were few and often isolated from downtown parishes by their involvement in fishing. Some, however, did reach important economic positions, and there was also an Italian consul at the port. Italy's alliance with the Axis in World War II faced some of Savannah's Italian Catholics with a shift in identity and the interpretation of events similar to that of the Germans in World War I, including the destruction of formal ethnic organizations. Informants recounted this period in pained detail.

Irish-American hegemony in the local Catholic church made Italians feel at a disadvantage in terms of ethnic organization as well. An activist member of an Italian-American family noted:

All the other ethnic groups—Jews, Irish, Greeks,—have used religion as a rallying point. Jews close in around the rabbis. Greeks have only one church. They may be split so they are not speaking but they meet under one roof. Italians can't do that. Irish have had the Knights of Columbus. Italians cannot rally around anything.

Italian heritage associations have been active in the 1980s but without the religious presence typical of northern ethnic parishes. These do appear, however, to have been the most open and successful of all heritage associations in incorporating new immigrants to the city, especially as those of Italian descent reach prominence in medicine, culture, and journalism.

The reminiscences of the Cajuns at the Savannah Sugar Refinery have been even more distinctively shaped by workplace and family. After immigration in the 1920s, Cajun life centered on the refinery as a total community with housing, recreation, and religious life. Savannah seemed distant and the Protestants surrounding the plant were perceived as unfriendly. Their distinctive religion, language, and cuisine became conflated with the factory as family, and this identity was passed on to new generations who lived on the grounds and were in turn hired by the company.

In discussions of their lives, members of these families let refinery events such as the construction of a parish church on land donated by the sugar mill in the 1940s or the closing of the mill village in the 1960s dominate their historical consciousness much more than citywide events or ties to their Louisiana homeland. Within this factory consciousness, racial divisions were nevertheless in force. The mill village was segregated and black Catholics there attended a nearby black parish rather than the church across the street from the entrance to the plant. For both groups, however, a company-based ethnic history has been supported by continued hiring in the family, as well as by formal anniversary celebrations and newsletters that intermingle factory and family history.[21]

Ethnic divisions appear to be less emphasized among southern Catholics than among their northern co-religionists because of the absence of national parishes, organizations, festivals, or neighborhoods. Still, ethnicity has both shaped differential perspectives on the past and has been particularly reinforced by this historical consciousness as maintained in families and networks. This in turn localizes the ethnic experience making it less open to those who might have similar claims of national heritage.

Yet it is also clear that ethnic labels are intertwined with the experience of workplace and opportunity. Cajuns were isolated at the sugar mill, Italians linked to fishing as both owners and workers, and the Irish worked on the railroad, at the port, or in foundries. Owners and workers also had different experiences and memories, for class remains an important division within the community as well as in its historical narratives.

Most of my informants came from families who were working class at the turn of the century, although they have moved upward within Savannah's economic and social framework in the course of the past eighty years. These individuals had intimate contact with religious discrimination and even violence.

Others, however, were scions of the upper-middle-class Catholics by the early twentieth century. For wealthy Irish Americans, the 1920s were not so significant as they were for coethnic members of the lower class. This elite was aware of prejudice, but understood it differently through both experience and interpretations of historical events. They often denied knowledge and experience of Klan activity in their lifespans. In more than one case, people complained of restrictions on upward social mobility, such as the "rules" that prevented them from entering elite social clubs of the city. Others recalled criticism from fellow Catholics who resented their attendance at "Protestant" schools, or their lace curtain social networks. The uppermost religious class boundary between Catholics and Episcopalians also concerned the elite, yet was irrelevant to most Catholics. Acceptance into an urban power group tended to outweigh a sectarian experience or interpretation of the past. The Italians and Cajuns seemed more united in their interpretations of the 1920s; the former were few, and the latter group had not yet developed extensive occupational and class diversity then.

This upper-class consciousness becomes particularly evident in areas of power within the Catholic church: governance and relationship to figures of the church hierarchy. One of the most consistent indices of class affiliation in interviews proved to be attitudes toward particular bishops (as diocesan leaders more than as theologians). A working-class Irish Catholic recalled a twentieth-century bishop as "a real arrogant son of a bitch. He was a Yankee—these Yankee bishops don't fit in here. He didn't think Southerners had a brain. . . . " This man remembered the bishop as an ally of the rich rather than a spiritual leader. Meanwhile, an upwardly mobile Catholic female said of the same figure that he "was magnificent. . . . He was outspoken so *some* people didn't like him. . . . " Other middle-class Catholics were shocked to hear that there had been any criticism of this bishop's tenure, attempting to refute it through their anecdotes of personal contact with him. Yet this contact was precisely what the working-class Catholics felt that they had lacked.

The versions of historical consciousness patterned by and patterning religion, national heritage, class and family experience still stand on one side of the great divide in southern society: race. White perceptions contrast sharply with the narratives of black Catholics in Savannah. The 1920s, for example, were hardly demarcated as a special time of prejudice for southern blacks. Instead, they fit into centuries of racially marked discrimination. As one older woman noted, "the Klan didn't care if you were Catholic if you were black."

Black reminiscences of earlier bishops, as reported by Society of African Missions (SMA) historian Josef Vogel, also suggest how alienation from power might be translated into historical animosity:

[Benjamin J.] Keiley's expression (to Father Lissner) remained famous for years: "I keep the whites, you take the niggers." Before this bishop there had been a Redemptorist, Bishop [William] Gross (1873-1885). He showed clearly—and shall we blush to say it—that the southern so-called white trash were not alone in hating Negroes; from the pulpit he dared speak of "those Niggers."[22]

Ethnic Catholics were rarely allies to black Catholics. Irish Americans competed with blacks for jobs and even neighbors attended different parishes. Indeed, the problems of the 1920s pointed to basic structural contradictions in the Catholic commitment to black conversion without their full inclusion in the social life of the universalist community. When the SMA fathers proposed a seminary for black priests and mentioned the possibility of a separate bishop for blacks in Georgia, Bishop Keiley responded negatively to his superiors, pointing out that he could hardly maintain his white flock against outside opposition to Catholicism itself, much less appear to favor black autonomy. The contradictions of historical recollection today are thus in direct relation to the structural contradictions of black and white Catholicism in the 1920s.[23]

The success of working-class immigrant families in their third and fourth generations coupled with recent migration of Catholics from the North have dramatically expanded the Catholic middle class and have decreased the experiential components that divided ethnic groups in the 1920s. For example, even as new ethnic heritage societies have developed in recent decades, intermarriage, social ties, and geographic mobility have linked Italians, Germans, Irish, and Cajuns. Indeed, families and individuals may be active in more than one such ethnic society without any social discord.

While these groups—ethnic and socioeconomic—varied in terms of their perceptions of the 1920s, many informants concurred in seeing the 1960s as another time of trouble and change. Older whites linked church reform, the problems in the cathedral, integration, the crisis of birth control, and the departure of many priests as a conjuncture of troubles that had fundamentally changed the church. Unlike the earlier period when challenges from the outside reinforced Catholic identity, here challenges came from inside the church and called that identity into question.

Age and education patterned variation in historical consciousness more than ethnicity or class. Older people found the internal and external adjustments in their identity as southern Catholics more difficult than did younger people less imbued with older traditions of both Catholic and southern life. The Catholicism of the 1920s forged a defensive mentality that made it harder to accept changes in the identity so long defended.

Education as well as activity in parish affairs also prepared people for the changes. Since innovations were spread out over years, continuing contact with church leaders and experts was important in understanding disruption. Involvement may correlate with class, as the discussion of contact with governance suggests. Yet upper-class and educated individuals also reacted emotionally in defense of traditions, especially when reforms to the cathedral were debated.

Changes may also influence the way new Catholics have been incorporated into the community. Many immigrants are younger than the older Savannah Catholics and have experienced innovations elsewhere. While statistics are not available for Savannah, in other areas these Sunbelt immigrants also have more education, which may leave them open to changes. Immigrants, at least, are not shaped in the same way by "the way we have always done things."[24]

Mobility has produced more dialogue among social groups within the white Catholic population, but white mobility also has contributed to the continuing differentiation of white and black memory. Although both Irish and black might have lived in the same poor neighborhood at the turn of the century, for example, the possibilities of advancement have been more limited for the latter, reinforcing gulfs of race and class that influence the interpretation of significant events. Economic and educational mobility also has been constrained for blacks.

The 1960s and 1970s witnessed crucial breaks in the life of blacks in Savannah. Although civil rights decisions began to change the laws on discrimination in the 1950s, their effects were felt only slowly in the city. Black Catholics are now found in all areas of Savannah life, including middle-class suburbs. Neighborhoods, however, continue to be segregated, particularly those that are poor *and* black. Integration has not erased the class divisions affirmed by generations of oppression in education, housing, and economic opportunity.

Civil rights activism also coincided with Catholic reforms that encouraged participation and "nationalization" of the parish in liturgy and social concerns.[25] Both were linked in a generally positive sense of the period. Yet other events intervened to shape a distinctive sense of history and identity.

Some local whites criticized the Roman Catholic church for being too quick or liberal in integration. In the 1960s, it was, for example, the only white-dominated institution to allow NAACP mass meetings to be held in its buildings. Yet the structure used was the still-segregated Catholic High School for blacks. This ambiguity was typical and blacks do not see the Catholic church as being rapid or liberal.

Catholic schools, elementary and high school, were effectively integrated in the 1960s, more or less at the same time as public schools. White Catholic leaders envisioned this as a liberal gesture, adducing equality of opportunity, improvement of facilities, and a commitment to universalism as the reason for closing black schools. Yet it is important here to observe the confrontations implicit in different interpretations of the same historical event.

Integration was effected by closing black parish schools and bringing students into formerly all-white programs. For blacks, the school was historically prior to the parish, and remained a social and cultural hub for the neighborhood. After consolidation, furthermore, black Protestant children, who had formerly composed the majority of students in the local parish school, took a lower priority in a system designed to reproduce the Catholic household, regardless of race.

Where whites, whether or not they supported the plan, saw integration as a way of bringing together black and white members of the church, black Catholics saw this plan as evidence of white disinterest or discrimination against neighborhood and racial patterns of association within the church.

Twenty years later, these school closings still evoke strong reactions from former teachers, students, and parents. A study of Catholicism among blacks in south Georgia written by a black nun who worked in Savannah at the time recalls that:

It was always the Black school that was closed rather than the White one. Black children were always to be absorbed into the White system, rather than vice versa. In some cases, particularly at the closing of Pius X, there was a strong protest from the leaders of the Black community.

Some time later, the closing of St. Mary's school was also the subject of bitter feelings among many of the Black community members. Here again, however, the reasons given for the closing were varied—a decrease in the number of religious sisters available to teach there, lack of financial resources and educational materials, the need for expensive structural repairs to the building.[26]

The contrast between official explanations and community perceptions are stark. These actions, in turn, reinforced older interpretations of social experience among black Catholics. Blacks were deeply aware of the prejudice against them in a population, including their fellow Catholics, that perceived them first and foremost according to race. A black Catholic teacher said about the closing of the black Catholic High School:

A Christian man loves God and doesn't worry about men but I still feel pangs when I go by there. Blacks get lost in white schools and parishes. But that group came in from Notre Dame and closed them down. Bishop ———came in, closed St. Benedict's, St. Mary's, St. Anthony's and St. Pius X, and then left. He was a hatchet man.

As in earlier class-linked examples, historical recollection includes denunciation of church leaders. A young black woman spoke of these events in similar terms:

I understood closing the elementary schools, but not St. Pius, which was so new and meant so much to us. Not just because it wasn't integrated . . . it might have become so in time the way people move. Everyone worked so hard. First they told us that the library wasn't good enough, so we found donors and raised money through sales, etc. Then they said it wasn't integrated. But 98% went to college—better than Benedictine. Do you close a school like that?

Both these blacks work closely with white Catholic and non-Catholic leaders. Nonetheless, their remarks reveal a pattern of perception of events distinct from that of the white leadership of their own church. While the church hierarchy saw incorporation as an advance, blacks could easily interpret it as an attack on their identity and development. This miscommunication, furthermore, laid the groundwork for continued suspicion and rumor about what the hierarchy might do.

A black perception of injustice in the 1960s counterbalances rather than coincides with the white "time of troubles." As with black perceptions of the 1920s, it is also overshadowed by those who have had more public voice in the church and city, although this imbalance has changed slowly in recent years. New arrivals in the community, especially if imbued with a northern view of segregation in the South, may in fact identify more strongly with the latter, and a few have joined predominantly black congregations or have expressed greater sympathy for blacks to me. In this sense, they, too, may be entering into and transforming historical consciousness and social categorization. At the same time, blacks are also participating in white congregations, potentially altering their experience of separation and history.

The experience of the 1960s and 1970s represents a transformation of the divisions of earlier Savannah society and the sense of history through which these divisions have been rehearsed. In the 1920s, different ethnic experience produced the differentiated memories rehearsed in the present. In the 1960s, ethnic divisions had been diminished in day-to-day experience, although the population remained differentiated by social and economic factors. Race, however, marks a more continuous theme of division and of power. That is, black Catholics not only have a different historical consciousness, but have been less likely to make this heard within the forum of the Catholic population of the city (even if the priests and hierarchy are attentive). The process of transformation, however, is one that potentially involves those who moved to Savannah by the 1960s, and those who have arrived since in reshaping church, social divisions, and history. As the number of immigrants increase, and the past fades away, new landmarks and narratives should enter into the dialogue of history.

My sense of where urban expansion may alter the future patterns of social division, religious life, and historical consciousness remains anecdotal, yet may suggest hypotheses for future examination. As new immigrants arrive, for example, we can observe how they adapt the systems of social categorization in their new home. I have suggested some possibilities of access to ethnic domains through public presentations (Irishness celebrations) or even heritage societies. This may be particularly true for groups who have had limited numbers in the past and may build new recognition in Savannah. Such groups include both northern ethnic Catholics and the new immigrants from Asia and Latin America who, with the exception of the Vietnamese, as yet play a small role in Savannah Catholic life.

Another possibility may be the incorporation of *local* and *outsider* as opposed categories within the social system of the city. The concept of the Yankee and the ethnic southerner on a national scale may be transformed by the presence of the former northerner as an apparently permanent resident. This may underlie in part the creation in Savannah of "Cracker Day," celebrating the native rural Georgian. As described by one reporter in 1982:

Last year more than 1,000 people turned out for Cracker Day, celebrated each year to honor "Georgia Crackers," described by supporters as hardy frontier folk with strong convictions about God and man and by detractors as ignorant, idle and more or less worthless.[27]

This is not to say that all such immigrants will understand or develop within this complex historical framework. A proposed suburban development of 40,000 inhabitants and related business and recreational facilities on the city's western suburban fringe, for example, has been christened "Savannah Quarters" by its South Carolina developers. Yet *quarters,* in traditional Savannah neighborhood usages, refers to slave dwellings or industrial/milltown dwellings generally associated with poor blacks, hardly the targeted population of the project.[28]

Moreover, these changes are related to changes in urban power. What impact will immigrants have on politics and economics and how will they influence old coalitions? As blacks moved into ever more active roles, for example, the local Irish Americans formed political action groups to lobby as an ethnic voice. Will this occur with other groups, reinforcing their sense of differentiation and being incorporated into new histories? Here analysis of Savannah certainly will profit from an understanding of other southern cities in flux.

The process of transformation will not take place merely on a local or ethnic scale. New urbanization links Savannah with changes throughout the South and the nation. Changes in the meaning of ethnicity in younger generations who depart northern cities, for example, will influence the transformations of southern life. Other social categorizations, at the same time, may emerge as self-conscious groups. For example, the changes opened up by the 1960s have led to continued redefinition of what it is to be Catholic. As George Tindall once proposed that southerners might be viewed as an ethnic group, so Father Andrew Greeley has suggested an emergent transformation in Catholic identity: the communal Catholic who is loyal to Catholicism without necessarily expecting leadership or even regular sacramental contact from it. That is, Catholicism, too, may emerge as a blurred category of ethnic and religious value nationwide. This status would not be unfamiliar within Savannah's idioms of social division.[29] These ideas are speculative. Yet if social division and historical consciousness have been in continual transformation in the past, they very likely will pose a tension of old and new in the future.

This chapter has concentrated on the past formation of social division among Roman Catholics in Savannah as an example of a process now open to adaptation in the context of new southern patterns of migration and urbanization. As such, it complements other studies in the volume that deal with the migrants themselves or the striking new social formations of

Sunbelt boomtowns. Such a balance is vital in understanding the South as a complex social tapestry, in which Sunbelt and old South are interwoven.

This chapter also attempts to draw together many aspects of the identity that are linked within Savannah life—religion, ethnicity, class, race, and history. Each term merits analysis on its own. Yet it is also important to synthesize them to explore the systematization and incorporation of social divisions within southern life.

Above all, this chapter has focused on urban life as a process. Developments in the past are keys to understanding the present and the future, whatever new factors may enter into the crucible of social life. If Savannah has new immigrants today, so it did a century ago. If those groups were incorporated into urban life and history, however painfully, so will those of the present and future. This analysis alone, and in comparison with other chapters in this volume, seeks to stimulate thoughts about the process and its ramifications, in Savannah and throughout the modern changing South.

NOTES

Author's Note: My field work in the study of Savannah Roman Catholicism has been conducted in both summer research since 1982 and a five-month stay focused on those who are black and Catholic in Savannah in 1985. This work has been funded by the University of South Florida and the NEH Summer Stipend Program. The theme of this chapter was stimulated by participation in an "Institute on Migration and Ethnicity in Post-World War II America" at the University of Florida in April 1984. At the same time, some themes of this paper have grown out of my personal experience of the transforming South in my native Louisville, in Atlanta, and in Sarasota.

Many people have commented thoughtfully on earlier drafts of this work, as well as the ideas on ethnicity and transformation I am working out here. I would particularly like to acknowledge the criticisms and insight of Karen O'Connor, Tony Andrews, Donald Moore, Chuck Rutheiser, Eugene Lewis, Liam Collins, Patrick Shinnick, Barbara Bennett, and Cindy Kelly, as well as the stimulating observations of the editors of this volume.

1. This sense of historical consciousness as a constitutional element in social life has been revivified in recent anthropological thinking by such works as Renato Rosaldo, *Ilongot Headhunting, 1883-1974: A Study in Society and History* (Stanford, 1980); Marshall Sahlins, *Historical Metaphors and Mythical Realities: Structure in the Early History of the Sandwich Islands Kingdom* (Ann Arbor, 1980); Karen Blu, *The Lumbee Problem: The Making of an American Indian People* (Cambridge, England, 1980); Richard Price, *First Time: The Historical Vision of an Afro-American People* (Baltimore, 1983), among others. These texts focus on how people tell and transform the past, as well as how this consciousness becomes an element in understanding and acting in the present.

The "histories" here rely on documents as well as interviews and general discussions. The narratives of the 1920s and 1960s are drawn from roughly 175 core informants, often with both formal interviews and repeated contacts. Of these, thirty are primarily Irish American; seven, Italian; ten, German; five, Cajun; sixty, black; and thirty, non-Catholic. Another thirty informants are priests or religious. All of these are anonymous. Although I have cited sections of individual interviews to give the flavor of local discourse, I have protected the identity of each individual collaborator. In addition to discussion of the past, the frequent contact I have maintained with these people and others with whom I have worked in Savannah has allowed me to discuss my interpretations and the logic of ethnic division with local Catholics and non-Catholics, whose comments have been weighed in this analysis.

This study also omits some ethnic groups and associations not intimately or historically linked to Catholicism, such as the Scottish St. Andrew's Society, founded in 1734 *(History of St. Andrew's Society, Savannah, Georgia* [Savannah], 1973); the primarily Lutheran German Friendly Society (C. A. Linn, *The History of the German Friendly Society* [Savannah], 1937); the small Greek Orthodox, Chinese, and Polish communities (Lee Griffen, "Woman to Woman," *Savannah Morning News* [October 18, 1959]; and Fannie A. Asselani, "The Greek Community in Savannah" [typescript, 1977]); and the recent Vietnamese Catholic parish, which numbers nearly 300 members (L. Moore, "Vietnamese Find Home in Savannah," *Savannah Morning News* [April 29, 1979]).

2. Population patterns are even more striking if we note that a century ago Savannah's population and importance still nearly rivaled that of Atlanta: 30,000 to the latter's 37,000. In recent years, as Atlanta's boom settles and migration moves elsewhere, population patterns show interesting similarities. Thus, according to the 1980 census, 20,803 of the Savannah SMSA's 135,185 inhabitants (15.4 percent) had lived in a different state in 1975; 5,825 (4.3 percent) came from north central or northeastern states. For Atlanta, 224,931 of its 1,414,753 inhabitants (15.8 percent) had lived elsewhere in the U.S. with 5.8 percent from northern states. Ten years earlier 11 percent of Savannah's population had come from elsewhere, while 35 percent of Atlanta's reported such a move.

Still, Savannahians think an even greater growth is under way. A recent popular history notes: "Savannah's economic vitality is favorably out of balance with the mere numerical weight of population figures which, at the beginning of 1984, showed the city proper at 143,708, while the combined Savannah-Chatham County total stood at 210,266": E. Chan Sieg, *Eden on the Marsh: An Illustrated History of Savannah* (Northridge, Calif., 1985), p. 149. The Fort Howard Paper Company in neighboring Effingham County now promises rapid suburban growth and the transformation of a rural sector in the SMSA.

In early 1987, county commissioners discussed another massive expansion of 18,000 single and multifamily homes, recreational facilities, and a business and research park in western Chatham County that would ultimately house 40,000 residents. This project, if completed, would be "the largest single development in the county's history." (Pamela Ramsey, "Commissioners to Weigh Changes," *Savannah Morning News* [February 27, 1987]).

3. J. Fallows, *The Water Lords: Ralph Nader's Study Group Report on Industry and Environmental Crisis in Savannah, Georgia* (New York, 1971), deals with these problems and the politics of older polluting industries. Sieg cites $100 million from

the port in 1984, $182 million from tourism, $100 million from the military and $50 million in revenues from the airport: Sieg, *Eden on the Marsh,* p. 149.

4. Kenneth Labish, "Gulfstream: The Turkey That Learned to Soar," *Fortune* 107 (May 30, 1983), 59-62; Eleanor Tracy, "The Dogfight for the Corporate Jet Market," *Fortune* 112 (December 23, 1985), 79. See Sieg, *Eden on the Marsh,* pp. 149-203.

5. The public celebration of history focuses on southern or local traditions yet does not ignore various groups in the city, exemplified in such diverse events as the *Georgia Salzburger Bicentennial Pageant* published for the Savannah Convention of the United Lutheran Church in America (Charles Linn, *Georgia S. B. Pageant* [Savannah, 1934]); the texts and annual anniversary celebrations surrounding the oldest independent black Baptist congregation in the city (E. K. Love, *The First African Baptist Church, from Its Organization January 20th, 1788 to July 1st, 1888, Including the Centennial Celebration, Addresses, Sermons, etc.* [Savannah, 1888]; J. M. Simms, *The First Colored Baptist Church in North America, Constituted at Savannah, Ga., January 20, A.D. 1788; with Biographical Sketches of the Pastors* [Philadelphia, 1888]); as well as annual anniversaries of the St. Patrick's Day parade (William Fogarty, *The Days We've Celebrated: St. Patrick's Day in Savannah* [Savannah, 1980]).

6. See Robert Perdue, *The Negro in Savannah, 1865-1900* (New York, 1973); and John Dittmer, *Black Georgia in the Progressive Era, 1900-1920* (Urbana, 1977) for past history. Recent developments are also discussed in my "Black and Catholic in Savannah," in James Peacock, ed., *Ethnography of the Southeastern Coastal Plain* (Athens, Ga., forthcoming).

7. Charles Hoskins, *Black Episcopalians in Savannah* (Savannah, 1983); Charles Linn, *Two Hundred Years of the Grace of God: A Sketch of the Life and History of the Lutheran Church of the Ascension* (Savannah, 1941); *History of the Independent Presbyterian Church and Sunday School* (Savannah, 1882); Orville A. Park, "The Georgia Scotch-Irish," *Georgia Historical Quarterly* 12 (January 1928), 115-35; Daisy H. Stubbs, "A History of Wesley Monumental Church, Savannah, Ga." (n.p., n.d.); James A. Lester, *A History of the Georgia Baptist Convention, 1822-1972* (n.p., 1972); Saul Rubin, *Third to None: The Saga of Savannah Jewry, 1733-1983* (Savannah, 1983); R. W. Gadsden, "A Brief History of the First Congregational Church, United Church of Christ, Savannah, Ga., April 1869-April 1969" (Ms., Georgia Historical Society); Georgia Writer's Project, *Drums and Shadows: Survival Studies Among Georgia Coastal Negroes* (Garden City, N.Y., 1972).

8. William Coleman, *The Church in South Georgia* (Savannah, 1967), p. 9. This theme has recently been revived with further investigations and interest in canonization of the Georgia Martyrs, which will thus establish an historical priority for Catholicism in this area. An alternative view of the Guale martyrs is presented in Carolyn Stefano-Schill, "The Gualean Revolt of 1597: Anti-Colonialism in the Old South," *Southern Exposure* 12 (1984), 4-9.

9. Fussell Chalker, "Irish Catholics in the Building of the Ocmulgee and Flint Railroad," *Georgia Historical Quarterly* 54 (1970), 507-16; Herbert Weaver, "Foreigners in Antebellum Savannah," *Georgia Historical Quarterly* 37 (1943), 1-17; Richard Haunton, "Savannah in the 1850s" (Ph.D. dissertation, Emory University, 1968); Edward L. Ayers, *Vengeance and Justice: Crime and Punishment in the 19th-Century American South* (New York, 1984), pp. 73-105. See also Dennis Clark, "The South's Irish Catholics: A Case of Cultural Confinement," in Randall M. Miller and Jon L.

Wakelyn, eds., *Catholics in the Old South: Essays on Church and Culture* (Macon, 1983), pp. 195-209.

10. Jerome Oetgen, "Oswald Moosmuller: Monk and Missionary," *American Benedictine Review* 27 (March 1976), 17; Jerome Oetgen, *An American Abbot: Boniface Wimmer, O.S.B., 1883-1887* (Latrobe, Pa., 1976). For Italians, see Sieg, *Eden on the Marsh*, p. 182, on the Maggioni family.

11. Michael Gannon, *Rebel Bishop: The Life and Era of Augustin Verot* (Milwaukee, 1964), pp. 115-44; William Osborne, "The Race Problem in the Catholic Church in the United States Between the Time of the Second Plenary Council (1866) and the Founding of the Catholic Interracial Council of New York (1934)" (Ph.D. dissertation, Columbia University, 1954), pp. 41-45.

12. Mary A. Ahles, *In the Shadow of His Wings: A History of the Franciscan Sisters* (Saint Paul, 1977), pp. 123-54; Brian De Breffny, *Unless the Seed Die: The Life of Elizabeth Hayes (Mother Mary Ignatius O.S.F.)* (n.p., n.d.), pp. 141ff.; Joseph Vogel, *Red and White Roses in Black Soil: The African Missions Society in Africa and the U.S. from 1856 to 1940* (n.p., n.d.); *Father Ignatius Lissner, S.M.A. (1867-1948): A Biographical Essay* (n.p., n.d.). See also McDonogh, "Black and Catholic in Savannah."

13. *Defamers of the Church* (n.p., n.d.), pp. 39-42; "Troops Avert a Riot: Ex-Priest Slattery Saved from Mob," and other articles in the *Savannah Evening Press* or *Savannah Morning News* (February 26-30, 1895).

14. Thomas Watson, *The Roman Catholic Church: Its Law and Its Literature* (Thomson, Ga., 1917); See also C. Vann Woodward, *Tom Watson: Agrarian Rebel* (Savannah, reprint ed., 1973, originally published, 1938).

15. *Savannah Morning News* (September 8-9, 1920); Edward Cashin, "Thomas E. Watson and the Catholic Laymen's Association of Georgia" (Ph.D. dissertation, Fordham University, 1960).

16. Arthur J. O'Hara, *Hibernian Society, Savannah, Ga., 1812-1912: The Story of a Century* (Savannah, [1912?]); Fogarty, *The Days We've Celebrated.*

17. "St. Patrick's Is Being Torn Down," *Savannah Evening Press* (July 31, 1941); "A Brief History of Our Lady of Lourdes Parish" (mimeograph, Savannah Diocesan Archives); Anne Ritzert, "History of St. James Parish" (mimeograph, Savannah Diocesan Archives); for black education, see Julian Griffin, *Tomorrow Comes the Song: The Story of Catholicism Among the Black Population of South Georgia, 1850-1978* (Savannah, 1978), pp. 70-73.

18. This issue is still recalled vividly in conversations. *New York Times* coverage reflected the issues of historical consciousness and ethnicity that were involved: K. Briggs, "Irish Americans in Savannah Dispute Plans to Renovate the Cathedral," *New York Times* (March 16, 1975). See also Debby Luster, "The Cathedral Renovated? The Laity Respond," *Savannah Morning News* (July 19, 1975).

19. The question of neighborhood, ethnicity, and historical memory is an important one. Yamacraw on the western flank of the city and the Old Fort on the east are now widely depicted as quintessentially Irish-American ghettos in contrast to the WASPish elegance of the city's central squares. In fact, both districts seem to have had long histories as marginal zones with lower-class populations who worked at the port or with the railroads. In the antebellum period, Savannah and other southern cities found "the city's new-found prosperity brought too many rough loud and often drunken newcomers and transients who crowded the most important streets and market areas; too many destitute Irishmen—'niggers turned inside out,' as the phrase

went, fraternized with too many blacks enjoying the relative freedom of the city; too many prostitutes beckoned to sailors in 'boardinghouses' too close to respectable neighborhoods." Ayers, *Vengeance and Justice*, p. 82. By the end of the century, these neighborhoods also had absorbed Greek and Jewish shipkeepers, as well as German immigrants. Blacks lived in separate sections or in the lanes behind the streets, but social interaction defined by class as much as race was possible—a situation captured in Savannah author Harry Hervey's *The Damned Don't Cry* (New York, 1939). After the Irish moved out in the 1910s and 1920s, the neighborhood took on a different value as a referent, emphasized by more recent historic renovation of the part of the Old Fort. Meanwhile, black sections of the Fort and Yamacraw have been bulldozed for housing projects, although a black Old Fort Association remains in the city.

20. Rubin, *Third to None;* Leonard Dinnerstein, *The Leo Frank Case* (New York, 1968).

21. This strong identity of workplace and historical consciousness was suggested to me by the work of Ignasi Terrades on Catalan milltowns: *Les colonies industrials: un estudi entorn del cas de l'Ametlla de Merola* (Barcelona, 1978). But what is the interaction of workplace and social identity for the new Sunbelt immigrant?

22. Vogel, *Red and White Roses in Black Soil,* p. 240.

23. Bishop Keiley to James Cardinal Gibbons, December 7, 1920; and Keiley to Archbishop Bonaventura Cerretti, December 7, 1920, Keiley papers (Savannah Diocesan Archives).

24. Gavin Wright, *Old South, New South* (New York, 1986), pp. 239-74.

25. See Joseph L. Howze et al., *What We Have Seen and Heard: A Pastoral Letter on Evangelization from the Black Bishops of the United States* (Cincinnati, 1984).

26. Griffin, *Tomorrow Comes the Song,* p. 79.

27. Alison Saussy, "Cracker Day!" *Savannah Evening Press* (July 31, 1982). See also George Tindall, *The Ethnic Southerners* (Baton Rouge, 1976). One Catholic informant defined "crackers" as an ethnic and political group by saying, "If you're not Irish or Jew or Greek but born in America, you're a Cracker."

28. Pamela Ramsey, "Commissioners to Weigh Changes," *Savannah Morning News* (February 27, 1987).

29. Andrew Greeley, *The American Catholic* (New York, 1977). This parallel was suggested to me by Douglas Langston's unpublished paper, "Fruit of the Vine: Modern American Catholicism."

5

Race, Ethnicity, and Women's Lives in the Urban South

Julia Kirk Blackwelder ⸻

World War II stimulated two related developments that transformed daily life in the South. Defense spending in the South and the Southwest touched off rapid economic expansion after the war and laid the groundwork for the industrial, commercial, and urban growth known as the Sunbelt phenomenon. The experiences of blacks in the military and in defense industries, as well as President Franklin D. Roosevelt's promises on civil rights, helped kindle the flames of the civil rights revolution. Economic development and the civil rights movement are twin themes in the historiography of the postwar urban South, but the impact of growth and change on the region's women has been virtually ignored. This chapter explores the roles that women played in the civil rights movement and, especially, the consequences of postwar economic change for women in the urban South.

Historically, urban residence provided particular employment options for women segregated by their ethnic and racial backgrounds. Towns and cities also offered women the opportunity to participate in a range of social and political activities that could lead to social change. In the urban South economic and social change had interactive effects on women's lives. After World War II, women in southern cities greatly enlarged their place in the work force. Simultaneously, black and white women cooperated to end racial segregation. Some white women, it should be noted, also stepped forward to resist desegregation.

Whatever their racial, ethnic, or regional heritage in the South of the 1980s, women face economic, social, and political situations that differ dramatically from those of prewar southerners. Despite economic growth and existing legal sanctions against racial and gender discrimination, not all women have shared equally in the bounty of the new southern prosperity. Both ethnic values and remaining habits of prejudice have preserved economic and social differences among women.

The one hundred years following the Civil War saw the South transformed from a prostrate, rural, and agricultural region to a land of thriving commercial cities supported by manufacturing as well as farming.[1] From Delaware to Texas, the economic development of the 1880s encouraged migration into towns and cities.[2] The growth of tobacco factories and textile mills, particularly in the Southeast, attracted women into the labor force. The commercial sector drew women into clerical occupations and janitorial employments. From the turn of the century until the Great Depression, southern cities expanded rapidly in population, physical size, and industry. Texas cities grew especially quickly, and in the teens and twenties the Lone Star State drew in thousands of political and economic refugees from Mexico.[3]

Urban areas disproportionately attracted blacks and women. Urbanization and the economic changes that fed this phenomenon dramatically affected women's lives. Women assumed new roles as workers. The female factory work force continued to grow during the early twentieth century and, after World War I, stores, offices, and consumer services opened new occupational opportunities for southern women. The employment of women in southern cities was highly segregated by race, and Mexican-American women were generally segregated from other white workers.

For most of the twentieth century, the factory, the office, and the store were workplaces that employed only white women, while black women worked in white homes or at domestic tasks in commercial establishments. Substantial numbers of black women also found employment in tobacco factories and commercial laundries. The sizable Mexican-American female population of Texas cities generally worked at either manufacturing or domestic jobs. Small groups of European immigrant women in the urban South followed the unskilled employment paths pursued by women of their nationalities in cities outside the South, although the domination of domestic work by black women somewhat discouraged their participation in household service.

From 1900 through 1920 married women in the South, urban and rural, had work rates significantly higher than married women anywhere else in the United States. From Reconstruction through the turn of the century, the high work rates of southern women can be explained by the unusually large numbers of black women in the work force. Rural black women typically entered field labor at a young age. Black town dwellers moved into domestic employment. Black women usually remained at work after marriage because of the poverty of black families and the demand for their labor. As the mill economy expanded in the early twentieth century, white women, single and married, entered the work force. Consequently, the female labor force was increasingly composed of town and city dwellers. Whether they were field hands, tenant workers, or mill hands, southern females remained members of families that labored together long after employment had segregated family members in most other areas. Child labor remained part of growing up in the South long after it had diminished elsewhere.[4]

The importance of urbanization for women as wage earners is reflected in the 1920 census. On the basis of 1920 returns, the census bureau reported that the percentage of gainfully occupied women ages sixteen and older in the South was 23.9 percent, or virtually the same as the national rate of 24.0 percent. The New England and Middle Atlantic states ranked far above the South with rates of 32.2 percent and 27.2 percent, respectively. When only urban populations were counted, however, southern women recorded higher work rates than the Middle Atlantic women and rates nearly as high as New England women. In 1920 the work rates of women in cities of 25,000 or more inhabitants were 36.5 percent in New England, 35.9 percent in the South, and 31.9 percent in the Middle Atlantic states.[5]

During the 1920s the South felt the effects of the technological and bureaucratic transformations that reshaped America. Growing corporations and commercial establishments such as banks enlarged their record-keeping functions and redefined office tasks in ways that created great demand for female clerical help.[6] Because employers of office workers demanded specific skills, the new female laborers differed dramatically from the farm and mill workers who had learned their skills through childhood employment and on-the-job training. Few white women from mill towns or tenant farms had the education to compete for such jobs. Racial prejudice and their lack of education kept black women out of store and office employment. Consequently these new workers came largely from the homes of white craftsmen, shopkeepers, landowners, and other groups who had been able to secure secondary education for their daughters. Middle-class black families produced the clerical workers for black-owned businesses. The vast majority of female clerical workers and professional women—unlike farm workers, domestics, and mill hands—retired from the labor force upon marriage.

At the same time that clerical work expanded as a major opportunity for white women in the urban South, industrial employment was in flux. During the 1920s and 1930s, light manufacturing and labor-intensive services such as commercial laundries opened and closed in response to changes in local economies and in the national economy. By the end of the 1930s, industrial and agricultural employment among women had declined markedly. The mill town, the garment factory, and the tenant farm persisted in the South, but none fully recovered the tenacious hold they had had on women's lives in an earlier era. Consequently, high school completion, which could provide entry into the clerical sector, became an increasingly important goal among white girls. Black women had few options, and they crowded the domestic sector, commercial laundries, the janitorial trades, and manufacturing outside textile production. Structural unemployment and racial prejudice, however, interacted during the Depression to drive black women from the work force.[7]

Although the demand for female workers increased with World War II, only the least desirable jobs were offered to black women. Even when black women did find work, they frequently suffered discrimination on the job. The experience of Anna Graves of San Antonio was typical. Graves was the first black clerical worker at nearby Kelly Field, but she did not secure her job until the end of the war and she was isolated by the refusal of white clerical workers to share the lunchroom and base transportation with her.[8] For southern white women, on the other hand, the war brought new job opportunities in traditional clerical jobs and high-paying nontraditional jobs in defense manufacturing. In the textile industry white women took over higher-paying jobs that had formerly been reserved for men.[9]

For white working women in the urban South, World War II presented temporary employment opportunities that permanently affected their lives. Women in traditional occupations tended to stay on the job after the war, but in the nontraditional and higher-paying occupations, women were generally replaced by men. For black women overall, the war highlighted racial injustice in southern towns and cities. Employment opportunities remained limited and breaking the color line was difficult. The 1950 census offers a final snapshot of the work and family patterns of southern women before the revolution wrought by Sunbelt development and the civil rights movement. This census snapshot shows that in 1950 women's work was strictly segregated by gender and race. The census revealed not only the glaring differences between black and white women but also significant differences among white women of various ethnic backgrounds.

Although more difficult to assess than differences between blacks and whites, cultural differences among southern white women are also significant in the modern South. With the exception of Mexican Americans, immigrants and their children comprised relatively small portions of southern cities in 1950.[10] Among non-western hemispheric immigrants, the largest number of women had come from Germany, with 25,495 German females aged fourteen and older residing in the urban South. The 109,460 second-generation German-American women outnumbered all other ethnic groups, including Mexican-American women, who were recorded officially at 94,175. Second most numerous among European immigrant women were Soviets, of unspecified national and ethnic heritages, who numbered 22,135. Patterns of family formation and of labor force behavior varied significantly among ethnic groups and between immigrants and the daughters of immigrants. In 1950 foreign-born white women and second-generation and immigrant women in the urban South were much more likely to labor for wages than were white women more than one generation removed from their immigrant roots. Labor force participation varied from a low of 17.4 percent among Italian immigrant women to a high of 35.4 percent among second-generation Italian women. The Irish distinguished themselves from others in several respects. As was true in earlier times, Irish women were more likely to emigrate as single women than were women of other nationalities. Despite Mexico's mutual border with the United States, single women were much less likely to have immigrated to the southern United States from Mexico than from Ireland. In 1950 31.8 percent of Irish immigrants and 12.0 percent of Mexican immigrants were single. The daughters of Irish immigrants also were the most likely to remain single of all second-generation ethnic women. Two fifths of Irish immigrant women aged 25 through 44 and one fifth of the women aged 45 and over had never married and one fifth of second-generation Irish women of these ages were single. Because more of them remained single, Irish-American women were more likely to be single and, consequently, to work outside their homes than were other white women. Overall, members of the second generation were more likely to work than were their mothers. Even among the Irish, young second-generation women were more likely to work than were immigrants of the same ages.

Among the small Chinese and Japanese communities of the urban South, female work rates were comparable to those of most white second-generation immigrant populations. One third of the working-age Chinese women and two fifths of Japanese females were in the labor force in 1950.

The occupational preferences that have been observed in other urban settings since the nineteenth century generally persisted among immigrant women residing in southern cities in 1950.[11] Black domination of domestic labor may have both influenced the job choices of immigrant women and limited their access to the domestic sector, but Irish, German, and Polish immigrant women frequently accepted positions in private households while Italian women almost never did so in the South, or anywhere in the nation for that matter. Among Mexican immigrant women domestic service was the leading employment sector with more than one fourth of their numbers working at these jobs. Regardless of national origin, the daughters of immigrants were much less likely to accept domestic work than the immigrants themselves. A significant proportion of immigrant women had owned or operated small businesses. The absolute numbers in like employment were generally greater among the daughters of immigrants but proportionally fewer of the daughters were proprietors or operators.

By 1950 clerical work predominated among female employments. White ethnic women were no exception in this regard as more women, immigrant and second generation, followed clerical or sales occupations than any other line of work. Again, the Irish differed from other groups in that professional work was the leading employment among immigrant women. The tendency of Irish women to postpone marriage or never to marry encouraged their career ambitions. Nearly one half of the Irish immigrant workers reported themselves as professionals, a status probably explained by the large numbers of Irish women who were teachers and nurses, either as members of religious orders or in nonsectarian capacities.[12] Among second-generation immigrants as well, professional workers accounted for a major share of Irish working women with more than one fifth of the women reporting themselves as professional persons. However, clerical and sales workers comprised more than half of the second-generation Irish work force while fewer than one in twenty female immigrant workers pursued a clerical or sales occupation.

Among European immigrant women in southern cities, domestic work was less commonly followed than elsewhere in the United States. Europeans either could not compete successfully with black women for this work or they chose not to compete. Congruent with patterns that have followed throughout the United States, the daughters of immigrants were less likely to enter household service than were immigrant women, and Italian Americans were the least likely of all European ethnic groups to serve in the homes of others. Among Mexican immigrant women, domestic service was the leading employment. However, as Mexican-American daughters had finally gained entree to pink-collar jobs during World War II, by 1950 the sales and clerical sector was the leading employer of U.S.-born Mexican-American women. Despite losses to the white-collar sectors, "ethnics" played major roles in the female factory labor force in 1950. Mexican, Polish, Italian, and German women filled more than 20,000 operative positions in southern cities with Mexican-American women predominating.

Although female work rates by age and by marital status are a critical dimension of the family experience, the 1950 census yielded little information on the subject. It is possible, although unlikely, that virtually all of the Irish-American working women were single. In contrast, among all other first- and second-generation ethnic women, the numbers of workers so greatly outnumbered the single women that significant proportions of married, widowed, or divorced women had to have been employed. Although the typical white working woman before World War II was young and single, immigrant workers have generally been an older group than native-born workers. By 1950 the typical white ethnic female worker was between the ages of 25 and 44 years. Among both first- and second-generation immigrants, work rates were highest during these middle years.

Regardless of ethnic origin, the children of immigrant families in southern cities had markedly different experiences from their parents. For most families immigration to the United States increased prospects for educating their children, but this was not the rule among all groups.[13] For American-born women of German descent, the median years of school completed was 8.9, which was slightly less than among German immigrant women. In contrast the median years of schooling for Mexican women was 2.1 while their daughters born in America remained at school twice as long. Among Italian-American women, the median years of schooling was 5.0 for the foreign born and 10.1 among the native born. Among the English Americans, place of birth had no relationship to years of schooling, while native-born Polish Americans and Irish Americans had more years of schooling than the immigrant women.

Increased years of schooling paid off for the immigrants' daughters in their ability to move outside the occupational sectors occupied by immigrant women. The one exception to the rule was Irish women, among whom an unusually large percentage (50 percent) of immigrant working women were professional. Consequently, the occupational status of second-generation Irish working women appeared markedly lower than that of the immigrants. A general pattern operating between immigrants and the daughters of immigrants saw the first generation concentrated in the domestic and industrial sectors, while the second generation entered clerical and sales jobs in high proportions. For the most part, ethnicity was not a barrier to employment in offices and stores among the second generation in the urban South. Roughly half of all American-born British, Irish, German, Italian, and Polish working women belonged to the clerical and sales sector. Lagging behind were Mexican-American women, of whom 31 percent held pink-collar jobs. The Mexican-American women were handicapped in competing for these jobs because of their inferior educational attainments. Among black women, however, racial prejudice played a major role in their failure to enter sales and clerical work in substantial numbers. Median years of schooling among black women were 12.2 in 1950, yet fewer than 5 percent of their numbers were sales or clerical workers and half (49.6 percent) were private household workers.

In terms of family composition, the ethnic or social groups of the urban South have not displayed characteristics markedly different from their counterparts elsewhere in the United States. Fertility has been generally higher in southern than in northern cities, but the pattern of differences among whites, nonwhites, and Spanish-surname whites remains constant regardless of region. Among married, widowed, and divorced women in the urban South in 1950, the lowest rate of childlessness occurred among Spanish-surname women, while the highest rate was among nonwhite women. In light of the low rate of childlessness among Hispanics, it is not surprising that Spanish-surname women also have the highest fertility of women in the urban South. However, completed fertility among black women is higher than among non-Hispanic white women. The lower rate of completed fertility among white women reflects smaller family size among whites and not a high incidence of childlessness. Among black women who did bear children, child bearing began earlier and ended later in life than among whites. Despite the high overall fertility of Spanish-surname women, black women also began their child bearing at slightly younger ages than Spanish-surname women.

When both sexes are considered together, the economic disadvantages of black families stand in sharp contrast to the fortunes of immigrants and their children. The median per capita earnings of all blacks at least fourteen years of age, including persons without income, was $861 in 1949. Closest to blacks in earnings but still substantially better off were Mexican Americans, for whom earnings were $1,164 among immigrants and $1,429 among the children of immigrants. At the high end of the earning scale were persons of Soviet extraction, with immigrants earning $2,737 in 1949 and immigrants' children earning $3,092. For every ethnic group, the second generation had more earning power than the immigrants.

The dire employment prospects that confronted southern black women encouraged them to leave the South. One of the most important differences between the work lives of black and nonblack women was the reality of employment-driven separations of black families as black women joined the labor force of northern cities. To cite one example: Twice during the 1950s Anne Bell Hodges of Tuscaloosa left her children with female family members in Alabama and accepted jobs as a governess in New York. Both unsatisfactory working conditions in New York and her sense of isolation from her children drew Hodges to return permanently to Alabama in 1963. Such interregional movement was not uncommon for black women during the 1950s and 1960s.[14]

The civil rights movement eventually stemmed the tide of black female migration to the urban North. Through the leadership and support they offered during the civil rights era, both black and white women in southern cities played parts in opening new options for black women in the urban South.

Historically, towns and cities provided a milieu that nourished achievement and leadership among southern women. Suzanne Lebsock has artfully demonstrated this phenomenon for the Civil War era in *The Free Women of Petersburg*.[15] Although urban places were important forums for women's economic and social leadership throughout the nineteenth century, southern women, partly through the influence of the club movement that swept America at the turn of the century, took on more visible roles of leadership in the early twentieth century. Through such groups as the National Federation of Women's clubs, Protestant Sunday school and missionary societies, the National Association of Colored Women, the Young Women's Christian Association (YWCA), the League of Women Voters, and the Business and Professional Women's Clubs, women learned how to accomplish their social, economic, and political goals.

Southern urban women, black and white, entered the post–World War II era with a legacy of important accomplishments and with the political and organizational skills to shape the destiny of the urban Sunbelt South. During the civil rights movement, women played crucial roles in easing racial strife and in promoting an equalitarian society. Rosa Parks, however, is one of the few female activists whose name remains indelibly etched in the public memory. The names of women like Septima Clark, Elizabeth Huckaby, and Dorothy Counts have been largely forgotten despite their courageous actions.[16]

The ability of some white women to break with southern traditions of racial oppression emanated both from the missionary zeal of southern Protestantism and from the realization that the white woman on the pedestal was both a myth and an oppressive ideal. This perception first bore important fruit in the Atlanta-based Association of Women for the Prevention of Lynching, founded in the 1930s.[17] The organizational skills that black and white women had developed through their clubs and church or civic groups were important assets in the movements for racial and gender equality. After World War II a few white southerners began to condemn segregation itself. Writer Lillian Smith was one of the first to do so. During the 1950s, more southern women joined the civil rights cause. As historian Sara Evans has documented, religious conviction was a driving force behind women's participation in the campaign for racial justice. Some of these organizations, such as the YWCA, provided a specific starting point for social change. Many women who became activists for either the civil rights movement or the women's liberation movement formed strong interracial friendships through the YWCA. The Y was also an environment in which women often questioned the accepted boundaries of race and gender.[18]

The YWCA in most southern cities had long served black clientele through segregated "Phyllis Wheatley" branches. Segregation within Y's was thus a deeply entrenched tradition at the outset of the civil rights revolution. Although service to black women was an important component of Y activities, the Phyllis Wheatley branches were generally underfunded and YWCA boards of directors were slow to repudiate their "separate but equal" philosophies. In 1953 the Atlanta YWCA allocated $167,435 to its Central (white) Branch and $47,029 to the Phyllis Wheatley Branch. Donors contributed to a branch rather than a joint operating fund. After its desegregation in the 1960s, the Atlanta YWCA took a more assertive role in promoting the economic independence of poor women. For most of its history, the Atlanta Y, like its sister organizations in other cities, had concentrated on classes in the social graces and job skills for domestic and factory workers and "business girls." In the early 1970s, however, the Y encouraged the formation of a craftworker cooperative known as Briar Patch Enterprises. Black and white women from depressed neighborhoods in Atlanta marketed their handicrafts through the organization. Rabbit Enterprises, Inc., a spinoff of the Briar Patch organization, marketed hand-sewn apparel and accessories during the 1970s. Half of the Rabbit Enterprises sewers were Cuban refugee women.[19]

Not all white southerners, of course, approved or even acquiesced in the face of desegregation attempts. When Virgil Blossom, superintendent of the Little Rock, Arkansas, public schools, announced a desegregation plan for his district, a group of segregationist women organized the Mothers' League of Central High School. The League tried unsuccessfully to block the token racial integration of Central High in 1957. In Little Rock the effects of the League were later countered by the Women's Emergency Committee

(WEC). The WEC campaigned to reopen the public high schools in Little Rock after Governor Orville Faubus had ordered them closed as a step to circumvent court-ordered desegregation.[20]

Although women of both races worked for social changes in the South and some white women worked to maintain the status quo, for most women and men in southern cities, change was something they accommodated and not something they led. For women of all races, the civil rights era ushered in a series of developments in which their views of themselves changed as much as their views of others. Partly because of their high rates of labor force participation, women in the urban South were most profoundly affected by the civil rights movement promise of improved employment. Economic and social forces in the Sunbelt coalesced to offer black women the prospect of liberation from a life in domestic service. Between 1950 and 1980 black women in the urban South posted substantial occupational gains, while black men were not so fortunate. During congressional debate over the Equal Employment Opportunity bill, white women working in southern offices and shops threatened to quit if black women were hired to work alongside them. By the 1970s, however, black women were working in banks, offices, and stores in southern cities without significantly disrupting white employment patterns.

For most of the South, interethnic concerns have been framed overwhelmingly in black and white terms, although the South is not simply a biracial society. In Texas, Mexican-American organizations had begun to press their cause vigorously. The economic disasters and political upheavals in Latin American and Southeast Asia over the past three decades have sent refugees to many southern states and changed the culture and the atmosphere of many southern cities. Eastern European immigrants, especially Russians and Greeks, have also established sizable communities in southern cities since 1950. As Deborah Dash Moore documents in her contribution to this volume, new Jewish migration to the Sunbelt has also enlarged the cosmopolitan dimension of women's lives in the urban South. Middle-class women from the Middle East, the Far East, and Western Europe have been part of the internationalization of the southern economy, moving to southern cities either as workers or as family members of employees in the textile, oil, and electronics industries.

As a consequence of the political, economic, and demographic changes that have occurred in the urban South since World War II, women have both enlarged their sphere of activities and faced new challenges to traditional ideals. Race was so important in defining southern society that it has frequently obscured the many facets of ethnicity. Although distinctive and separate from the Protestant majority, Jewish and Catholic women historically meshed into the caste system on the basis of race. Religious prejudice is also a southern tradition. In Texas the emphasis on black and white has unfortunately worked against solidarity among immigrants from Mexico.

Women who claim a pure Spanish heritage often still shun the "black" Indian women of Mexican peasant stock.[21]

The new immigrant women also have behaved differently from the European and Mexican women whose work and family lives were glimpsed in the 1950 census. In Miami, the primary terminal point of Cuban emigration, Cuban immigrant women have maintained far lower birthrates than other Hispanic women in the United States, rates even lower than the native white population. As the Cuban immigrants have been older than the native population, lower birthrates are to be expected, but completed fertility among the Cuban women is also lower than among native whites.[22] In 1970 and 1980, Spanish-origin women of Miami held proportionally more professional positions than Spanish-origin women in Houston, a situation explained by the generally high educational levels of Miami's Cuban immigrants and the low educational achievement of Mexican Americans, and the relative youth of the Mexican-American women.

The earnings differentials between any two immigrant groups reflect not simply the relative success or failure of national groups in adapting to the United States. The rapid economic rise of Cuban as opposed to Mexican immigrants reflects the reality that the Cubans were better educated. Cuban-American migrants enjoyed more economic success in prerevolutionary Cuba than had Mexican Americans in their native land.

In 1970, whether or not they lived in cities, virtually all working women in the South were employed in occupations outside agriculture.[23] Although the occupational impact of the civil rights movement had only recently begun, black women's work had diversified considerably by 1970. Black women remained the vast majority of private household workers, but household service constituted fewer than one quarter of the jobs black women filled. Overall, service jobs accounted for slightly more than one half of the positions held by black women. By way of comparison, one fourth of all jobs held by women of Spanish heritage and by all southern women in 1970 were in the service sector. Black women had moved into clerical and sales positions in significant numbers, but their progress did not keep pace with that of Hispanic women, who held about the same proportion of sales and clerical jobs as Anglo women. Significantly, black women were more successful in obtaining clerical jobs than in finding sales jobs in which employers put a premium on workers' making a favorable impression on the public. Hispanic women were not similarly handicapped in finding sales jobs. Black women had achieved numerical parity with other women in industrial jobs by 1970 and Hispanic women continued to be overrepresented in these same occupations.

Over time, newcomers to the South have fared better in the labor force than have native blacks. In 1980 both Spanish-surname and Asian-American female workers had a higher occupational status than black women despite the considerable advance of black workers since the civil rights revolution.[24]

While no statistics have been compiled for the urban South in 1980, census reports for individual cities suggest the comparatively high occupational status of nonblack minority women. Three southern cities—Atlanta, Houston, and Miami—had distinctly different nonblack minority populations in 1980. In all three cities, however, Spanish-origin and Asian-American women recorded higher occupational status than black women. In all three cities, Asian-American women had a higher proportion of their numbers in professional and managerial occupations than did white women. Asian-American women also had achieved parity with black women in the pink-collar sales and clerical sector, though white women continued to dominate these jobs. Spanish-origin women in Houston (largely Mexican-American) and in Miami (largely Cuban-American) had not caught up with blacks in management and the professions, but in Atlanta the relatively small Spanish-origin female labor force surpassed black women's attainments in these occupations. In both Houston and Miami, Spanish-American women were highly concentrated in production jobs and held a disproportionate share of skilled manufacturing jobs as well. In none of the cities were nonblack minority women as concentrated in service jobs as were black women. In Houston, 24 percent of Mexican-American women versus 29 percent of black women were employed in service jobs and in Atlanta 19 percent of Asian-American women versus 27 percent of black women were service workers. In the one job most strongly linked to black women in a segregated society, the position of household domestic, nonblack women were not strongly represented.

The decline of household service has been a revolutionary change in the lives of black women. At the end of World War II, approximately one fourth of all black working women in southern cities were household workers, and about one half were employed in unskilled service jobs outside homes. In Atlanta, Houston, and Miami in 1980, only 5 to 8 percent of black women were domestic workers, and the service sector overall (including domestics) accounted for only one fourth to one third of all the jobs held by black women. In all three cities, the numbers of women in the clerical and sales sectors exceeded the numbers in service occupations. Black women in the urban South have come a long way since the war, but they still are far from achieving equality. The progress of the newer Asian, Mexican, and Cuban women in the labor force reveals that black women still bear the consequences of an earlier biracial caste system.

In adapting to new economic and family roles in post-World War II America, immigrant women in the urban South were as much influenced by their socioeconomic roots as by their nationality. Women from elite or middle-class families coped more easily with their new environments. Their husbands and fathers moved into stable employment more readily than other immigrants. In the case of Cuban immigrants, many women had previous business experience themselves and rapidly became productive members of the American economy.[25] The ability of middle-class immigrants to achieve economic security in America quickly mitigated pressures on the family that are experienced by many poor Americans, immigrant and native alike. In immigrant families in which integration into the American economy has proved difficult, family relationships suffer great stress. Even among Cuban immigrants, the economic adjustment has been difficult.

Consider the case of Esther Bolanos. Shortly after the Cuban revolution, Esther Bolanos came from Cuba to Miami with her husband and children. By 1980, the Bolanos family had established economic security, but they struggled mightily in their first few years in the United States. They faced challenges shared by most recent immigrants. Unlike many immigrants, particularly non-Cubans, the Bolanoses met these challenges with their family intact. During their first three months in Miami, the Bolanoses survived with the help of *Refugio,* an immigrant aid group. During this period, Esther's husband sought employment but failed in his efforts. After their assistance ran out, the family was evicted from their apartment. Friends donated $75 to rent the family a motel room for one month. As is frequently the case among today's immigrants, the woman rather than the man was the first to find employment. The motel owner offered Esther a job as a maid, a job she accepted with a mixture of relief and disappointment. With her meager earnings, the family barely subsisted. As Esther remembers:

We solved the problems of shelter, but the problem [was] a new refrigerator in the room, which was empty except for the last of the canned meat we had brought with us. It was our only source of protein. We ate it a teaspoon at a time, with beans and cornmeal. I would go to sleep thinking of food. . . . One day, cleaning one of the rooms, I found a salami and some cheese. We had a banquet that night.[26]

Among Southeast-Asian immigrants in the South, steady income has been a more difficult achievement than it was for the political refugees of World War II and the 1960s exiles from Cuba. The service orientation of the contemporary economy has interacted with a sex-segregated occupational structure to produce greater demand for female than for male workers in unskilled and semiskilled jobs. Consequently, the immigrants of the 1970s and 1980s, regardless of their skills, have met different employment prospects from those that existed in the 1940s, 1950s, and the early 1960s. In families where women and not men were able to secure employment readily, traditional patriarchal family values have been challenged with husbands and fathers losing self-respect and the esteem of their families as well. Family disorganization has been high among recent immigrants. For many women, loss of respect of male authority figures has exacerbated their own stress in adapting to roles as paid workers.[27]

Both the cultural and the economic environments of the United States challenge the ability of ethnic groups to preserve traditional family ways. Although black Americans have proved most vulnerable to family stress, all other groups have also experienced high levels of family disorganization in the recent past. In the South in 1980, 83 percent of white children (including Spanish-origin whites) under age eighteen years lived with both parents; but only 48 percent of black children (including Spanish-origin blacks) enjoyed similar circumstances. Asian Americans have proved more successful than whites at raising children in two-parent households, while Spanish-origin families have suffered considerable disruption. It is universally true that one-parent households are much more likely to be headed by women than by men. A sizable portion of American children do not live with either parent. Within the South, 12 percent of black children were living apart from both parents in 1980. Overall, southern children are more likely to live outside parental circles than children elsewhere in America, which is largely but not totally explained by the higher proportion of blacks in the South than in other regions.

Overall, the economic, demographic, and social changes that have oc- curred since World War II have diminished the differences between women in the urban South and women in other American cities. In the South and na- tionally, women marry later and bear smaller families in the 1980s than they did in the 1950s. Proportionally more women work for wages in the 1980s than were employed in the 1950s. White women have left the factories and black women have left domestic work for clerical, sales, and nondomestic service jobs. After a day's work at the office, Anglo, Asian, black, and Latin women alike go home to cook and clean for their families. Although family headship is still more common among black females than among any other group of women, female headship has risen for all ethnic groups over the past three decades. For black women especially, but also for other women, occupational advancement has been partly or totally offset by the loss of hus- bands' earnings. Women who have immigrated recently from Latin Amer- ica and from Southeast Asia have often been widowed or separated. More commonly, the stresses of high unemployment among black and immigrant males have destroyed marriages and left women to raise families on the slen- der rewards of their and their children's unskilled labor. Native-born Anglo women have fared better than other groups in occupational terms, but ris- ing divorce rates among Anglo couples also have increased the likelihood of poverty and family headship for these women.

For women in America, the years since World War II have brought dramatic changes in work and family life as married women's work rates and mother-headed families have increased. Because of the historically high work rates of women in southern cities, the rise in the proportion of women working has been smaller in the South than elsewhere. Working women in the urban South, however, felt the imprint of the civil rights movement more deeply than women outside the South. Because southern black and Mexican-American women faced more occupational barriers than did black and Mexican-American women outside the South, the breaking of these barriers has been especially meaningful for women in southern cities. Because Anglo women had previously worked in totally segregated employments in the urban South, the racial changes that occurred in the 1960s and 1970s appeared more threatening to them than to their northern counterparts.

Ultimately, however, employment changes in the South have occurred relatively peacefully. In comparison with the receptions that awaited young black women who broke the color barrier at southern schools and colleges, black women entered white offices, nursing and teaching staffs, and production jobs with little protest. Mexican-American and Cuban-American women in the urban South faced less discrimination than blacks in entering traditional Anglo employments. Cuban Americans, however, have advanced occupationally much more rapidly than Mexican Americans, who continue to be held back by low educational achievement. The new Asian immigrant women represent a different phenomenon from past immigration to the South. They have disproportionally entered jobs at the upper reaches of income and occupational status. The historical experiences of women in the urban South, where working female family heads have always been numerous, indicate that the struggle for survival for female-headed families has been difficult. Ironically, important strides toward racial and gender equality in our society have been accompanied by a significant rise in poverty among single or divorced mothers and their children and the urban South has led the march toward this new dilemma.

NOTES

1. In this chapter the U.S. Bureau of the Census definition of the South is used. The South includes the states of Alabama, Delaware, Florida, Georgia, Kentucky, Louisiana, Maryland, Mississippi, North Carolina, Oklahoma, Tennessee, Texas, and Virginia, and the District of Columbia.

2. Howard Rabinowitz, "Southern Urban Development, 1860-1900," in Blaine Brownell and David R. Goldfield, eds., *The City in Southern History: The Growth of Urban Civilization in the South* (Port Washington, N.Y., 1977), pp. 92-122.

3. Blaine A. Brownell, "The Urban South Comes of Age," in ibid., pp. 123-58.

4. Farm women were much less likely to be counted as wage earners by the census bureau than were town dwellers. Consequently, the work of rural women has been seriously underreported. For a thorough analysis of women in manufacturing in the urban South, see Dolores E. Janiewski, *Sisterhood Denied: Race, Gender, and Class in a New South Community* (Philadelphia, 1985).

5. Joseph A. Hill, *Women in Gainful Occupations, 1870 to 1920*, U.S. Bureau of the Census. Census Monographs, 9 (Washington, D.C., 1929), Table 130, p. 142; Table 4, p. 9; Table 5, p. 11.

6. Alice Kessler-Harris, *Out to Work: A History of Wage-Earning Women in the United States* (New York, 1982), pp. 217-49.

7. Julia Kirk Blackwelder, "Women in the Work Force: Atlanta, New Orleans and San Antonio, 1930 to 1940," *Journal of Urban History* 4 (May 1982), 337-44.

8. Anonymous interview by the author, San Antonio, May 16, 1978.

9. Mary Hardy Phifer, *Textile Voices* (n.p., 1943).

10. The demographic, educational, and occupational statistics on women in the urban South in 1950 that are presented in this chapter were extracted from U.S. Bureau of the Census, *Seventeenth Census of the United States, 1950 Population: Detailed Characteristics and Special Reports* (Washington, 1953-1957). In these volumes, statistics were reported for the urban South as a whole and not for individual cities.

11. For a general description of immigrant workers in nineteenth-century America, see Kessler-Harris, *Out to Work,* pp. 123-38.

12. These findings parallel those found by Hasia R. Diner for the nineteenth-century United States: Diner, *Erin's Daughters: Irish Immigrant Women in the Nineteenth Century* (Baltimore, 1983), pp. 70-105, 130-37.

13. The contrasts in schooling attainments between the foreign born and the native born are not a reflection of the older ages of the immigrants. The differences persist when controlled for age.

14. Interview, Tuscaloosa County Oral Biography Project, 1978 (University of Alabama, Tuscaloosa).

15. Suzanne Lebsock, *The Free Women of Petersburg: Status and Culture in a Southern Town, 1784-1860* (New York, 1984). See also Jean Friedman, *The Enclosed Garden: Women and Community in the Evangelical South, 1830-1900* (Chapel Hill, 1985), who argues that evangelical women engaged in feminist-related reform in the late nineteenth century as part of their own adaptation to urban life.

16. For those who have forgotten or never knew, Septima Clark, presently a resident of Charleston, South Carolina, worked alongside Martin Luther King, Jr. in the Southern Christian Leadership Conference and in other civil rights groups. Elizabeth Huckaby was a white teacher who worked for the acceptance and academic success of the first black students at Little Rock Central High School. Dorothy Counts was the first black student to enter a previously all-white high school in Charlotte, North Carolina.

17. The work of Jessie Daniel Ames and the Association of Southern Women for the Prevention of Lynching is eloquently documented by Jacquelyn Dowd Hall in *Revolt Against Chivalry: Jessie Daniel Ames and the Women's Campaign Against Lynching* (New York, 1979).

18. Sara Evans, *Personal Politics: The Roots of Women's Liberation in the Civil Rights Movement and the New Left* (New York, 1979), 27-55.

19. Records of the Atlanta YWCA, Box 40B (Special Collections, Robert W. Woodruff Library, Emory University).

20. Elizabeth Jacoway, "Taken by Surprise: Little Rock Business Leaders and Desegregation," in Elizabeth Jacoway and David R. Colburn, eds., *Southern Businessmen and Desegregation* (Baton Rouge, 1982), pp. 20-22, 30-31.

21. Interviews by the author with Mrs. G. J. Moore, San Antonio, May 23, 1979, and Adela Navarro, San Antonio, May 29, 1979.

22. Thomas D. Boswell and James R. Curtis, *The Cuban-American Experience: Culture, Images, and Perspectives* (Totowa, N.J., 1984), pp. 107-11.

23. Statistics for 1970 are from U.S. Bureau of the Census, *Nineteenth Census of the United States, 1970 Population: Detailed Characteristics* (Washington, D.C., 1973).

Statistics for the urban South were not reported in 1970. The analysis for 1970 is based on the South as a whole.

24. Statistics for 1980 are based on three cities: Atlanta, Houston, and Miami. U.S. Bureau of the Census, *Twentieth Census of the United States, 1980 Census of Population: Detailed Population Characteristics: Florida; Georgia; Texas* (Washington, D.C., 1983).

25. Marie La Liberitad Richmond, *Immigrant Adaptation and Family Structure among Cubans in Miami, Florida* (New York, 1980), pp. 30-67; Rafael J. Prohias, *The Cuban Minority in the United States: Preliminary Report on Need Identification and Program Evaluation and Final Report for Fiscal Year 1973* (Washington, D.C., 1974), pp. 61-64, 90-91.

26. Jose Llames, *Cuban-Americans: Masters of Survival* (Lexington, Mass., 1980), pp. 45-46.

27. Boswell and Curtis, *The Cuban-American Experience,* pp. 182-83.

6

The Changing Face of Neighborhoods in Memphis and Richmond, 1940-1985

Christopher Silver

The influx of "new immigrants" into Memphis and Richmond in the past two decades has drawn far less attention than did the arrival of the "old immigrants" in the nineteenth and early twentieth centuries. A "golden age" of the Irish in Memphis between 1865 and 1890 witnessed the creation of a cohesive, albeit impoverished, neighborhood known as the "Pinch" north of the downtown along the Mississippi, the establishment of three churches and a host of social clubs that catered to the Hibernians, and a citywide celebration of ethnicity through a grand St. Patrick's Day parade. In contrast, the influx of nearly 3,000 refugees from Southeast Asia and nearly twice that number of Hispanics since the early 1970s has gone virtually unnoticed in Memphis, apart from occasional articles in the local press discussing the challenges of assimilation confronted by these new immigrants.[1] If we were to compare the experiences of the Germans in Richmond in the late nineteenth century to those of the same array of new immigrants in the 1970s and early 1980s, the same sort of contrasts would be evident.[2]

Census counts of foreign born and (as the 1970 census termed their children born in the U.S.) "foreign stock" indicate the absence of anything approaching a critical mass of nonnative ethnics in either city. Out of a total population of over 600,000 in 1970, Memphis boasted only 5,111 foreign-born residents. In the case of Richmond, the foreign-born contingent barely cracked the 1 percent of the total population mark in 1970. By counting the foreign stock, the percentages of "ethnics" increased more than threefold in both cities, although the numbers remain too paltry to bolster the spirits of any numbers-conscious southern ethnologist. If a sufficiently long time perspective is employed (let us say from 1900 to 1980), population figures confirm the steady erosion of the ethnic base of Memphis and Richmond despite recent increases in the number of "new immigrants."[3]

If, however, we broaden our approach to ethnicity in Memphis and Richmond to include race as well as national origin, it is possible to argue that the diversity of culture implied by an ethnic component has been a dominant characteristic of both cities over the past four decades. Yet in neither city can the ethnic component be understood simply in terms of a separation between a dominant white community and subordinate black community. The notion of a "community" implies an integrity to the two racial worlds that simply could not be sustained within a constantly changing city. Rather, blacks and whites identified not only with race, but also with place, class, occupation, and culture, making both Memphis and Richmond amalgams of microworlds that are best grouped under the notion of neighborhoods.

Prior to 1940, the neighborhood pattern in both cities was rather loosely constructed because limitation on residential space required native white, the foreign born, and blacks to exist side by side, except for those affluent enough to live at the fringes of the city. The rapid expansion of both cities after 1940 altered neighborhood patterns in a number of ways. First, demarcations between white and black neighborhoods became more visible. Second, the remaining pockets of white ethnics dispersed into the many areas of the periphery, thereby becoming more fully absorbed into the white world of both cities. Similarly, the new immigrants who arrived during the 1970s and 1980s eschewed the center city for settlement along the periphery.[4] Finally, the revamped neighborhood structure in both cities between 1940 and 1985 not only distinguished the black world from that of the white, but also pointed to a noticeable stratification along class lines. As both cities developed a formal process for addressing the issue of neighborhood preservation by the 1970s, it became clear that class differences mattered in allocation of scarce resources. As neighborhoods experienced transformation in the post-1940 period, so too did the city as a whole. This did not represent simply an erosion of ethnicity in Memphis or Richmond but rather a redefinition of the diversity of lifestyles in both cities on the basis of class as well as race in its neighborhood substructure.

It is the intent of this chapter to examine the neighborhood development process in Memphis and Richmond after 1940 as a window through which to observe and to describe the perpetuation of an ethnic dimension in the modern southern city. Memphis and Richmond offer an appropriate comparative perspective on neighborhood change in the urban South since the 1940s for several reasons. First, the black proportion of the total city population in Memphis and Richmond was comparable in 1940. Moreover, the pattern of black settlement in these two cities at the end of World War II was dispersed through a wide area of urban core, as compared to southern cities where a concentrated racial residential pattern already existed. Of the two cities, however, Richmond possessed the most physically cohesive black community.

Finally, Memphis and Richmond hired the same planning consultant, Harland Bartholomew, who prescribed a similar development strategy for both cities that placed significant emphasis on neighborhood planning to counter the inimical effects of racial coexistence at the neighborhood level. While working with a basically similar strategy, the contrasting styles of Memphis and Richmond in addressing residential change after 1940 point to the determining impact of local priorities in explaining the evolving pattern of ethnic neighborhoods in the southern city. While it is true that federal housing and renewal programs influenced development in the two cities after 1940, federal policy induced change but did not produce a transformation in local approaches to black community needs. Neighborhood planning ideas and practices in Memphis and Richmond flowed directly from the local political environment.

The relatively dense residential structure of both Memphis and Richmond on the eve of World War II fostered a considerable degree of overlapping among native white and nonnative and black neighborhoods. Indeed, it may be somewhat of an exaggeration to use the term *neighborhood* to denote the settlement patterns of the foreign born in either city in 1940, although native whites and blacks tended to cluster in distinct geographical areas in both cities.

According to the 1940 census, there were only 4,458 foreign born among Memphis's 292,942 inhabitants. More telling was that not one of the city's seventy-five census tracts had a foreign-born contingent in excess of 3.8 percent of the total tract population. The only semblance of a white ethnic concentration in Memphis was in seven contiguous midtown census tracts extending eastward from the fringe of the central business district. These tracts alone accounted for over one third of the city's foreign-born population. Yet in the two tracts located adjacent to the central business district with the highest proportion of white ethnics, blacks actually accounted for the majority of the residents.[5]

By 1950, however, the foreign-born population in these two tracts had been halved, thereby signaling the dispersion of the city's amorphous white ethnic population even more widely throughout the metropolitan area (see Figure 6.1). As Richard Thomas noted in a 1970 study of the residential patterns of Memphis's white immigrants, the midtown area had served as home for the bulk of the immigrants who had come to Memphis primarily from Ireland, Italy, Germany, Greece, Poland, and Russia beginning in the late nineteenth century. The exodus of immigrants from the neighborhood known as the "Pinch" just north of downtown exemplified the Memphis neighborhood transition pattern. Originally developed by poor Irish families in the nineteenth century who accepted the misery of its substandard housing in order to live close to their jobs along the riverfront, the twelve-block area later drew a cross section of the Memphis immigrant community. As the downtown business district expanded northward after 1900, its immigrant

Figure 6.1
Census Tracts of 1950 Containing 200 or More White Ethnics
by 1960—Memphis

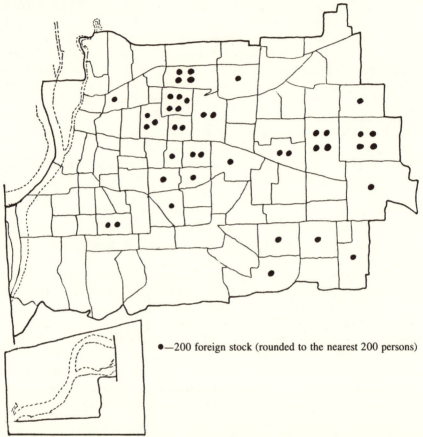

●—200 foreign stock (rounded to the nearest 200 persons)

inhabitants inched eastward, usually on a block-by-block basis so as "to keep their old neighborhood in view." Encroachment by the rapidly expanding black community also may have prompted the drift of the white ethnics to the periphery of the midtown area. Whatever the motivation, "every twenty-five years," according to Steve Stern, "they put a synagogue [or a cathedral] on wheels. They kept moving further east."[6]

In Richmond, as late as 1960, it was still possible to discern a clustering of white ethnics in neighborhoods extending westward from the city's center. In 1940, white ethnics resided principally in two areas, Shockoe Valley and adjacent Church Hill in the city's east end and in the Fan neighborhood to the west of the central business district (CBD). Over the next twenty years, however, blacks replaced all but a few white ethnics in the east-end

Table 6.1
Census Tracts Containing 200 or More White Ethnics* in Memphis, 1960

Census Tract	Total Population	Ethnic Population	Black Population
7	7,007	875	3,836
9	7,222	219	4,910
16	3,131	484	90
17	5,144	925	11
20	5,386	260	391
25	5,633	660	176
26	3,677	324	98
29	6,876	705	38
30	5,794	310	1,902
31	4,613	220	23
32	5,227	314	372
33	3,349	224	49
34	3,193	228	258
35	4,366	235	157
59	6,573	301	2,801
62	4,174	207	476
79	6,985	263	5
80	6,561	246	302
81	9,067	237	31
83	7,219	250	6
85	3,985	271	329
86	7,676	744	15
87	6,635	248	11
92	8,104	648	228
93	6,553	341	4
94	5,663	271	Annexed 2
95	7,271	288	in the 481
96	4,291	306	1950s 171
99	6,784	265	22
100	4,784	290	59
101	11,051	393	38

Source: U.S. Census of Population and Housing: 1960, Memphis Census Tracts, PHC(1)-89, Table P-1.

*White ethnics were recorded in the census as "foreign stock" and broken down into foreign born and native born of foreign or mixed parentage. The figures here represent the total foreign stock in selected census tracts.

neighborhoods. Apart from a handful of ethnic businesses, most notably some Italian-run wholesale produce establishments in the "Valley," white ethnics had disappeared from the working-class neighborhoods in the city's east end by 1960. Indeed, the westward migration by white ethnics produced a neighborhood pattern physically more cohesive than that existing when they first arrived in the city.[7]

Beginning in the Fan neighborhood and extending westward in a five-mile wedge to the Richmond-Henrico boundary, lived approximately 5,500 of the city's 9,702 foreign stock. More than one third of Richmond's white ethnics resided in the five contiguous census tracts that made up the bulk of the city's affluent West End (see Figure 6.2). Leading the westward drift of white ethnics was the city's substantial Jewish community, a mixture of Germans, eastern Europeans, and Russians. As late as 1986, Richmond's Jewish community numbered approximately 8,000 and supported six synagogues, four of which are located in the West End, with one remaining in the heart of the Fan. It is also significant to note that adjacent Henrico County boasted more than 7,000 white ethnics in 1960, the largest proportion of whom were German Jews living in the West End.[8]

It is apparent that the pressure of black population growth prior to 1940 accounts in large measure for the neighborhood transition process in central Memphis. Between 1900 and 1940, the black population of Memphis grew from 49,910 to 121,498, with the greatest concentrations located in the mid-town area and extending both north and south of the central business district. The spectacular growth of the Memphis-Shelby County black community in the 1930s by nearly 28,000 occurred exclusively through migration from the countryside to the city.[9]

To accommodate such a substantial population increase necessitated the dispersion of blacks through a large number of neighborhoods. The 1940 census reveals that blacks in Memphis occupied more than 20 percent of the housing units in forty-eight of the city's seventy-five census tracts. Nearly 94 percent of black households in Memphis resided in those forty-eight census tracts. Although a clear demarcation separated the black neighborhoods clustered around the central city from the predominantly white neighborhoods that extended eastward toward the urban fringe, there was a substantial degree of racial intermingling at least at the census tract level. A telling indication of this was that in only thirteen out of the seventy-five city census tracts did blacks make up 5 percent or less of the total number of households. In other words, there were relatively few exclusively white census tracts in Memphis in 1940. The dispersed pattern of black residence in Memphis had been observed first by sociologist Thomas J. Woofter in the mid-1920s and cited as a distinguishing feature of southern urban demographic patterns. Obviously, the pattern persisted through the period of enormous growth in the black community in the 1930s.[10] Indeed, it became an issue of public policy in the decades after 1940 to devise a strategy to

Figure 6.2
Census Tracts of 1950 Containing 200 or More White Ethnics
by 1960—Richmond

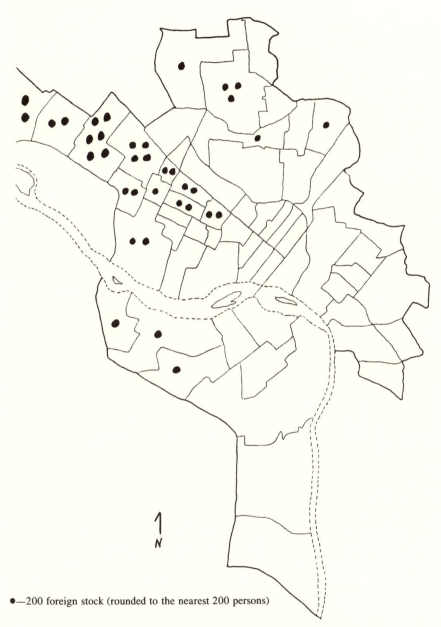

●—200 foreign stock (rounded to the nearest 200 persons)

Table 6.2
Census Tracts Containing 200 or More White Ethnics* in Richmond, 1960

Census Tract	Total Population	Ethnic Population	Black Population
N-10	3,476	221	1,161
N-12	4,885	281	70
N-15	6,408	572	20
N-17	4,263	246	5
S-5	5,473	297	398
S-6	3,400	224	8
S-7	6,120	251	119
W-9	4,762	346	20
W-12	4,327	329	7
W-13	4,977	393	28
W-14	3,544	363	9
W-15	2,895	200	2
W-16	2,322	349	11
W-17	3,313	420	2
W-18	6,015	837	22
W-19	6,103	1,211	28
W-20	3,802	417	287
W-21	4,890	417	51

Source: U.S. Census of Population and Housing: 1960, Richmond Census Tracts, PHC(1)-126, Table P-1.

* White ethnics were recorded in the census as "foreign stock" and broken down into foreign born and native born of foreign or mixed parentage. The figures here represent the total foreign stock in selected census tracts.

contain black residential expansion within a more carefully defined sphere and to delineate more precisely the boundaries between the black and white worlds of Memphis.

The pattern of black community expansion in Memphis between 1940 and 1980 exemplifies the merging of two distinct residential concentrations into a single expansive and segregated enclave. According to Woofter's research on Memphis in the 1920s, black residential areas were confined largely to the core of the city but hardly could be regarded as a continuous black belt. Scattered pockets of black housing were located north of the central business district, with the largest concentrations situated south of Poplar Avenue and adjacent to the city's industrial area. As late as 1940 this dispersed settlement pattern still persisted with most blacks living either north of Jackson Avenue or south of Poplar in the tracts located closest to the Mississippi River. The tracts in between ranged from less than 10 percent to as high as 55 percent black both directly north and south of Poplar Avenue. Figure 6.3 plots the expansion of Memphis census tracts

Figure 6.3
Census Tracts with 70 Percent or Greater Black Population—Memphis,
1940 to 1980
(indicates census in which first became 70 percent black)

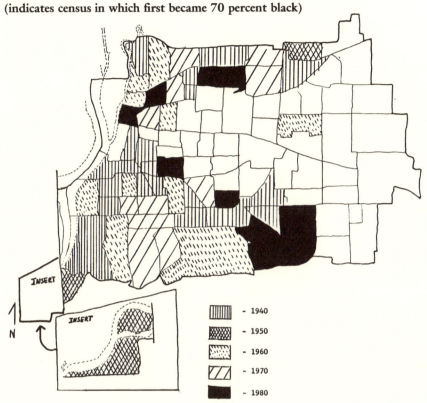

that had a predominantly black population (70 percent or more) from 1940 through 1980. Between 1940 and 1950, there was relatively little change in the locus of black residential areas in the city. During the 1950s, the number of predominantly black census tracts increased from twenty-one to thirty-three, representing an increase of six in both the north and south Memphis black communities. After 1960, however, the area of greatest expansion of the black community was in South Memphis where in two decades an additional seventeen census tracts shifted from a racially mixed to a predominantly black status. In North Memphis, only four census tracts underwent a similar racial transition during this period. In the face of an expanding black community, inner-city white neighborhoods coalesced into a residential wedge extending eastward from the CBD that proved to be impervious to black in-migration. As will be discussed later, the controlled character of black neighborhood expansion was a product of a carefully orchestrated housing development process.

The spatial configuration of the black community points to a geographic gulf between those residing in North and South Memphis. In terms of socioeconomic status, the division between the two areas was just as wide, especially when home-ownership rates and income are used as determinants of variation. The home-ownership rate among blacks in the six predominantly black census tracts in North Memphis in 1950 was 53 percent, with several exceeding 60 percent. In contrast, the home-ownership rate within the thirteen predominantly black census tracts in South Memphis was only 29 percent (see Table 6.3). Public policy decisions, particularly in the area of public housing, fostered the significantly higher incidence of black renters in South Memphis. Of the 3,337 units of public housing constructed prior to 1950, 2,220 units were built in South Memphis and all were designated for black occupancy. Only 280 units of public housing for families were built in the North Memphis black census tracts over the life of the program.

Income data from 1950 confirm that North Memphis boasted the greater proportion of the city's more affluent blacks. Five of the ten census tracts

Table 6.3
Homeownership/Renter Rates among Blacks in Memphis, 1950
(by tract and section)

Census Tract	Total Housing Units	Black Owner Occupied	(%)	Black Renter Occupied	(%)
		North Memphis			
1	972	223	(27)	602	(73)
5	331	99	(62)	61	(38)
6	1,119	629	(69)	279	(31)
10	314	220	(73)	80	(27)
18	954	436	(46)	504	(54)
90	862	513	(60)	345	(40)
	TOTAL	2,120	(53)	1,871	(47)
		South Memphis			
40	2,494	198	(9)	2,038	(91)
41	2,523	82	(4)	1,900	(96)
43	345	34	(11)	287	(89)
44	736	66	(9)	635	(91)
45	1,316	265	(21)	987	(79)
48	1,585	267	(18)	1,256	(82)
49	1,647	449	(34)	856	(66)
51	1,708	135	(10)	1,218	(90)
53	1,717	1,004	(71)	408	(29)
54	1,654	580	(36)	1,021	(64)
60	703	451	(78)	124	(22)
61	478	280	(62)	172	(38)
67	1,924	1,011	(59)	690	(41)
	TOTAL	4,822	(29)	11,592	(71)

Source: U.S. Census of Population: 1950, Memphis Census Tracts, P-D30, Table 3.

in North Memphis had a black population that was predominantly middle class (more than 80 percent of the median city family income). Blacks in the census tracts to the east of downtown (which were largely integrated) were poorer. None of the fifteen had a majority of blacks with annual incomes above the city median, and twelve contained a black component that was more than 70 percent low to moderate income. Of the twenty-eight census tracts with a sizable black population in South Memphis, all but three were more than 60 percent low to moderate income. Only in one census tract did the majority of blacks have an annual income above 80 percent of the median (see Table 6.4). Thus, while poverty was a trait pervasive among

Table 6.4
Black Families, 80 Percent or Less of Median Income* in Memphis, 1950
(by tract and section)

	North Memphis				South Memphis		
Census Tract	Total Black Families	Black Families 80% or less	(%)	Census Tract	Total Black Families	Black Families 80% or less	(%)
1	960	690	(72)	40	3,070	2,095	(68)
2	770	390	(51)	41	2,965	2,295	(77)
3	980	345	(35)	42	750	655	(87)
4	890	535	(60)	43	465	380	(82)
5	175	90	(51)	44	1,090	880	(81)
6	1,155	720	(62)	45	1,595	1,105	(69)
7	620	270	(44)	46	820	610	(74)
9	860	420	(49)	47	470	320	(68)
10	335	205	(61)	48	2,030	1,395	(69)
14	235	145	(62)	49	1,650	1,100	(67)
18	1,115	685	(61)	50	910	645	(71)
90	900	630	(70)	51	1,585	1,140	(72)
TOTAL	8,995	5,125	(57)	52	675	490	(73)
				53	1,810	1,100	(61)
	Central Memphis			54	2,165	1,445	(67)
				55	835	515	(62)
19	720	505	(70)	57	815	545	(67)
20	420	335	(80)	58	475	290	(61)
21	830	625	(75)	59	155	115	(74)
22	595	480	(81)	60	640	295	(46)
23	1,535	1,105	(72)	61	555	305	(55)
24	1,625	1,210	(74)	62	265	145	(55)
28	1,055	610	(58)	63	340	235	(69)
30	285	155	(54)	65	855	550	(64)
32	155	125	(81)	66	300	180	(60)
34	185	135	(73)	67	1,775	1,235	(70)
35	325	260	(80)	68	910	570	(63)
36	285	240	(84)	76	665	475	(71)
37	155	130	(84)	TOTAL	30,635	21,110	(69)
39	315	245	(78)				
TOTAL	8,485	6,160	(73)				

Source: U.S. Census of Population: 1950, Memphis Census Tracts, P-D30, Table 4.

*Eighty percent of median income in Memphis in 1950 was $1,881.

most blacks in Memphis in 1950, there is clear evidence that a growing and largely impoverished ghetto in South Memphis was separated from more affluent black neighborhoods north and northwest of the downtown.

The changing distribution of blacks in Memphis must be viewed in the context of the city's expansion through annexation from 1900 through the 1960s. Even though the black community pushed both northward and southward from the city center toward the outer boundaries after 1900, the city's aggressive annexation campaign continuously expanded those boundaries. Figure 6.4 shows annexation from 1940 to 1970. While the black community in North Memphis extended to pre-1951 boundaries, the addition of thirty-five square miles of territory, much of it directly to the north of Wolf River, provided space for white expansion and placed black

Figure 6.4
Memphis Annexation, 1940 to 1970

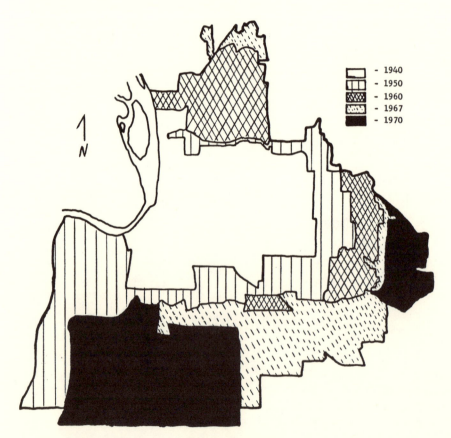

Source: Memphis-Shelby County Planning Commission.

neighborhoods within the center, rather than along the fringe of the city. The persistence of the "white residential wedge" extending eastward from the downtown area connected the center with the area annexed between 1901 and 1950. By encouraging black residential expansion southward from the city center, the potential for change in these suburbs was minimized.

The growth of the black community in Richmond both prior to and in the following four decades of 1940 differed in some respects from the process in Memphis. Richmond's black population was slightly smaller than that of Memphis in 1900, although it represented nearly the same proportion of the total city population. Concern over the spread of black residences into white neighborhoods, which became a consuming issue in Memphis in the 1950s, surfaced as early as 1911 in Richmond and led to enactment of a racial zoning ordinance. Although the state court denied a challenge to the constitutionality of racial zoning in 1915, the Supreme Court decision in *Buchanan* v. *Warley* in 1917 undermined the local initiative. Further attempts during the 1920s to draft a legally viable racial zoning ordinance failed to gain court sanctions. Nevertheless, Richmond remained "a hotbed of strong opinion favoring the preservation of the strict integrity of both races." According to the editor of the *Virginia Municipal Review,* writing in 1930, "a gradual and natural encroachment of the colored population into white neighborhoods" would confront Richmond with "a problem of increasing significance . . . whose solution deserves the thought and discussion of leaders of both races."[11]

Indeed, there was some movement of blacks into predominantly white neighborhoods both before and after the trial run with racial zoning, but not to the extent suggested by proponents of racial zoning. Slow growth in the city's population after 1900, especially when compared to that of Memphis, enabled most newcomers to find accommodations in already established black neighborhoods. Expansion of black neighborhoods tended to occur in those areas undergoing a change from residential to commercial or industrial land uses. The most vivid example of this in Richmond was in Jackson Ward where expansion of the central business district led to abandonment of the area by middle-class whites, among whom there was a healthy sprinkling of white ethnics. The result was that as early as 1920 in Richmond, "a centralized ghetto, or something very like it, appeared first in its most highly articulated form."[12]

The contrasts between Richmond and Memphis in the pre-1940s era are instructive and help to explain, at least in part, the variations in neighborhood patterns and neighborhood development policies that marked the post-1940 period. As noted above, Memphis's black population in the 1920s and 1930s was considerably more dispersed than that of Richmond. The Memphis black community, which was only slightly greater in population than that of Richmond, spanned an area almost three times that of the black community in Richmond. Memphis blacks boasted 21 persons per acre as compared with

46 persons per acre in Richmond. Whereas black neighborhoods in Richmond were constricted within less than 10 percent of the city's residential acreage, black Memphians occupied nearly 28 percent of the city's residential space. In Memphis, it was the black community, not the white, that was displaced by business expansion in the city's core. One outcome of this was that blacks were pushed into outlying wards where home-buying opportunities were better. Between 1910 and 1920, the number of black home owners in Memphis increased by 70 percent. In Richmond, the number of black home owners increased by only 22 percent during the same period.[13]

After 1940, expansion of Richmond's black neighborhoods was eastward and northward, whereas the direction of new residential development was westward and southward. This was particularly the case in the 1950s when Richmond's black community, which had previously concentrated in the census tracts constituting Jackson Ward, extended their neighborhood core northward and eastward (see Figure 6.5). By 1970, the black community dominated all but one census tract east of Chamberlayne Avenue (the major north-south axis that passed through the city center) from the northern to southern borders of the city. Like in Memphis, there was a predominantly white-occupied residential wedge that linked the city center to the exclusively white fringe neighborhoods north of the James River. This white wedge did not constitute the barrier between major segments of the black community as it did in Memphis. If there was a geographic divide within Richmond's black community, it was the line of Interstate 64 extending eastward from the central business district. To the north of I-64 were the formerly white-occupied neighborhoods to which middle-class blacks migrated during the 1950s and early 1960s. To the south, especially in Church Hill, resided the largest concentration of working-class blacks. The concentration of low to moderate income blacks in the Church Hill area was not surprising since 1,848 (64 percent) of the 2,885 public housing units built prior to 1970 were located in that neighborhood. As figure 6.5 indicates, the major change in the black neighborhood pattern after 1970 was the filling out of the northeast sector (Highland Park) just to the north of the I-64 corridor and the spreading out of predominantly black neighborhoods in south Richmond. Displacees from urban renewal areas probably accounted for much of the change in both areas, although the site selection process for public housing accounts for neighborhood change in the Southside area. The development of nearly 500 new units of public housing in the Bainbridge-Hull Street area, coupled with the transition of Hillside Court (402 units opened for occupancy in 1952) from white to black occupancy, increased substantially the proportion of low-income blacks in the area.

Census data for 1960 indicate the highest proportion of Richmond's black home owners lived in selected Eastend and Northside neighborhoods, and the largest proportion of renters resided in the traditional center of the black community in Jackson Ward. The proportion of black renters to

Figure 6.5
**Census Tracts with 70 Percent or Greater Black Population—Richmond,
1940 to 1980***

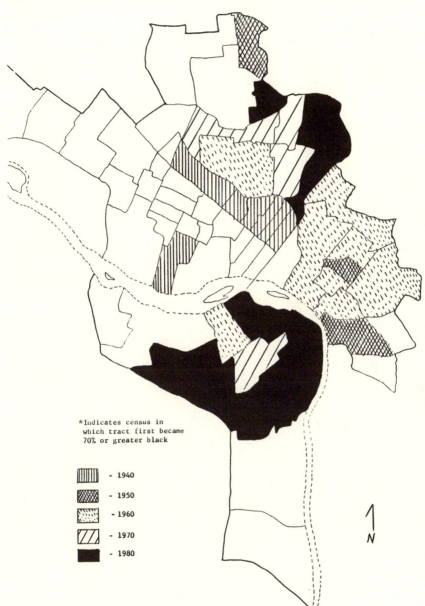

*Indicates census in
which tract first became
70% or greater black

|||||| - 1940

▨ - 1950

░ - 1960

▨ - 1970

■ - 1980

N

home owners was also high in the neighborhoods adjacent to Jackson Ward to the north. It is evident that as late as 1960, the black community in Church Hill still possessed a substantial number of black home owners but that Jackson Ward had become poorer and more transient in nature (see Table 6.5). After 1960, as the black middle class sought better housing outside of the traditional boundaries of the black community, Church Hill lost its appeal as a mixed-income black neighborhood, while the Northside lured a substantial proportion of the black middle class. The middle-income neighborhoods in the Northside (and not Church Hill) would become the

Table 6.5
Homeownership/Renter Rates among Blacks in Richmond, 1960
(by tract and section)

Census Tract	Total Housing Units	Black Owner Occupied	(%)	Black Renter Occupied	(%)
		East			
E-2	1,258	519	(51)	503	(49)
E-3	1,202	610	(55)	489	(44)
E-4	1,172	402	(36)	708	(64)
E-5	1,147	342	(32)	707	(68)
E-6	1,067	160	(18)	722	(82)
E-7	1,352	702	(55)	583	(45)
E-8	1,161	292	(28)	760	(72)
E-9	1,208	279	(35)	527	(65)
TOTAL		3,306	(40)	4,999	(60)
		Central			
N-1	653	129	(20)	494	(80)
N-2	774	171	(25)	523	(75)
N-3	1,215	227	(20)	926	(80)
N-6	1,234	129	(11)	1,047	(89)
N-7	695	196	(29)	473	(71)
N-8	458	161	(36)	286	(64)
TOTAL		1,013	(21)	3,749	(79)
		North			
N-4	1,029	426	(52)	393	(48)
N-9	1,279	534	(53)	471	(47)
N-10	1,036	226	(44)	287	(56)
N-11	1,097	195	(59)	137	(41)
N-12	1,759	10	(67)	5	(33)
TOTAL		1,391	(52)	1,293	(48)
		West			
W-7	1,691	897	(55)	723	(45)

Source: U.S. Census of Population and Housing: 1960, Richmond Census Tracts, PHC(1)-126, Table P-3.

focus of neighborhood preservation and rehabilitation programs initiated in the 1970s, while core neighborhoods such as Church Hill would receive only minimal attention.

The demographics of neighborhood change in Memphis and Richmond after 1940 point to several trends in the evolution of urban ethnicity. First, the dispersion of white ethnics to outlying neighborhoods was a trend observable in both cities by 1960. White ethnic neighborhood identification, which had been decidedly weak in both cities throughout the twentieth century, was effaced by the general phenomenon of white migration from core city neighborhoods. Ethnic institutions followed residential dispersion as evidenced in Richmond by westward relocation of Jewish synagogues. Indeed, white ethnics who traditionally resided in core city neighborhoods prior to 1940 generally relocated to those areas where black in-migration was least likely to occur. As the blacks pushed their neighborhoods eastward and northward, white ethnics moved their residences and their social institutions westward.[14]

In Memphis, for example, the Memphis Italian Society, which had built a meeting hall downtown in 1905, sold the hall in 1947 and moved its social life to a country club developed in the South Memphis suburbs. A main feature of the fifty-acre club was twelve bocce alleys, a baseball diamond, playgrounds, and plenty of space to present "an inviting retreat from the city." Some 3,000 Italians in Memphis attended the opening festivities at the club in 1949.[15] In 1963, as the spread of urban neighborhoods encroached upon their suburban retreat, the Italians moved their club farther out, and while retaining several bocce lanes, on its 120 acres the club incorporated an eighteen-hole golf course, tennis courts, and a swimming pool. The club persisted as the social focus of Italian life through the early 1980s, although linked to the new dispersed settlement in suburbs rather than the cohesive ethnic neighborhood of the early 1900s around Second Street in the city's core.[16] Neighborhood change for Jews in Memphis after 1940 followed the same pattern of dispersal to the white fringe communities.[17]

White ethnic neighborhood dispersion was accompanied by (and was perhaps fostered by) a significant realignment in the neighborhood boundaries of the black community after 1940. The patterns of change varied somewhat in the two cities, although both Memphis and Richmond experienced a consolidation of fragmented black residential areas into a continuous zone of settlement. Rapid growth in the black population, more so in Memphis than in Richmond after 1940, explains the process of racial transition. Yet it is also important to note the effects of black displacement in both cities resulting from a range of public improvement projects during the 1950s and 1960s. Clearly, public housing development and the accompanying removal of slum housing caused a transition in the racial and class occupancy of neighborhoods in the 1940s and 1950s. Urban renewal and new highway construction merely exacerbated an already difficult problem of increasing the housing stock for blacks while safeguarding white neighborhoods from black encroachment. As the evidence for Memphis and Richmond reveals, racial transition occurred in a substantial portion of center city between 1940 and 1980.

In both cities, this process engendered efforts to establish constraints on black neighborhood expansion. Neighborhood planning was one means of controlling population movement. The demographic transition in black neighborhoods fostered first a response from white neighborhoods to hold the line against further change and then a counter response from black leaders to address their unmet housing needs. By the 1970s, both cities had initiated a neighborhood planning process to address the decline in core city neighborhoods. In the process of creating a neighborhood planning framework in both cities, however, conflicts between poor and more affluent black neighborhoods emerged. By the 1970s, the black community in Memphis and Richmond was divided along class lines. The process for addressing neighborhood needs that emerged was slanted decidedly toward the more affluent members of what could no longer be regarded as a single, cohesive black community.

White ethnic residential clusters in both cities were also a victim of the process of creating separate and distinct racial worlds after 1940. Certainly, the lack of an infusion of new members into the old immigrant neighborhoods eroded ethnic identity. Yet dispersal in the face of rapid racial change at the neighborhood level hastened the process. Moreover, it is significant that the new immigrants of the 1970s and 1980s, especially the Hispanics and Southeast Asians, settled largely along the urban fringe rather than in center city neighborhoods. For example, the clustering of Southeast Asians in Richmond created an Asian community numbering approximately 6,500 persons by the mid-1980s, which was located in three major apartment complexes in predominantly white suburban areas. In Memphis, most of the area's established 15,000 Hispanics found housing during the 1970s and early 1980s outside the city limits.[18] The settlement patterns of the new ethnics suggest that the process of recasting neighborhood boundaries since 1940 did more than just accentuate demarcations between the black and white communities. To a significant extent, the creation of a neighborhood configuration based largely on race closed off the possibility for urban neighborhoods to continue to function as staging grounds for new white ethnic community settlement. In their quest to resolve the race issue, both cities effectively "planned away" one key attribute of healthy urban life, that is, neighborhood diversity. While the following discussion of neighborhood planning since 1940 underscores the attention given to black residential expansion, the overall effect was to undermine ethnic vitality in both Memphis and Richmond.

On the eve of World War II, the social geography of both Memphis and Richmond was the amalgam of a score of separate neighborhood units.

Differentiated from each other by factors such as architecture, ethnicity, class, and race, the patchwork pattern of neighborhoods attested to the social diversity within the southern city.[19] Over the next four decades, however, the organic process of neighborhood formation was irreparably altered by major reorganization in the physical and social structure of both cities. As planning replaced the unplanned approach to neighborhood formation after 1940, the demarcations between individual neighborhoods gave way to broader divisions in each city along class and race lines. Both Memphis and Richmond used planning to reinforce the separateness of the class and race worlds that had been sustained loosely in the traditional neighborhood fabric.

The neighborhood planning approach employed by both cities after 1940 was remarkably similar. For one thing, both cities made use of the same federal urban redevelopment programs to guide and finance the neighborhood planning process. Public housing constructed in Richmond was identical in size and design to complexes built in Memphis. Likewise, urban renewal efforts followed a common set of federal guidelines and produced similar consequences in both cities. Yet it is important to recognize the broad degree of local discretion allowed by federal policymakers from the 1940s through the 1960s in the use of urban redevelopment funds. Moreover, federally sponsored urban initiatives were not mandatory. Cities determined the level and timing of their participation. It was, in fact, these two factors—the level and time of participation—that account for some of the differences between Memphis and Richmond in neighborhood planning after 1940.

Concern over residential expansion by a growing black population, coupled with efforts to eliminate the blighting influence of substandard housing in minority neighborhoods, fueled the neighborhood planning movement in Memphis and Richmond after 1940. Similarities in their approach to these shared concerns were owed in large measure to the influence of Harland Bartholomew, the planning consultant retained by both cities in the late 1930s to draft a master plan for future urban development. For both clients, Bartholomew prescribed a brand of neighborhood planning that called for strict separation between classes and races. The sort of neighborhood planning that Bartholomew and others in the planning fraternity propagated in the 1940s coincided with prevailing local attitudes toward the proper social division of cities. Only a few critics, such as Chicago planner and community activist, Reginald Isaacs, regarded neighborhood planning as an insidious "instrumentation for segregation of ethnic and economic groups." For most urban leaders, especially those in Memphis and Richmond, Bartholomew's approach spoke directly to an enduring social problem that seemed to be getting worse.[20]

Bartholomew's initial relationship with Memphis occurred in the early 1920s when he was hired by Mayor Rowland Paine to prepare a comprehensive plan for the city's expanding street system and for implementation of the city's recently enacted zoning scheme. Although the 1924 Memphis plan made no direct reference to neighborhood concerns per se, a similar plan drafted for Knoxville in 1929 referred to the comprehensive plan as a guide for "the proper direction of new growth and the rehabilitation of the older sections of the city." According to Memphis historian Robert Sigafoos, the revised street system set forth in the 1924 plan established physical and functional divisions that would serve as neighborhood boundaries in both the older and newly developed sections of the city. Sigafoos maintained that "the form of Memphis" (in the 1970s) was "a product of the recommendations of the Bartholomew organization" dating back to the 1924 plan.[21]

When Bartholomew went to work on plans for Memphis and Richmond in the late 1930s, he was convinced that neighborhood preservation should be the cornerstone of effective city improvement strategies. In the Memphis plan of 1938, as well as in the Richmond plan of 1946, Bartholomew warned city leaders to eschew excessive decentralization through new residential development in favor of preserving, or if necessary rebuilding, already established neighborhoods. For one thing, neighborhood preservation would eliminate the necessity of costly annexation to sustain the white residential base within the city. Bartholomew was particularly concerned about the migration of whites from the core to the periphery that over the past three decades frequently had compelled urban leaders in both cities to annex the suburbs to hold onto their population. Given the expanded size of both cities in the early 1940s, Bartholomew felt that there was enough space to provide for residential growth if established white neighborhoods could be preserved.[22]

Equally important for retention of white residents was the need for careful planning of black residential expansion. In the case of Memphis, neighborhood planning could serve as a strategy to consolidate the city's dispersed black population and prevent further incursions by blacks into established white neighborhoods. Bartholomew called for slum clearance to eliminate pockets of black poverty because of their "depressing effect" on adjacent established white neighborhoods. He proposed that "the bulk of the negro population . . . be confined to definite districts" through planned development of public and privately constructed housing.[23] As both cities turned to public housing as a substitute for substandard low-income housing in the late 1930s, they did so on Bartholomew's premise that neighborhood boundaries should be recast to accommodate black residential expansion in specified areas. The organic neighborhood pattern was to be replaced by planned separation of the urban population on race and class lines.

In the case of Richmond, as noted previously, efforts to contain black residential growth dated back to the 1911 racial zoning ordinance and continued throughout the 1920s. In the mid-1930s, however, the issue of black containment reemerged in conjunction with a project to replace slum housing with a 300-unit apartment complex financed through the federal government's limited dividend housing program. The original site for the Sunshine project on vacant land adjacent to Virginia Union, a black college located northwest of the central business district, was opposed vehemently by nearby white residents. Northside whites argued that it transgressed traditional racial boundaries and extended the black community of Jackson Ward too close to their neighborhoods. The alternate plan was to clear 150 existing structures in the heart of Jackson Ward for the needed land. Black home owners in Jackson Ward objected just as strongly to the alternate site. According to resident George W. Howell, who headed the neighborhood's Home Owners Committee, "to deprive us of our homes, reduce us to the status of renters, . . . is most inconceivable on the part of our Government. . . .We are well satisfied where we are and do not wish to depart from the homes we own, since after this area is rebuilt, we have no possible chance to buy in the rebuilt area."

The refusal of black residents to relinquish options on their homes during the summer of 1935 delayed the site acquisition. In September, the Sunshine project backers learned that the federal commitment for the project had been rescinded. With the backing of black community leaders, Richmond tried to salvage the project by proposing a third site that required removal of only four structures, but to no avail.[24]

The failure of the Sunshine project was to have a profound significance on neighborhood planning for black residential expansion in the future. Despite close cooperation between white and black representatives on the Mayor's Advisory Committee on Housing to find a mutually acceptable site, opposition from white neighborhoods forestalled use of the most appropriate location. Moreover, it was clear from the Sunshine experience that blacks would oppose neighborhood clearance as a strategy if they were given a voice in the site selection for subsidized housing. Consequently, when the city initiated a public housing program in the early 1940s, the open dialogue between whites and blacks over site selection no longer operated. Less than a year after the creation of the Richmond Housing Authority in October 1940, construction workers were pouring footing for the twenty-six buildings that would make up Gilpin Court, the city's first public housing project. The site cleared for Gilpin Court was the same area rejected by blacks six years earlier and safely within the boundaries of the established black neighborhood. Black residents were informed of the public housing site only after the decision was made to build Gilpin Court. When the Housing Authority announced its plans in November 1954 to expand Gilpin Court, black residents living adjacent to the public housing project launched a protest, but to no avail. As in the early 1940s, the speed with which the Housing Authority pushed the 388-unit extension through city council negated the dissent of the black community. Although Richmond's conservative city council was not enamored with the idea of additional public housing, the controversial program was acceptable as a substitute for slum housing in areas of the city already relegated to black residency.[25]

The negative experiences of blacks in planning for residential development carried over into a generally critical posture toward the city's planning agenda in general. The black response in Richmond to neighborhood planning from the 1940s through the 1970s is best characterized as a critical and defensive posture. More often than not, blacks opposed the housing and neighborhood programs devised for them by well-meaning but misguided white reformers. Ironically, black opposition to an array of neighborhood rebuilding schemes and related planning ventures required them to join forces with whites whose antiplanning sentiments were complemented by an equally intense desire to maintain the racial status quo. Blacks and conservative whites not only opposed slum clearance and public housing in the 1930s and 1940s, but teamed up to fight highway development in the early 1950s, and urban renewal throughout the 1950s and 1960s. Not until the late 1960s did blacks in Richmond possess sufficient voting strength to form an independent political bloc capable of offering their own planning agenda. Yet by the late 1960s, as will be shown later, the transition of Richmond from a city of diverse neighborhoods to one bifurcated along racial lines was nearly complete. Whereas blacks and whites had competed for neighborhood space in various parts of the city in the 1940s, a maginot line between sprawling black and white sectors had nearly obliterated traditional neighborhood lines by 1970.[26]

Neighborhood change and black response to that change in Memphis after 1940 followed a somewhat different course from that of Richmond. Unlike black Richmonders, who had some initial involvement in planning for residential development, their counterparts in Memphis had little opportunity for participatory decisionmaking under the autocratic rule of Edward Crump. No biracial discussion preceded the city's aggressive public housing program initiated in 1934 under the Public Works Administration program. By 1938, the Memphis Housing Authority (MHA) had cleared a few hundred slum housing units to provide space for 1,124 new units in two separate complexes, one for whites and the other for blacks. Indeed, Richmond was still debating the issue of creating a housing authority while Memphis was completing construction of three more projects.

Public housing stock in Memphis numbered 3,337 units by 1941, of which more than one half were designated for black occupancy. The initial absence of controversy in Memphis's public housing program was probably due to more than local unwillingness to criticize the work of Crump's hand-picked housing czar, Memphis Housing Authority Director Joseph A. Fowler. For one thing, the existence of a severe problem of substandard housing was unquestionable. A 1940 survey of local housing conditions financed by the Works Progress Administration disclosed that 46,753 of the city's 83,540 homes were substandard. Moreover, the slum clearance associated with public housing construction in the 1930s involved largely sparsely populated, blighted areas adjacent to the central business district. Neither slum clearance nor public housing construction posed a direct threat to established black or white neighborhoods.

While Memphis apparently acquiesced to these initial slum clearance efforts, by the early 1950s neighborhood resistance to further activity began to appear. Formation in 1952 of the Bluff City and Shelby County Council of Civic Clubs, a confederation of more than two dozen black neighborhood civic groups, was intended to give blacks a collective voice over neighborhood concerns. One of its members, the Eleventh Ward Civic Club, openly protested the MHA-proposed urban renewal project in the Railroad Avenue area on the grounds that neighborhood residents had recently spent money to remodel homes slated for demolition. Yet it was also in 1952 that white opposition to changing racial boundaries prompted city officials to regulate black neighborhood expansion. Members of the A. P. Hill Civic Club posted signs in their neighborhood in November warning real estate agents that houses were "not for sale to Negroes" and warned the city commissioners that violence would ensue if blacks attempted to move into the neighborhood. The commissioners responded by barring further black housing development in the area and requiring developers of a nearby black subdivision to erect a steel fence to separate it from white residential areas.[27]

Neighborhood racial tensions that first appeared in 1952, but which persisted throughout the decade, were a direct result of an aggressive postwar development drive involving both white and black entrepreneurs to satisfy the enormous demand for new black housing. With the support of the Federal Housing Administration (FHA), several major private housing projects for blacks were initiated in postwar Memphis. A. L. Thompson, race relations advisor for the FHA (and a former black school teacher in Memphis), urged black developers to promote new housing opportunities but to do so in consultation with city officials and in conformity with local preferences regarding the location of black residential expansion. It was white builders, however, who took the lead in constructing new housing for blacks, as exemplified by the 170-unit Vandalia Homes constructed in the Binghampton neighborhood in 1948. The necessary rezoning for the project was secured, and initial white opposition appeased, with assurances that Cyprus Creek would remain a buffer between the new project and the adjacent white neighborhood. Black businessman Dr. J. E. Walker also participated in the housing development boom with several large single-family subdivisions for blacks.[28]

The construction boom in postwar Memphis stood in marked contrast to the new housing market available to Richmond's black community. Except for the Eastview subdivision, with its more than one hundred moderately priced homes located less than one mile from downtown, blacks in Richmond secured new homes principally by moving into units abandoned by whites or moving into one of the 1,736 public housing units built in the 1950s.[29] Moreover, many of the black home seekers were not voluntarily looking for a new place to live but were victims of displacement. Approximately one tenth of the black population in Richmond was forced to move to make way for publicly sponsored development during the 1950s. Displacement of nearly 20,000 blacks, the limited number of new housing units built to compensate for the demolitions, and an increase in the black population of Richmond dispersed blacks not only into other blighted central-city areas, as local reporters Ed Grimsley and Larry Weekly noted, but also "into attractive neighborhoods farther from the core city."[30]

Census figures for 1950 and 1960 confirm the dramatic racial turnover in neighborhoods in the northeast and near West End (see Table 6.5). However, the census data on housing also indicate that housing units lost because of demolition in neighborhoods that were predominantly black in 1950 would have been enough to accommodate one half to two thirds of the black population growth during the decade. In other words, displacement and a failure to replace demolished units, not population growth alone, hastened the process of neighborhood change. Although many blacks secured better housing and established new neighborhoods that would remain cohesive for decades, the shock wave of the large influx of blacks into traditionally white neighborhoods prompted the mass exodus of whites that neighborhood planning was supposed to avert. What was most surprising about such radical neighborhood transition was the relatively muted protest from whites in Richmond. The fact that black neighborhood expansion posed no threat to vast numbers of new suburban subdivisions built after World War II may explain this.

Not so in the case of Memphis. Despite an aggressive private construction effort to accommodate black housing demand, the debate over where to allow new black housing became a subject of intense debate by 1957. The issue first surfaced in February when a proposed public housing project met with stiff opposition from the Real Estate Board, the Home Builders' Association, and residents of the host neighborhood adjacent to the Crump Boulevard site. According to opponents of the project, including approximately fifty black home owners, the neighborhood's recent investment in repairs through the city's code enforcement program would be lost if the public housing project was built there. While debate over the public housing project site lasted for more than a year, it was the broader issue, as *Commercial Appeal* reporter Mike McGee observed, of "what to do with the Negro families" that was at stake in the controversy. In a five-part series in the *Commercial Appeal* in July of that year, McGee examined the effects of demolition of black neighborhoods as a result of proposed urban renewal, highway construction, and code enforcement programs. It had been estimated that approximately 20,000 persons, the large proportion of whom were black, would be required to move in the next three years, as a result of public projects. McGee explored a number of alternatives being considered to alleviate the housing shortage and to minimize the impact of black residential change on white neighborhoods. The Real Estate Board favored creation of a biracial committee with the authority to determine which areas of the city to convert from white to black occupancy. But there were also those, McGee concluded, "who feel that transition has gone far enough and should be stopped." From their vantage point, annexation of additional land was the best approach since it would enable new black housing to be built "in the corporation" without disturbing existing white neighborhoods.[31]

Mayor Edmund Orgill recognized the increasing neighborhood tensions that resulted from unplanned shifts in black neighborhoods. Indeed, it was Orgill's unflinching support of the MHA urban renewal program that explains why five major projects were initiated during his brief tenure as mayor, and why there was so much residential instability. In a letter to Planning Commission Chairman, William "Billy" Galbreath, Jr., Orgill criticized the Bartholomew zoning plan for rezoning black neighborhoods to industrial use "when we need residential Negro areas pretty bad." In his view, the Planning Commission should address immediately "the need for additional areas in which Negro subdivisions can be developed without controversy." Yet the principal strategy employed by the city, with the strong backing of Orgill, was to annex new territory to recapture suburban-bound whites as well as to provide space in the city for new black residential development. Overall, between 1951 and 1960, twenty-five square miles were added to corporate Memphis. Between 1961 and 1967 an additional thirty-three square miles of land were annexed, thereby enlarging the city by 55 percent over a sixteen-year period (see Figure 6.4).[32]

The Real Estate Board's idea of creating a biracial committee to monitor and guide racial change in city neighborhoods was modeled after the work of the Westside Mutual Development Committee (WMDC) established by Mayor William Hartsfield in Atlanta in 1952. The objectives of the WMDC were to preserve racial homogeneity in existing neighborhoods by fighting block busting, planning for new black residential development, and identifying white neighborhoods where transition to black occupancy should be allowed to operate. The WMDC operated as a steering mechanism to counter the potential for unregulated neighborhood change through block busting. In Memphis, where the local real estate board did not allow its members "to sell property to Negroes in white areas," such a group would enable real estate agents to broaden their activities in transitional neighborhoods. In June 1957, and with real estate interests in support, Orgill floated the idea of encouraging two local independent race relations committees, one representing whites and the other blacks, to merge into a single group similar to the WMDC.[33]

After studying the Hartsfield plan, however, Orgill chose not to pursue any formal dialogue between black and white neighborhood leaders over such a sensitive issue as the future racial character of neighborhoods. Instead, Orgill and his successors opted for an alternative strategy. Rather than regulating change in existing city neighborhoods, Memphis would simply grow out of the problem. Through annexation, the city would recapture whites who had fled to the suburbs and, at the same time, secure additional space in which to plan carefully new black residential development. In a lengthy memorandum to the Memphis city commissioners in July 1957, Orgill offered a number of annexation options, all of which centered on the issue of accommodating black neighborhood expansion within the city boundaries. The proposed area for expansion in South Memphis afforded "an area in which Negro subdivisions can be developed without causing a controversy. I do not see how anybody could ever complain about Negro housing in this area." Although Orgill favored a more sweeping annexation that would push the city boundary south to the Mississippi state line, the immediate need was space to accommodate new black housing.

Along with annexation, Memphis expanded its stock of public housing by construction of 600 units in two complexes in 1959 and 1960, respectively. These were the last new units constructed in Memphis until the 1970s, however. Despite the urging of MHA Executive Director Walter Simmons in 1958 that the city's $70 million urban renewal program was in jeopardy of being cut by the federal government unless housing for 4,800 displaced black families was provided, city leaders, under pressure from white neighborhoods, were willing to accommodate only a few hundred more public housing units. To real estate interests, who consistently opposed more public housing, to most neighborhood groups, and to the post-Orgill city administrations, the lines of black settlement had been stretched far enough.[34]

Tensions in the overcrowded and dilapidated core black neighborhoods mounted during the 1960s in the face of such an abrupt end to the discussion over black housing needs. A bitter conflict between black sanitation workers in early 1968, the assassination of Dr. Martin Luther King on the balcony of a Memphis motel in April of that year, and the ensuing violence that swept through Memphis forced city leaders to confront seriously the neighborhood and housing issues that had been left to fester over the previous ten years. Formation of the Memphis-Shelby County Citizens' Advisory Committee late in 1968 to bring blacks and whites together to discuss neighborhood concerns was a belated and tentative step toward a citizen-based biracial planning process. Concurrently, under the leadership of Memphis Housing Authority Commission Chairman Paul Borda, the city's dormant public housing program was resuscitated, and despite continual opposition from white neighborhoods, over 2,500 federally assisted low-rent housing units were constructed throughout the city between 1968 and 1971.[35]

The battle over the location of public housing in Memphis neighborhoods that erupted during the summer of 1968 focused on a proposal by the MHA to build a 300-unit turn-key housing project in Frayser, a predominantly white, blue-collar neighborhood. Borda pressed city leaders in the postriot months to seek federal housing assistance aggressively to address the city's black housing problem, which he saw as a contributing factor in the violence. Yet when the MHA announced plans to construct public housing in Frayser, nearby residents not only banded together to pressure the city council to reject the necessary zoning change, but also filed a court suit to prevent any future use of the property for low-income housing. According to Mayor Henry Loeb, who openly opposed the Frayser location, public housing should be built "in a place where it is wanted" and the Frayser residents were justified in their opposition. Council member Lewis Donelson told a mass rally of 700 persons sponsored by the East Frayser Civic Club that the turn-key project was "nothing more than enforced blockbusting." He favored building such projects in minority areas rather than having the federal government "become an agency of social experimentation." Bowing to neighborhood opposition, the city council rejected the zoning amendment necessary to build the project on September 24 on a seven-to-five vote but agreed to seek HUD approval to allow the units to be shifted to an alternative site. As proponents of the project noted, however, the council action not only delayed needed low-income housing, but established a precedent for neighborhood protest that jeopardized the future of low-income housing in the city.[36]

In late September 1970, Borda expressed his frustration to Loeb over the difficulty of securing city support for public housing. In particular, he noted that the postriot Operation Breakthrough program submitted to HUD in 1968 to address the severe Memphis housing problems had not received a "show of confidence and support of the 'City Fathers.'" Since the Frayser controversy, he continued, "we have not been able to get enough sites approved for the authorized 2,000 units on our books." The major impediment was site selection, with only ten of the forty-three sites submitted by developers approved by all city agencies. "On this basis," Borda concluded, "how can we get sites for the next 2,000 units we have asked to be authorized?"[37]

In June 1969, the MHA went back to the city council with an alternative site for the 300-unit project and, again, neighborhood residents registered a strong protest. The 300 persons who showed up at the council to protest the action were nearly equally divided among white and black residents. This time, however, the council voted (with only one dissenter—Wyeth Chandler) to approve the rezoning of the forty-acre parcel in the newly annexed area of South Memphis. Unlike Frayser, which was an exclusively white community, the transitional nature of the southwest Memphis neighborhood made it a prime candidate for public housing. Memphis continued to place the burden of public housing in black neighborhoods.[38]

An interesting and significant outcome of the 1968 debate over a renewed public housing program was that blacks now joined whites to criticize the process of designating locations for low-rent housing without neighborhood input. Besides clamoring for an end to segregation, black representatives on the city council after 1968 also lent support to neighborhood revitalization efforts to preserve rather than displace the black community. These demands would directly influence the new neighborhood planning process devised by the city in the mid-1970s.

In comparison to the volatile character of neighborhood change in Memphis during the 1960s, Richmond's process was devoid of any intense public debate over the direction of expanding black settlement. It was not the desire to guide neighborhood change but to recapture the suburbanites who had fled the city in the 1950s that motivated Richmond's leadership. The dramatic proportional increase of blacks in the city's population, as pointed out in the 1960 census, rekindled interest in annexation. Not since 1943 had Richmond enlarged the corporate boundaries. It was hoped that consolidation with adjacent Henrico County would resolve the city's demographic imbalance. The failure of the consolidation movement left the boundaries of the city intact and generated a new sense of urgency to address finally the problems of neighborhood transition and neighborhood deterioration.[39]

Richmond's sudden willingness to embark upon a massive urban renewal program in 1965 was because of the failure of the traditional annexation strategy and a belief that redevelopment would ease the pressures of black migration into white neighborhoods and the subsequent flight of whites beyond the city borders. Urban renewal was a strategy of desperation, and it became clear that black residents of the three major target areas (Fulton, Randolph, and Washington Park) were not going to support the program unless the city proved willing to plan with and not for the neighborhood. Unwittingly, the experiences the urban renewal program laid were a solid foundation for the neighborhood planning and conservation program that would dominate local policy by the mid-1970s.[40]

Beginning in 1973, as black political power became a reality throughout the urban South, the neighborhood planning movement gained accelerated momentum. This was most evident in Atlanta with the victory in 1973 of Maynard Jackson over Sam Massell in the city's mayoral race. As the numerous analyses of the Jackson-Massell contest indicate, the pro-neighborhood platform espoused by Jackson forces drew unanimous support not only from blacks but also from a substantial number of whites. Acknowledging his commitment to the neighborhood movement, Jackson pushed through a city charter change in 1974 that established a citywide network for neighborhood planning and citizen input into the policy-formation process.[41]

Although Atlanta served as a showcase for neighborhood planning enthusiasm after 1973, Memphis also responded to neighborhood needs with an ambitious plan of its own. Like so many cities, Memphis's neighborhood planning approach flowed directly from the prerequisites of the Community Development Block Grant (CDBG) program. In conjunction with the city's newly created Division of Housing and Community Development (which stripped the MHA of its neighborhood planning function) the forty-member Action Program Advisory Committee developed a ranking system to determine which neighborhoods would receive priority for CDBG funds. The greater proportion of neighborhoods deemed eligible for assistance were in the black community, but there was a catch. The ranking system was weighted heavily toward moderate-income neighborhoods with a relatively high proportion of home owners and effectively bypassed the poorer and neediest areas. It was a strategy geared toward preserving and upgrading the more substantial and successful black neighborhoods. There was, of course, a fiscal logic behind this approach: Under the block grant program there simply was not adequate money to fund needed improvements in the most deteriorated areas.[42]

As a result, neighborhood planning in Memphis during the 1970s and early 1980s did little to touch the fundamental income, housing, and poverty problems of the most depressed black neighborhoods. Only one bona fide lower-income black neighborhood, New Chicago, received community development aid, but only after intense political lobbying. On the other hand, the Douglass neighborhood in north Memphis, where middle-class blacks had settled in the early 1900s (and which had been a showcase for city-sponsored rehabilitation since the 1950s), received a substantial commitment from the city's CDBG funds. The city's commitment to neighborhood planning produced a significant redistribution of resources to the black community, however. All but one of the nine neighborhoods selected for funding were black. Moreover, between 1975 and 1982, the city committed more than $80 million to neighborhood improvement efforts. Yet, by the 1980s, the city's planners were still unable to document that their efforts had made a difference, especially in the most deteriorated core neighborhoods.[43]

In Richmond, neighborhood planning involved a two-pronged process: supplying a significant citizen voice in the four ongoing urban renewal projects and, after 1976, adhering to a distribution process for CDBG funds that mirrored the Memphis approach. The city's 1976 Housing Action Plan (which was never officially adopted by the city council) supplied the framework for a revitalization effort that channeled most of the federal and local resources into relatively stable black neighborhoods. Whereas some cities made low-interest loans and grants to rehabilitate houses available to eligible families on a citywide basis, the Housing Action Plan called for targeting exclusively to "conservation areas." Those neighborhoods with serious housing deterioration were bypassed on the assumption that limited city resources could most effectively be used in so-called transitional areas.[44]

Even though Richmond's policy-making structure underwent a dramatic transformation in 1977 with the election of a black majority on the city council and the appointment of the city's first black mayor, the unofficial neighborhood strategy devised in 1976 nevertheless remained the cornerstone of its neighborhood planning efforts. Black leaders voiced regularly their commitment to the most depressed black neighborhoods and yet accepted the constraints of the approach set forth in the 1976 plan. The one exception was Jackson Ward. This deteriorated symbol of black community cohesiveness gained the precious designation of a conservation area largely through black political backing. Yet it should be noted that Jackson Ward also possessed unique attributes that other dilapidated black neighborhoods lacked. As a dense collection of mid-nineteenth-century brick structures adjacent to the city's emerging civic center, it was ripe for gentrification.[45] Public investment merely accelerated a rehabilitation process fueled by speculation, although it did supply necessary resources so that blacks could compete with affluent whites in the process. Although attention by black leaders also focused on deteriorated sections of Church Hill, only those areas that qualified under the existing neighborhood strategy received assistance. It can be shown that the targeting neighborhood strategy in Richmond enhanced the livability and the property values in selected areas. But as in Memphis, the benefits of recently acquired black power redounded principally to moderate- and middle-income black neighborhoods. Sensitive and caring leadership proved incapable (and, in a sense, unwilling) to tackle head on the severest problems that had plagued the black community for decades.

In Memphis and Richmond the neighborhood movement, launched in the era of protest and brought to fruition as black power increased, did make some notable contributions. Especially after 1974, black neighborhoods were the major recipients of a comprehensive improvement program in both cities. Neighborhood preservation rather than neighborhood removal had become the cornerstone of public policy; but then the urban context had changed substantially since the 1940s.

Neighborhood planning had been initiated in the post-Depression period in response to a radical restructuring of the community fabric in Memphis and Richmond. Concern over unregulated expansion of black residential areas into white neighborhoods made neighborhood planning an attractive, albeit ineffectual, public policy option. Urban leaders recognized that neighborhood change was an inevitable by-product of urban growth and that whites were leaving older inner-city neighborhoods as much because of the lure of new suburban residential development as because of real or perceived encroachment by blacks on their turf. What lent such urgency to the neighborhood planning process was the magnitude of the transition and the fear that uncontrolled change would result in a wholesale abandonment of the city by whites.

By the 1970s, however, the demographic revolution had essentially run its course in both cities. Memphis and Richmond were now more rigidly divided along race and class lines than they had been in 1940. Large portions of the city that had once been exclusively white had become exclusively black neighborhoods. While neighborhood change continued to occur in the 1970s, it in no sense approached the magnitude of the previous three decades. In fact, the 1970s witnessed the beginning of a much exaggerated but nevertheless significant "return to the city" movement by a handful of descendants of those whites (ethnic and nonethnic) who previously fled the center city. In one section of Church Hill in Richmond, the "gentrification" process transformed a low-income black neighborhood into a showcase of nineteenth-century elegance when white middle- and upper-income investors rediscovered the charm and utility of its historic structures. As noted previously, a similar process was initiated in Jackson Ward, although in that case the black middle class was every bit as involved as whites. In other Richmond neighborhoods, such as the Fan, which had held the line against black encroachment after 1940 but which had accommodated whites too poor to escape to the suburbs (some of whom were the vanishing ethnics), the same sort of class transformation occurred during the 1970s. Memphis also boasted its share of revitalized neighborhoods, especially in that residential wedge extending eastward from the urban core that had been so vigilantly protected from takeover by an expanding black population.

The terms of the neighborhood planning process changed as class was added to race and ethnicity as the determinants of neighborhood identity in the 1970s. Neighborhood preservation was no longer preoccupied with excluding blacks (although racism certainly had not disappeared altogether); it increasingly focused on preserving the economic stability of the new neighborhood patterns that had been formed. If there was a thread of continuity between neighborhood planning as it was fashioned in the 1940s and the neighborhood revitalization efforts of the 1970s and 1980s, it was its relationship to the larger problem of retaining (or recapturing) the urban middle class. In the final analysis, the experiences in Memphis and Richmond indicate the futility of a neighborhood planning process conceived on such a limited vision. As evidenced in the changing face of neighborhoods in both southern cities between 1940 and 1985, planning cannot dictate the character of urban neighborhoods in seemingly perpetual change. It can (and should) offer a means to respond to the range of debilitating factors affecting urban neighborhoods, to stabilize communities rather than accelerate the process of change. Rather than fostering the erosion of neighborhood diversity as it did in Memphis and Richmond over the past two generations, the challenge to urban planners in the 1980s is to assist the new waves of immigrants from Southeast Asia, from Latin America, and, indeed, from their own suburban backyards and deteriorated ghettos, to reestablish a basis of community life. Planning for social diversity will aid immensely in restoring vitality to the urban South.

NOTES

1. For a brief description of Southeast Asian immigrants in Memphis since 1975, see Memphis *Commercial Appeal* (January 7, 1979; April 9, 1979; February 19, 1984;

April 27, 1985). For a brief description of the estimated 15,000 Hispanic immigrants in the Memphis area in 1980, see Memphis *Press-Scimitar* (May 15, 1980).

2. See Myron Berman, *Richmond's Jewry, 1769-1976: Shabbat in Shockoe* (Charlottesville, 1979); Klaus Wust, *The Virginia Germans* (Charlottesville, 1969), p. 249.

3. U.S. Census Bureau, *U.S. Census of Population and Housing 1970: Final Reports,* Table P-2, Richmond, Virginia, PHC(1)-173 (Washington, D.C., 1972); U.S. Census Bureau, *U.S. Census of Population and Housing, 1970: Final Reports,* Table P-2, Memphis, Tennessee, PHC(1)-127 (Washington, D.C., 1972).

4. Evidence from the 1980 census confirms that the largest clusters of new immigrants settled outside the center city of both Memphis and Richmond. In the Richmond SMSA, for example, suburban Henrico and Chesterfield counties boasted 2,500 residents of Asian descent in 1980 as compared with only 976 in the city.

5. U.S. Bureau of the Census, *Population and Housing. Statistics for Census Tracts, 1940,* Memphis, Tennessee, Table 1 (Washington, D.C., 1942).

6. Richard K. Thomas, "The Residential Distribution of Immigrants in Memphis" (M.A. thesis, Memphis State University, 1970), pp. 48, 50, 88, 97-98, 103, 107; Steve Stern, "Echoes of the Pinch," *Memphis Magazine* 8 (March 1984), 66-73, 80-85.

7. Berman, *Richmond's Jewry,* p. 286; U.S. Bureau of the Census, *Population and Housing Statistics for Census Tracts, 1940,* Richmond, Virginia, Table 1 (Washington, D.C., 1942).

8. Cindy Gricus, "The Jewish Community: A Century of Success," *Richmond Style Weekly* 4 (July 1, 1986), 28-29.

9. Leigh D. Fraser, "A Demographic Analysis of Memphis and Shelby County, Tennessee, 1820-1972" (M.A. thesis, Memphis State University, 1974), 25, Table 5. Fraser demonstrated that there was actually a net natural decrease in the black population of Shelby County (which includes Memphis) of 162 during the 1930-1940 decade.

10. 1940 Census, Memphis; Thomas J. Woofter, *Negro Problems in Cities* (Garden City, N.Y., 1928), p. 60.

11. *Ordinances and Resolutions of the City of Richmond, September 1910-August 1912* (Richmond, 1913), pp. 166-67; Roger Rice, "Residential Segregation by Law, 1910-1917," *Journal of Southern History* 64 (May 1968), 179-99; Barbara J. Flint, "Zoning and Residential Segregation: A Social and Physical History, 1910-1940" (Ph.D. dissertation, University of Chicago, 1977), p. 302; *City of Richmond et al.* v. *Deans* 37F. (2nd) 712-13 (January 14, 1930); *Virginia Municipal Review* 7 (February 1930), 27.

12. Charles Knight, *Negro Housing in Certain Virginia Cities* (Richmond, 1927), pp. 38-39; Zane L. Miller, "Urban Blacks in the South, 1865-1920: The Richmond, Savannah, New Orleans, Louisville and Birmingham Experience," in Leo Schnore, ed., *The New Urban History* (Princeton, 1975), pp. 201-2.

13. Woofter, *Negro Problems in Cities,* pp. 137, 139-40.

14. See Gricus, "The Jewish Community," 28-29.

15. Memphis *Commercial Appeal* (October 10, 1949); Memphis *Press-Scimitar* (October 12, 1955).

16. Memphis *Press-Scimitar* (July 19, 1963; May 18, 1981; October 6, 1982). See also *St. Joseph's Church, Memphis: A Hundred Years 1878-1978* (Memphis, 1978).

17. See *One Hundred Years of B'nai B'rith* (Memphis, 1958); Samuel Shankman, *Baron Hirsch Synagogue* (Jackson, Tennessee, 1957); Lawrence C. Meyers, "Evolu-

tion of the Jewish Service Agency in Memphis, Tennessee: 1847-1963" (M.A. thesis, Memphis State University, 1965).

18. Susan Abramson, "Rebuilding Life from Zero," *Style Weekly* (July 1, 1986), 34-35; Memphis *Press-Scimitar* (May 15, 1980).

19. See John Harkins, *Metropolis of the American Nile: Memphis and Shelby County* (Woodland Hills, Calif., 1982); Thomas, "The Residential Distribution of Immigrants in Memphis"; Lisa K. Jorgensen, "Binghampton, East of the Park: A History of Binghampton, Tennessee" (Honors Thesis, Memphis State University, 1984); Charles Williams, Jr., "Two Black Communities in Memphis" (Ph.D. dissertation, University of Illinois—Urbana, 1981); Roger Alan Bates, "The Relationship Between Socio-Economic Status and Religious Behavior in a Mid-South Suburb" (M.A. thesis, Memphis State University, 1968); Mary W. Scott, *Old Richmond Neighborhoods* (Richmond, 1950); Charles Wallace, *The Boy Gangs of Richmond in Dear Old Days* (Richmond, 1938).

20. Norman J. Johnston, "Harland Bartholomew: His Comprehensive Plans and the Science of City Planning" (Ph.D. dissertation, University of Pennsylvania, 1964); Harland Bartholomew, "Neighborhood Rehabilitation and the Taxpayer," *American City* 53 (February 1938), 57; Reginald Isaacs, "The Neighborhood Unit as an Instrument for Segregation," *Journal of Housing* 5 (August 1948), 215-19.

21. Robert A. Sigafoos, *Cotton Row to Beale Street: A Business History of Memphis* (Memphis, 1979), pp. 150-52; Harland Bartholomew and Associates, *A Comprehensive City Plan, Knoxville, Tennessee* (Knoxville, 1930).

22. Harland Bartholomew, *A Report Upon the Comprehensive City Plan, Memphis, Tennessee* (St. Louis, 1940), p. 88; Bartholomew, *A Master Plan for the Physical Development of the City, Richmond* (Richmond, 1946); Bartholomew to Mayor Walter Chandler, February 5, 1940, Mayor's Files (Memphis-Shelby County Public Library Archives, Memphis).

23. Bartholomew, *City Plan,* Memphis, pp. 307, 311, 317, 331, 337.

24. See Christopher Silver, *Twentieth-Century Richmond: Planning, Politics and Race* (Knoxville, 1984), pp. 131-40.

25. Ibid., pp. 150-54.

26. Memphis Housing Authority, *Ten Years in Housing: Memphis Housing Authority, 1947-48 Annual Report* (Memphis, 1948), p. 18; Sigafoos, *Cotton Row to Beale Street,* pp. 179-80, 182; David Tucker, *Memphis After Crump: Bossism, Blacks and Civic Reformers, 1948-1968* (Knoxville, 1980), especially Chapter 1.

27. *Memphis World* (June 10, 24, November 18, 28, 1952).

28. *Memphis World* (February 28, 1947; October 22, 1948; May 10, August 12, 1955); Gloria B. Melton, "Blacks in Memphis, Tennessee, 1920-1955: A Historical Study" (Ph.D. dissertation, Washington State University, 1982), 308-9.

29. Richmond *Times Dispatch* (July 4, 1961); Richmond *New Leader* (June 27, July 4, 5, 6, 1961).

30. Richmond *Times Dispatch* (January 14, 15, 19, 1957).

31. Memphis *Commercial Appeal* (July 7, 8, 10, 1957).

32. Edmund Orgill to W. D. Galbreath, Jr., and Fred Davis, undated, in Memphis-Shelby County Planning Commission, 1959 Folder, Mayor's Files (Memphis-Shelby County Public Library Archives, Memphis); Memphis *Commercial Appeal* (August 25, 1957; *Annexation: A Must for a Growing Memphis,* (Memphis, September 1967), p. 4.

33. See Edmund Orgill Papers, especially Orgill to Edward R. Richmond, June 6, 1957 (Mississippi Valley Collection, Memphis State University). Detailed records and correspondence related to the Westside Mutual Development Committee (including correspondence with Memphis leaders) is in the Atlanta Historical Society, Atlanta, Georgia. Also see William B. Hartsfield Papers (Emory University, Atlanta).

34. Edmund Orgill to Commissioner Claude A. Armour, July 9, 1957, Orgill Papers; Memphis *Press Scimitar* (February 25, 1958); Tucker, *Memphis After Crump*, pp. 65-78, 95, 98-99.

35. See Henry Loeb Papers, correspondence with Paul Borda, Chairman of Memphis Housing Authority (Memphis-Shelby County Public Library Archives, Memphis); and the Public Record and Oral History Collection of Memphis Sanitation Strike and M. L. King Assassination (Mississippi Valley Collection, Memphis State University).

36. Borda to Loeb, September 21, 1970; Loeb to Mrs. Paul Kramer et al., August 22, 1968, Loeb Papers; Memphis *Press-Scimitar* (August 14, September 25, 1968).

37. Borda to Loeb, September 21, 1970; Jesse Turner to Loeb, undated (probably late 1968), Loeb Papers.

38. Loeb to Wyeth Chandler and Billy Hyman, September 21, 1970, Loeb Papers.

39. See Silver, *Twentieth-Century Richmond*, Chapter 8.

40. Richmond's three major urban renewal projects dealt with recommended areas in the 1965 Community Renewal Plan, although the final shape of the program owed to citizen protest over housing clearance by RRHA. In all but the Fulton project, rehabilitation was a major component of the plans that eventually followed.

41. Mack H. Jones, "Black Political Empowerment in Atlanta: Myth and Reality," *The Annals of The American Academy of Political and Social Sciences* 439 (September 1978), 90-117.

42. See Division of Housing and Community Development, *APAC Recommendations, 1978-1981* (Memphis, March 1978).

43. Interview with neighborhood planning staff, Memphis, August 1981.

44. Raymond, Parish, Pine, and Plavnick, *Housing Action Plan* (3 volumes, Richmond, 1976).

45. See Department of Planning and Community Development, *Central Wards Conservation Area Plan* (Richmond, 1975); Silver, *Twentieth-Century Richmond*, Chapter 10.

7

Race, Ethnicity, and Political Change in the Urban Sunbelt South

Ronald H. Bayor _____

Ethnic political competition, bloc voting, and coalitions have usually been associated with politics in northern cities. In these urban centers, various ethnic and racial groups often fiercely competed for power, each trying to find a niche in the city hierarchy. While competition sometimes resulted in violence, eventually competing groups reached a resolution that led to some sharing of the political spoils. There was a tendency for groups, after initial resistance, to make room for others, to accept an adjustment of the ethnic power structure.[1] This did not mean that equality was achieved in the North, but only that other groups were considered to be legitimate competitors and were due some recognition. While competing groups, conflict resolution, and accommodation usually described the ethnic political patterns in the North, the South evolved a different system. In this region a caste structure developed and society was rigidly split between only two groups—whites and blacks. Very often violence and the legal system determined relations between these groups. There was little room for the negotiation and compromise to meet group demands that was evident in northern ethnic relations. This was true both for the rural and urban South. As one historian of the urban South has noted, "rural values dominated southern cities."[2] In a sense then, in describing intergroup contacts, one could speak of a northern and southern model.[3]

Since World War II, the South has been experiencing a change in its intergroup patterns. Black-white relations have undergone major shifts since 1945, and the region has become the destination point for large numbers of immigrants.[4] An analysis of the impact of these ethnic and racial changes on politics in four southern Sunbelt cities (Atlanta, Miami, San Antonio, and Houston) reveals a "New South" emerging by the 1970s with fundamental

changes in the character and dynamics of urban politics. These four cities
were chosen because they illustrate various sections of the region and contain
large black and/or Hispanic populations. While not representative of all
southern cities, they do exemplify the Sunbelt urban South—cities showing
population and economic growth, a concern with maintaining that growth,
and a legacy of civil rights activities.

The history of the urban South until well into the twentieth century fits the
pattern of the southern model. With rare exceptions, whites made little effort
to acknowledge black demands or in any way to see them as a legitimate
competing group. While blacks have held minor offices in a few southern
cities since Reconstruction into the early twentieth century, for the most
part blacks did not emerge as a group due any political recognition until at
least the World War II period.[5] Beginning in the 1890s, the law carefully
determined how whites and blacks acted toward each other in public settings.
A caste system developed throughout the South with blacks being treated as
inferiors. A Jim Crow system denied blacks voting rights, access to public
accommodations, city services, and educational funds, and it presented the
constant fear of violence. Segregation in all phases of white-black contact
was the law.[6]

The other "ethnics" in the South—for example, Jews, Italians, and
Chinese—were generally forced to fit into either the white or black group.
If part of the black caste, as were the Chinese, ethnics were treated in a
similar inferior manner.[7] But even Italians and Jews, though somewhat accepted into the white majority, were never considered equals. The violence
against Italians in New Orleans in 1891 and the lynching of Leo Frank
in 1915, as well as Klan attacks and general discrimination against both
groups, indicate their limited acceptance. The southern model of urban intergroup contacts provided little room for differences; consequently, stronger
pressures to assimilate totally into the favored white Protestant majority existed. By assimilating, or at least muting differences, white ethnics tried to
find acceptance in the white, largely Anglo-Saxon Protestant majority. But
ethnic differences were never a major concern in the South as long as racial
diversions held primacy.

In the immediate post–World War II period, there is some evidence of the
northern model beginning, on a limited scale, to appear in the urban South.
In the 1880s and 1890s, in an effort to deny blacks any political power,
politicians instituted a white primary. Whoever won the primary—restricted
to whites—won the general election, so blacks were in effect disfranchised.
In some cases, blacks were able to retain some degree of political power
through their ability to vote in general elections. This meant little in terms
of political office or state and city elections but did play a role in votes
on such things as bond issues. In Atlanta, for example, black support for
passage of bonds was sought and resulted in trade-off benefits for the group
in terms of funding for schools. A 1921 bond vote resulted in the building

of the first high school for blacks in the city.[8] Still, blacks were mostly ignored politically, although they fully understood the importance of the vote. As the *Atlanta Daily World* (a black newspaper) noted in 1932, while urging blacks to vote: "With it [the vote] they have something with which to bargain. A people with nothing with which to bargain cannot be surprised reasonably when economic and industrial opportunities pass on by their doors."[9] This situation prevailed until the mid-1940s when the Supreme Court ruled against the white-only primary in the South and blacks began to participate in this important election. The white politicians now had to deal with blacks as a legitimate group with some power, for, as Hubert Blalock has observed, in race relations, "power considerations lay beneath all minority relationships.[10] This was the beginning of the end of the caste system and the repercussions were felt very quickly.

The experience of Mayor William Hartsfield of Atlanta, who had not considered black demands before, illustrates white political adaptation to the new political circumstances. The All-Citizen Registration Committee began to register blacks in 1946 (black registration tripled in Fulton County in three weeks). When the Atlanta Negro Voters League presented a united front of black Democrats and Republicans after 1948, Hartsfield and other white politicians became convinced that some black demands had to be met. Hartsfield had earlier noted that if blacks could register and mobilize 10,000 votes, he would be willing to listen to their concerns. Within a few years black police had been hired in the city, housing needs were considered, and, most importantly, black leaders now had access to city hall to present their grievances.[11] Yet problems in race relations were far from being solved. Although a black was elected to the Atlanta Board of Education in 1953, it was not until the mid-1960s that blacks won election to the state senate or city council. School segregation remained, many black Atlantans continued to live in slums, and access to public accommodations occurred slowly and mainly through the efforts of the federal government. Blacks were starting in the 1940s to "compete, bargain, and come to agreements in a style familiar . . . from northern urban politics," although still from a weak position.[12]

A political coalition of the white business and economic elites and blacks eventually developed in Atlanta. Beginning in the early 1950s and continuing through the 1960s, these two groups decided mayoral contests; indeed, whites elected to office often owed their success to black supporters. In an effort to maintain the economic growth of the city, and wary of the economic problems caused by racial unrest in Little Rock and Birmingham, the white business group, although slowly and often reluctantly, gave in to many black demands. White leadership was faced with a choice between economic growth and the racial status quo particularly during the civil rights movement. Economic needs finally took precedence over racial concerns in many southern cities. As Ivan Allen, two-term mayor in the 1960s, commented, "I wasn't so all-fired liberal when I first moved into City Hall, but when I saw what the race-baiters were doing or could do to hold back the orderly growth of Atlanta, it . . . swung me to the extreme end opposite them." With the recognition that traditional handling of the race issue could destroy Atlanta, and with black-white contacts and coalitions formed in the political arena combined with a growing black population in the city (51.3 percent by 1970), an effort was made to resolve other related problems—public school desegregation, public transportation desegregation, and similar situations—through negotiation and compromise.[13]

The same process of change occurred in a number of other southern cities, although not always with the same speed. In Miami it was not until the mid to late 1960s that blacks secured some power in metro and city politics, and in Houston and San Antonio, as in Miami, progress was slowed due to at-large council or commission voting long after the white primary was eliminated. In the Texas cities, annexation also played a role in weakening black and other minority voting strength.[14] It was clear that change was coming slowly even with the Voting Rights Act of 1965 and civil rights movement, but also clear that there was now room for negotiation and a beginning adjustment of the racial power structure. After the race relations upheavals of the 1950s and 1960s, most southern white business and political leaders apparently realized the need for racial harmony and political accommodation in order to maintain economic and political stability. But the white elite also tried to change as little as necessary.[15] The end of the caste system and the emergence of northern style racial politics, therefore, is an ongoing process, still unfolding in the South today.

The development of a competitive, conflict-resolving race relations system based on the northern model is only one of the changes taking place in the South. Due to large-scale Hispanic and Asian settlement and the recognition of their ability and right to compete for power, the urban South has also experienced the beginnings of a pluralistic intergroup pattern. In the urban South it is no longer possible to focus on white or black categories alone since other groups are now legitimized and a new awareness of coalition politics exists. In Georgia, for example, although only about 1.1 percent of the state's population is Hispanic and .5 percent Asian, these groups are heavily concentrated in the Atlanta area. The Hispanic population, consisting of various nationalities, rested at 13,000 in metro Atlanta in 1970 and numbered over 50,000 by 1979. Koreans, Chinese, Indians, and Vietnamese also have emigrated to this area. Many of these people are middle class, educated, upwardly mobile, and interested in securing and protecting their rights.[16]

White and black politicians have been forced to pay attention to these new groups. In the 1970s as Atlanta city leaders began to become aware of the city's growing Hispanic community, a report (financed by city, state, county, and private funds) was prepared for the Atlanta Regional Commission in an attempt to identify the location and needs of this ethnic group. The report made a number of recommendations to ease Hispanic integration into the city. For example, the study called for employment training programs, the provision of bilingual information, and the hiring of some Spanish-speaking police officers in neighborhoods with large Hispanic populations.[17] City leaders had already made efforts to facilitate Hispanic adjustment (treating all Hispanics as one group) and continued to do so after the report was issued.

When the first Hispanic organizations appeared in the 1970s, the Atlanta Community Relations Commission, in response to their needs, was able to secure the translation of driver's license applications and all city documents into Spanish.[18] Atlanta has a Mayor's Task Force on Hispanics, and a Hispanic Advisory Council meets once a month with the police department to deal with this community's problems. In addition, the city administration has developed plans to begin cultural awareness training for the police so that greater understanding of the Hispanic community can be achieved.[19] The city also has made attempts to hire Hispanic police officers. Andrew Young's mayoral administration has expressed its desire to "see that Hispanics get a fair share of the [city] contracts." Mayor Young noted that he does not wish to see this group become alienated. The Asians also have been the subject of attention by city officials. The mayor has been active in trying to hire Asian police officers.[20]

Southern blacks, who, like southern whites, previously viewed the South in only black and white, have had to come to terms with pluralism. After many years of fighting for equality and recognition, blacks are the leaders in cities such as Atlanta who are having to deal with recognition of other groups. This has not been always easy. Hispanics and Asians are recognized as distinct groups with whom accommodation must be reached, but, as elsewhere in the Sunbelt South, there are tensions. An indication of how Atlanta politicians must now be careful about saying anything that might be perceived as an ethnic slur comes from a statement by Mayor Young. The mayor had to apologize to Korean doctors in the Atlanta area after he made a remark comparing the poor working conditions of the Atlanta zoo veterinarian to those of a doctor in Korea. "Actually I was thinking of MASH" and battlefield conditions, Young said, and did not mean to disparage Korean doctors. Nonetheless, in a city with about 15,000 Koreans, the remark did not go unchallenged.[21]

Other groups have also taken note of the new situation in the city. Metro Atlanta's Jewish community, experiencing a sixfold increase in size since 1945, had made an effort to form coalitions with other ethnics (Asians as well as Hispanics) in an attempt to organize conflict-resolution committees. Most successful, however, has been the Black-Jewish Coalition initially organized by the local chapter of the American Jewish Committee in 1982 to mobilize support for the extension of the Voting Rights Act. The Coalition is indicative of the attempts to develop working relationships across ethnic-racial lines in the urban South in order to discuss issues pertinent to the two communities, and strengthen ties. Issues at meetings have included KKK activity in Georgia, the Martin Luther King, Jr., holiday, the Leo Frank case, minority issues in political campaigns, apartheid, and affirmative action. Black and Jewish political, business, and religious leaders have formalized their contacts through this organization, which meets about every other month. Although not directly involved in political campaigns, the Coalition has defused volatile issues and kept communication open between Atlanta's blacks and Jews regarding such volatile issues as Louis Farrakhan's anti-Semitic remarks and the response of Atlanta's black leaders to them.[22]

Atlanta has witnessed coalition building and efforts to reach out to recently arrived and growing groups that are not yet seriously competing for political power due to their relatively small size and newness to the city. The Miami area, however, illustrates the intense pluralistic political competition over interests and values between non-Latin whites, blacks, and the various Hispanic groups that also define the "New South" Sunbelt city. The controversy over official bilingualism is one indication of this conflict. The county commission voted in 1973 to make Dade County officially bilingual. By 1980 an opposition in the form of the Citizens for Dade United was successful in securing enough petition signatures to put the issue of bilingualism on the ballot. The proposal called for the elimination of funding for the 1973 bilingual resolution by forbidding the use of county money for the purposes of promoting "any language other than English or for the promotion of 'any culture other than that of the United States.' " The measure was inspired by resentment against growing Cuban economic and political power. A poll taken at the time of the vote indicated that among various groups, Jews gave the antibilingual resolution the strongest support. The leader of the petition drive, a post-World War II immigrant from Russia, asked "How come the Cubans get everything?" and expressed her desire to bring Miami back to "the way it used to be." The resolution passed with 71 percent of non-Latin whites supporting it, while blacks and Cubans opposed it. The blacks' opposition was based on their view that the measure was discriminatory. Although the Cubans saw in this vote the possible formation of a black-Hispanic coalition, there were tensions between these two groups over jobs, politics, services, and government funds.[23]

Blacks had been barred from participating in Miami politics until 1945 by the white primary and after that by the procedure of at-large city commission elections. It was not until the 1960s that blacks began to see the end of the caste system and were able to compete with whites. Hence, they resented the appearance of Cubans, a third group with whom to share political power.[24] In Miami, in 1981, blacks were the major group responsible for the defeat of the Cuban candidate for mayor Manolo Reboso and the re-election of Maurice Ferre (of Puerto Rican background), supported also by non-Latin whites and the small percentage of non-Cuban Hispanics in the city. Latins made up 36 percent of the voters, blacks 30 percent, and non-Hispanic whites 34 percent.[25] The Miami area, which represents one of the most ethnically diverse areas of the Sunbelt South, illustrates the northern model of ethnic competition-conflict, ethnic bloc voting, coalition formation, and resistance-accommodation. There is no caste system or simple black-white split here but rather a number of competing groups (including at times intragroup Hispanic rivalries), an awareness of a multiethnic society, and an effort to compete through nonviolent means.

This competition will continue as the Hispanic population increases and adds to its political power in the city and county. The first Cuban on the City Commission was elected in 1973, and on the Metro Commission, the first was elected in 1982. By 1985 Cubans (with 40 percent of the registered voters in Miami) were the majority on the Miami City Commission and a Cuban had been appointed metropolitan county manager by the Dade County Commission, indicating growing Hispanic strength beyond the city of Miami. One black, Miller Dawkins, also sits on the Miami City Commission. Defeating a Cuban opponent, Victor DeYurre in 1985 in a campaign in which an issue was whether Dawkins represented only black interests to the detriment of the rest of the city's population, Dawkins won a majority of the black and non-Latin white vote and DeYurre captured the Latin vote. Also by 1985, a Cuban, Xavier Suarez, was elected mayor over another Cuban candidate, Paul Masvidal, in a run-off election. Maurice Ferre, Miami's six-term incumbent had lost in the earlier vote due to his alienation of black voters—he had previously aided in the ouster of Howard Gary, Miami's city manager and the "highest ranking black official in the area." Ferre received 96 percent of the black vote in 1983 and only 10 percent in 1985. In the run-off the black vote became the battleground between the two Cuban candidates.[26] However, with the two top aspirants for the mayoral position being Cuban and the City Commission secured by this group, it is obvious who is winning the ethnic political battles; yet the three groups are clearly still contending for political power and influence. Within the competition there is also some evidence of efforts to forge new coalitions. As in Atlanta, the American Jewish Committee in Miami is involved in an attempt to reach ethnic understandings. The boards of the Committee and the Cuban National Planning Council in Miami meet two times a year to work out "joint approaches . . . on local issues" and cooperate on such concerns as immigration and bilingual education.[27]

The appearance of a northern model and a fundamental change in urban politics is also evident in other parts of the urban Sunbelt South. San Antonio represents a city in which whites (made up of those of Anglo, German, and French background) have controlled the city politically since antebellum days. Blacks had little or no political power and subsequently were often ignored in regard to city services and group needs. As in Atlanta, blacks retained the vote in general elections and were at times solicited by the white power structure to support certain candidates but had little real power due to the white primary. Also, the black population remained small throughout the twentieth century (7.8 percent in 1930 and 7.6 percent in 1970). Mexican Americans, always a large segment of the population (over 50 percent in 1970), fared better and were recognized as part of a multiethnic machine coalition in the latter part of the nineteenth century. However, with the migration into the city of numerous Anglos and Germans by the turn of the century, their increasing political and economic influence, and the emergence of new machines and various reform movements in the twentieth century, the Chicanos received little attention from the political leaders as these other groups (particularly the Anglos) came to completely dominate the political scene. Chicanos were provided only with token political power until the 1970s, and less in terms of city services. The recent shift in the racial/ethnic intergroup pattern came mainly as the result of outside forces. The end of the white primary, the civil rights movement, the Voting Rights Act of 1965 and its amendments in 1975, and other federal government reforms hastened the needed change and inspired other reforms.[28]

The first black was elected to the city council in 1965. For the Mexican Americans, their political emergence came with the outside impetus toward change coupled with community activism. Mexican Americans had organized as early as 1921 in an effort to secure full political, economic, and social rights. La Orden de Hijos de America, founded in 1921 in San Antonio, worked for these goals. As an assimilationist, middle-class group, its members wanted to be considered good American citizens and worked to secure their full rights as citizens. Other Mexican-American organizations appeared afterward with the same general thrust. The League of United Latin American Citizens (LULAC) was founded in 1929 to encourage Americanization and a political role for the Chicano community and to fight discrimination particularly in the schools. The American G.I. Forum began in 1947 to push for veterans' rights and political involvement. An increasing attention to the need for political action is indicated by these groups as well as those organized in the 1960s—Mexican Americans for Political Action and the Viva Kennedy clubs.[29]

In 1974 San Antonio Chicanos started a new neighborhood-based, grassroots group called Communities Organized for Public Service (COPS) whose goal was to "gain recognition as an equal in the bargaining process." This group engaged in massive voter registration efforts and pressured the city government for the delivery of more services to the Mexican-American areas of the city. Also involved in registration work was the San Antonio-based Southwest Voter Registration Education Project, started in 1974 to increase Mexican-American political involvement in Texas. In 1976 the Atlanta-based Voter Education Project (VEP), which had been concerned primarily with black registration, joined with the San Antonio group to foster all minority voting in Texas. The announcement of the joint cooperative effort noted that "we are working to show that a minority political coalition, composed of black and Mexican Americans who have, until recently, been denied access to the political process, can have a positive impact for all the citizens of Texas." According to John Lewis, executive director of VEP, the objective was "to foster a sense of cooperation and unity between these two minority groups which have historically followed separate paths of development." The demand from both organizations was for full minority access to all "social, political and economic arenas." Active also was the Mexican American Legal Defense Fund (MALDEF), which challenged at-large district elections in San Antonio and worked to secure and enforce the 1975 Voting Rights Act.[30]

The organizational work of Chicano and coalition groups was very effective in increasing the number of registered voters and in changing the ethnic make-up of the city government. The Southwest Voter Registration Education Project has been able to increase dramatically Hispanic registered voters in the Southwest during the late 1970s, and COPS during a three week period in 1984 registered 16,000 Chicanos in San Antonio. Combined with an end to the poll tax in 1966, state provision for Spanish language registration and voting forms as of 1975, and federal action, changes came quickly.[31]

The first indication of the ethnic shift came with city council elections. Traditionally, council members were elected by an at-large vote, which weakened the strength of the Mexican Americans concentrated on the south and west sides of the city. As the Mexican-American voting population increased in San Antonio, the city leaders in 1972 annexed surrounding Anglo-dominated areas and thereby further diluted the Chicano vote. Under the Voting Rights Act of 1975, the U.S. Department of Justice threatened to nullify retroactively the annexation unless a new single-member council district plan rather than the old at-large system was developed. The vote in 1977 on whether to change to single-member council districts split along ethnic lines with Chicanos carrying the vote for the new plan. With the 1977 elections, Mexican Americans, who previously had never secured more than three seats on the nine-member council, and blacks gained a majority of the positions on the new eleven-member council. A coalition of blacks and Chicanos, therefore, wrested control of the council from the non-Latin whites. Temporarily losing control in 1979, the minorities regained their majority on the council in 1981. After the series of confrontations between the Anglo establishment and the minorities, an accommodation was worked out with the realization that little could be accomplished in the city without Anglo-minority cooperation. After 1977, according to political scientist Thomas A. Baylis, "the outlines of a pattern of working cooperation between moderate Anglo businessmen, city officials and council members on the one side, and COPS members and several minority councilmen on the other, centering on a common concern for economic development, seemed to begin to emerge." This cooperation "was reaffirmed in . . . 1980 with the . . . formation of an organization called United San Antonio." This group brought together the various racial/ethnic and other elements in order to strive for economic growth in the city.[32]

The cooperation between competing groups was also realized in the mayoral elections where ethnic political alliances have been formed. As Tucker Gibson observed, "Through 1979, no candidate who relied predominantly on the Mexican-American vote had won." Henry Cisneros, a Mexican American and a councilman, captured city hall in 1981 with 90 percent of the vote on the city's Mexican-American west side. However, Cisneros also won a number of Anglo votes. He had worked with the Anglo leadership before through the Good Government League, described in a *Texas Monthly* article on San Antonio's politics as the "political arm of the downtown establishment." Having ties with both COPS and the Anglo establishment, Cisneros was the perfect choice to secure a resolution of the ethnic-based political battles. He campaigned on a consensus platform and was successful in bringing the various groups together behind him. Winning with 62 percent of the total vote in 1981, he was easily re-elected in 1983, drawing support from all segments of the city. Cisneros became a strong supporter of the economic growth of the city as well as minority rights and thereby embodied the perfect Sunbelt coalition of interests. As one student of San Antonio politics noted, by 1981 "San Antonio had apparently passed from an Anglo elite-dominated machine system to a coalition system in which no single class or ethnic group held complete power over political decisions." A pluralistic political system had developed in which power was shared by competing groups.[33]

Houston had a similar history. Mexican Americans and blacks had little power and were mostly ignored by city officials. Blacks had been largely disfranchised around the turn of the century with the imposition of the white primary. To support Mexican rights, particularly in regard to the police, the community organized La Asamblea Mexicana in 1924. This group was successful in securing the hiring of Mexican-American policemen to patrol Chicano neighborhoods. At times the Mexican and black communities formed coalitions, as, for example, during the 1920s to fight Klan activity in the city.[34]

Mexicans began to organize politically during the 1930s. In 1935 the Latin American Club was formed in Houston to register eligible Mexican-American voters and to represent group interests before the city leaders. This club eventually became a chapter in LULAC and continued to work for Mexican-American rights as citizens. After World War II, LULAC and the American G.I. Forum, as in San Antonio, fought for "social, political, and economic equality." Further political interest and activism was evident with the formation of Viva Kennedy clubs, the Political Association of Spanish Speaking Organizations (PASO), and La Raza Unida Party. For blacks, according to one analyst of Houston politics, "regular political participation began with the abolition in 1944 of the . . . white primary."[35]

Initially, as elsewhere, the white primary, poll tax, at-large council voting, and annexation prevented blacks and Hispanics from competing equally with whites for political positions. The end of the white primary in 1944 and the poll tax in 1966 brought the minorities fully into political competition. With the abolition of the poll tax, the number of black and Mexican-American registered voters increased with every year. In 1944 blacks were "20 percent of the voting age population [but] they made up only 5 percent of the electorate." With the organization of the Harris County Council of Organizations in the late 1940s to register and mobilize the black vote, the situation changed. By 1967 blacks represented almost 17 percent of the registered voters, and as with the Atlanta Negro Voters League, white candidates eventually sought endorsements from this organization.[36] The growing strength of the minorities soon became apparent in a number of ways. The initial indication of their strength was the appointment of a black policeman in 1947. In 1958 the first black was elected to the school board in Harris County and represented the first black to win any public office there since Reconstruction. The first black administrator in the Houston school system was appointed in 1963, and in 1969 the Houston Teachers Association had its first black president. The police department appointed its first Hispanic captain in 1980.[37]

The first black mayoral candidate, Curtis Graves, while capturing only 32 percent of the vote in 1969 and losing to the incumbent Louis Welch, did well in black and Mexican-American neighborhoods and began to awaken more fully the white leadership to the emerging minorities. Mayor Welch, who received less than 6 percent of the vote in black areas and faced the possibility of opposing Graves again in two years, began to cultivate the black voter. As he said, "I have heard this vote and I sympathize with it. It is my sincere hope that during the next two years I will be able to let these people know that their problems represent the problems of the entire community." The mayor then stated he would ask the city council to pass a minimum housing code so as to improve slum housing. The strong vote Graves received, according to Welch, represented a desire of blacks for a "more active voice in government," and he would support that active voice.[38]

By 1970 blacks were 25.7 percent and Mexican Americans 15.1 percent of Houston's population, and made up about 35 percent of the registered voters in 1971. Once again, these communities were playing an important role in the mayoral election. In 1971 Welch opposed Fred Hofheinz, who was getting significant black and Chicano support due to his pledge to set up a police review board. The contest was thrown into a run-off election which Welch won, but only after the campaign had been racially polarized. Although Welch said he would try to win over more black votes in the run-off, his supporters called for a turnout of white voters to stop the minority bloc vote. Hofheinz did well in minority areas and set the stage for his future victory. More significant were the actual minority victories in 1971. In the school board election a black and a Mexican American won positions; in the city council vote, Judson Robinson, Jr., became the first black elected to the council, and a Mexican American, Leonel Castillo, was elected city controller. Hofheinz accurately noted after the election that it "showed that no future Mayor could be elected unless he listened to the needs of 'all of Houston.' " He was right. In 1973 and again in 1975, Hofheinz was elected mayor with strong support from the black and Mexican-American communities, and they have figured prominently in campaigns since then.[39]

In one area, however, the minorities still had little power. The city council was chosen on an at-large basis, and therefore up to 1979, only one black and no Mexican Americans had been elected to that board. The U.S. Department of Justice rectified this situation when it suspended city elections in 1979 in order to study compliance with the Voting Rights Act. Houston had annexed six mainly white areas in 1977, and the issue, as in San Antonio, was whether that annexation had diluted the minority vote. Due to Justice Department pressure, the city developed a new plan to elect the council. Five of the fourteen were to be elected at-large and the others on a single-district basis. The 1979 council vote elected three blacks and one Mexican American. The minorities now were in an effective position to compete, negotiate, and secure concessions in a way similar to northern ethnic politics. The business elite in Houston was willing to accept some division of power with the minorities in an effort to prevent potential conflict that would limit economic growth.[40]

These four cities represent the political alterations brought about as a result of the civil rights movement, federal intervention, immigration, and political organization within the minority communities. White flight has also played a role, as indicated in the efforts to annex surrounding white areas in San Antonio, Houston, and as early as the 1950s, in Atlanta in an attempt to dilute the burgeoning minority vote. Nonetheless, in these cities of the Sunbelt South a northern model of ethnic/race relations has emerged and urban politics has been fundamentally changed. The different cities represent variations of the change but are far removed from the rigid, violent, and politically noncompromising white-black caste system of earlier years. From the intense competition for power in Miami, to the accommodations worked out in Atlanta, San Antonio, and Houston, and the coalition building and recognition of a multiethnic society found in all these cities—a "new South" is evident. This is not to say that all southern cities have shifted to a northern model. During the civil rights movement, those cities that had "little or no population or economic growth in the postwar period . . . typically experienced considerable racial turmoil" and resistance to change as compared to cities which had both population and economic growth and successfully sought new industry and migrants.[41] The cities of postwar burgeoning economies and populations where business and political leaders understood the connection between racial/ethnic accommodation and stability were the urban centers that saw the northern model emerge. The functioning and economic development of these cities had become dependent on the cooperation of the various ethnic/racial communities (Hispanic, black, white, Asian). The establishment of single-district rather than at-large council voting in a number of Sunbelt cities by itself suggests the greater importance neighborhoods and racial/ethnic coalitions will have in the future of this region. As in northern cities, civic renaissance and future economic growth ultimately will depend on the ability of many interest groups to work together. This has already been realized in Atlanta, San Antonio, and Houston, with Miami likely to follow suit in the near future. As one social scientist noted, "situations most conducive to the growth of new understandings and realistic adjustments will be those in which highly important outcomes are unavoidably dependent upon long-continued cooperation among individuals (and groups) no one of whom has overwhelming power."[42] The importance placed on civic and economic improvement in Sunbelt cities, the continued immigration of Hispanics and Asians, and the willingness to deal with all groups in order to enhance the city will result in the northern model becoming firmly entrenched in the urban Sunbelt South. Whether the sharing of political power leads to equality, the end of neighborhood segregation, and the opening up of job opportunities is a question for the future. Certainly northern cities still have not reached that point. What we see is an ongoing process whose resolution is still being worked out, but a process increasingly based on the acceptance of pluralism and conflict resolution.

NOTES

1. See, for example, Ronald H. Bayor, *Neighbors in Conflict: The Irish, Germans, Jews and Italians of New York City, 1929-1941* (Baltimore, 1978).
2. David R. Goldfield, *Cotton Fields and Skyscrapers: Southern City and Region, 1607-1980* (Baton Rouge, 1982), p.4.
3. The northern and southern models are discussed in Nathan Glazer and Daniel Moynihan, *Beyond the Melting Pot: The Negros, Puerto Ricans, Jews, Italians and Irish of New York City*, (2nd ed., Cambridge, Mass., 1970), pp.xxiii-xxiv; Nathan Glazer, "Ethnicity—North, South, West," *Commentary* 73 (May 1982), 73-74, 78; Nathan Glazer, "Politics of a Multiethnic Society," in Lance Liebman, ed., *Ethnic Relations in America* (Englewood Cliffs, N.J., 1982), pp.128-49. Glazer and Moynihan in their 1970 second edition suggested that the northern model was moving south and was particularly evident in Atlanta, and that the southern model could be seen in the North. However, Glazer in his later works suggested that a third model—a western model—developed out of the southern and has been extended to all other parts of the country. The western model grew out of the government's effort to regulate intergroup relations through laws and mandate equality by specifically providing

special benefits and protection to certain minority groups. I would argue that the northern rather than the southern, or its variation the western model, became the norm in intergroup relations.

4. Franklin J. James, Betty L. McCummings, and Eileen A. Tynan, *Minorities in the Sunbelt* (New Brunswick, N.J., 1984), pp.4-5.

5. Blaine A. Brownell, "The Urban South Comes of Age, 1900-1940," in Blaine A. Brownell and David R. Goldfield, eds., *The City in Southern History: The Growth of Urban Civilization in the South* (Port Washington, N.Y., 1977), p.153; Don H. Doyle, *Nashville Since the 1920s* (Knoxville, 1985), p.225.

6. Howard N. Rabinowitz, *Race Relations in the Urban South, 1865-1890* (New York, 1978).

7. Robert Seto Quam in collaboration with Julian B. Roebuck, *Lotus Among the Magnolias: The Mississippi Chinese* (Jackson, Miss., 1982), pp.45-51.

8. E. Bernard West, "Black Atlanta-Struggle for Development, 1915-1925" (M.A. thesis, Atlanta University, 1976), pp.15, 17-24.

9. *Atlanta Daily World* (March 21, 1932).

10. Hubert M. Blalock, Jr., *Black-White Relations in the 1980s* (New York, 1979), p.156.

11. *Atlanta Journal* (April 25, 1956); Atlanta Negro Voters League to voters, September 2, 1949, Box 10, William B. Hartsfield papers (Emory University Special Collections); interview with John C. Calhoun, August 7, 1985. Calhoun was active in founding the Registration Committee and the Voters League. He was also co-chair of the Georgia Voters League and executive director of the Atlanta chapter of the NAACP in the 1960s.

12. Glazer, *Beyond the Melting Pot*, p.xxiv.

13. Ivan Allen, Jr., with Paul Hemphil, *Mayor: Notes on the Sixties* (New York, 1971), pp.87, 219; Interview with Ivan Allen, Jr., July 29, 1985; Ronald H. Bayor, "A City Too Busy to Hate: Atlanta's Business Community and Civil Rights," in Harold Sharlin, ed., *Business and Its Environment* (Westport, 1983). For a discussion of the economic factor's impact on racial change in various southern cities, see Edward F. Haas, "The Southern Metropolis, 1940-1976," in Brownell and Goldfield, eds., *City in Southern History*, pp.171, 181-83; and Elizabeth Jacoway and David R. Colburn, eds., *Southern Businessmen and Desegregation* (Baton Rouge, 1982), pp.6-7, as well as essays on particular southern cities, such as Atlanta by Alton Hornsby, Jr., pp.120-36.

14. Raymond A. Mohl, "Miami: The Ethnic Cauldron," in Richard M. Bernard and Bradley R. Rice, eds., *Sunbelt Cities: Politics and Growth Since World War II* (Austin, Texas, 1983), pp.82-83; Barry J. Kaplan, "Houston: The Golden Buckle of the Sunbelt," in ibid., pp.205-6; Robert Brischetto, Charles L. Cotrell, and R. Michael Stevens, "Conflict and Change in the Political Culture of San Antonio in the 1970s," in David R. Johnson, John A. Booth, and Richard J. Harris, eds., *The Politics of San Antonio: Community, Progress and Power* (Lincoln, Neb., 1983), pp.76, 78, 86-87, 90; John A. Booth, "Political Change in San Antonio, 1970-82: Toward Decay or Democracy?" in ibid., p.195.

15. See note 13.

16. *Atlanta Constitution* (February 26, 1984; February 15, 1979). "The Assessment of Special Service Needs Among the Hispanic Population of the Atlanta Area"

(a report to the Atlanta Regional Commission, prepared by the Center for Urban Research and Service, Georgia State University, 1979), p.3.

17. "The Assessment of Special Service Needs," pp.xiv-xv.

18. Interview with Mayor Andrew Young, February 13, 1986.

19. *Atlanta Constitution* (February 14, 15, 1979).

20. Interview with Young.

21. Ron Arias, "In Search of El Dorado," *Atlanta Weekly* (December 4, 1983), 28. *Atlanta Constitution*, (August 24, 1985; January 25, 1986).

22. Atlanta Jewish Federation, *Metropolitan Atlanta Jewish Population Study: Summary of Findings* (Atlanta, 1985), pp.2-3. "The Black-Jewish Coalition, a Brief History, 1982-1986" (mimeographed) in the author's possession; observations of the author who is a member of the Coalition and has attended a number of meetings.

23. *New York Times* (September 17, 1980; November 2, 1980; November 9, 1980). See also Hall Tennis and Dewey W. Knight, Jr., "Minorities and Justice in Greater Miami: A View from the Metro Courthouse," *Urban Resources* 2 (Spring 1985), 14, 22, 24.

24. *Washington Post*, (May 23, 1980); Raymond A. Mohl, "Race, Ethnicity, and Urban Politics in the Miami Metropolitan Area," *Florida Environmental and Urban Issues* 9 (April 1982), 6, 23-24; *New York Times* (April 28, 1980; May 23, 1980).

25. *New York Times* (November 11, 1981, November 4, 1985).

26. *New York Times* (November 11, 1981; January 31, November 4, 7, 12, 1985); Mohl, "Ethnic Cauldron," 84; Mohl, "Ethnic Politics in Miami, 1960-1985" (paper presented at the 1985 Organization of American Historians meeting), pp.12-13; *Miami Herald*, (November 6, 1985); *Atlanta Constitution* (November 13, 1985).

27. Edwin Black, "Hispanics and Jews: A Hopeful New Alliance," *B'nai B'rith International Jewish Monthly* 100 (May 1986), 16.

28. John A. Booth and David R. Johnson, "Power and Progress in San Antonio Politics, 1836-1970," in Johnson et al. eds., *Politics of San Antonio*, pp.25-27; Haas, "The Southern Metropolis," 183; U.S. Department of Commerce, Bureau of the Census, *1970, Characteristics of the Population*, Vol. 1, Part 45, Texas.

29. Brischetto, Cotrell, and Stevens, "Conflict and Change in the Political Culture of San Antonio in the 1970s," p.76; Ralph C. Guzman, *The Political Socialization of the Mexican American People* (New York, 1976), p.133; Rodolfo Acuña, *Occupied America: The Chicano's Struggle Toward Liberation* (San Francisco, 1972), pp.189-90; Matt S. Meier and Feliciano Rivera, *The Chicanos: A History of Mexican Americans* (New York, 1972), pp.240-48.

30. Brischetto, Cotrell, and Stevens, "Conflict and Change in the Political Culture of San Antonio in the 1970s," p.85; Carl Abbott, *The New Urban America: Growth and Politics in Sunbelt Cities* (Chapel Hill, 1981), pp.232-33; Voter Education Project Press Release, July 12, 1976, Clarence Bacote Papers (Atlanta University Woodruff Library, Special Collections); F. Chris Garcia and Rudolph O. de La Garcia, *The Chicano Political Experience: Three Perspectives* (North Scituate, Mass., 1977), pp. 180-83.

31. Brischetto, Cotrell, and Stevens, "Conflict and Change in the Political Culture of San Antonio in the 1970s," pp.78, 86-87; William Dunn, "The Growing Political Power of Blacks and Hispanics," *American Demographics* 6 (September 1984), 26, 29; "A Surge of Hispanic Power," *Macleans* 97 (May 14, 1984), 32-33.

32. *New York Times* (January 17, 1977; April 4, 1977; March 29, 1981; April 6, 1981); Brischetto, Cotrell, and Stevens, "Conflict and Change in the Political Culture of San Antonio in the 1970s," pp.75, 87, 90; Booth, "Political Change in San Antonio," pp.195, 197-98; Thomas Baylis, "Leadership Change in Contemporary San Antonio," in Johnson et al., eds., *Politics of San Antonio*, pp.102-4.

33. Tucker Gibson, "Mayoralty Politics in San Antonio, 1955-79," in Johnson et al, eds., *Politics of San Antonio*, p.127; Nicholas Lemann, "First Hispanic," *Esquire* 102 (December 1984), 480, 484; Paul Burka, "Henry B and Henry C," *Texas Monthly* 14 (January 1986), 222, 224, 226: *New York Times* (April 6, 1981); "A Surge of Hispanic Power," 33; Brischetto, Cotrell, and Stevens, "Conflict and Change in the Political Culture of San Antonio in the 1970s," pp.92-93; Booth, "Political Change in San Antonio," p.194.

34. F. Arturo Rosales, "Mexicans in Houston: The Struggle to Survive, 1908-1975," *Houston Review* 3 (Summer 1981), 228-30, 237,239; Charles Davidson, *Biracial Politics: Conflict and Coalition in the Metropolitan South* (Baton Rouge, 1972), pp.15-16.

35. Rosales, "Mexicans in Houston," 241-44, 247; Davidson, *Biracial Politics*, p.84.

36. Davidson, *Biracial Politics*, pp.41-43, 55-57, 84-85; Kaplan, "Houston," 205.

37. Davidson, *Biracial Politics*, pp.85, 121; David G. McComb, *Houston: A History* (Austin, 1981), pp.171-72.

38. *New York Times* (November 22, 1971; November 9, 16, 17, 1969).

39. Ibid. (November 14, 22, 1971; December 9, 1971; December 3, 1973; December 3, 1975; November 23, 1977; November 21, 1979; November 16, 1981); Davidson, *Biracial Politics*, p.18; U.S. Department of Commerce, Bureau of the Census, *1970, Characteristics of the Population*, Vol. 1, Part 45, Texas.

40. *New York Times* (March 28, 1979; November 21, 24, 1979); Kaplan, "Houston," 205-7. Before a 1955 charter revision, of the eight city council members, five had been elected by ward. After 1955, all were elected at large. See Davidson, *Biracial Politics*, p.60.

41. Jacoway and Colburn, eds., *Southern Businessmen and Desegregation*, p.11.

42. Robin M. William, Jr., *Strangers Next Door: Ethnic Relations in American Communities* (Englewood Cliffs, N.J., 1964), p.351.

8

Ethnic Politics in Miami, 1960-1986

Raymond A. Mohl ───────────────────

Traditional interpretations of immigration history generally have asserted the importance of the open and democratic American political system in the assimilation of immigrant and ethnic groups. More than thirty years ago in *The Uprooted*, Oscar Handlin suggested that for the newcomers democracy in America meant power and the ability to achieve some control over their destiny. As immigrants became citizens, they became voters; and as ethnic groups emerged as residential and cultural units, they became useful voting blocs for the nineteenth-century political machine and the modern-day political party. The traditional view holds that participation in American politics—even machine politics—facilitated the Americanization of the immigrants over time. If ethnic politicization initially stimulated group identity and organization, the political process ultimately eased group tensions and accommodated conflicts of interest. The American democratic system, this argument runs, encouraged the economic and political integration of the foreign born into the American mainstream. Taking this argument a bit further, one scholar has asserted that "politics was on the leading edge of the Americanization process."[1]

Recent scholarship has modified these views somewhat. We now know, for instance, that the melting pot did not work exactly as believed, that ethnicity has remained a vital force in twentieth-century American life, and that political participation often strengthened ethnic identification.[2] Numerous studies of ethno-cultural voting persistence suggest the pervasive influence of ethnic voting in American history. Long after the close of mass European immigration, poll watchers can still make accurate election predictions on the basis of ethnicity, religion, and similar ethno-cultural factors. Political scientists have demonstrated that ethnicity remains "an important independent vari-

143

able in voting behavior" and an "important predictor of political behavior."[3] Even the most ardent pluralist would probably agree that it is a rare case in which ethnicity remains immutable before the powerful forces of American culture. But it seems equally clear, as historian Lawrence Fuchs put it, that "politics in America has been an important factor in promoting the persistence of ethnic identity."[4] This is certainly the case in Miami, where Cubans and other new immigrants from Latin America and the Caribbean have settled in massive numbers since 1959.

Just a bit of background about Miami is in order. Beginning as a small tourist haven in the mid-1890s, the city grew quickly in the early twentieth century through the efforts of its chief urban booster, Henry M. Flagler. Miami boomed in the twenties with the rest of south Florida, almost doubled in population in the Depression thirties, was positively affected by World War II military spending, and zoomed still further ahead in the fifties as the widespread availability of air conditioning drew new population and economic activities to the area. Today Miami is the central city in a metropolitan area rapidly approaching two million in population. Although the population of the city itself is relatively small (just over 380,000 in 1985), Miami is the vibrant economic, social, and cultural center not only of the Dade County metro area but of the entire Caribbean basin. Miami has emerged as one of the booming and rapidly changing metropolitan areas of the American Sunbelt.[5]

Three further bits of background information are necessary for understanding the nature of ethnic politics in the city. First, the city and the larger metropolitan area are both often described as "tri-ethnic" in character—with blacks, Hispanics, and non-Hispanic whites (or Anglos, as they are called in Miami) competing for a share of political power and decisionmaking. Blacks comprised a substantial portion of Miami's early population, particularly Bahamian blacks who worked in the local construction industry and in agriculture. Between 1940 and 1980, the percentage of blacks in the total metropolitan population declined marginally from 18.5 percent in 1940 to 17.2 percent in 1980. Hispanics were less numerous historically, totaling about 20,000 or 4 percent of metropolitan population in 1950; most of them were Puerto Ricans, with only a small Cuban community.[6]

The Cuban Revolution in 1959 changed all this. A massive exodus of Cuban exiles began in 1959 and continued sporadically over the next two decades. Between 1959 and 1980, more than 800,000 Cubans left their homeland for the United States. Despite federal government efforts to relocate Cuban exiles throughout the United States, a large proportion eventually settled in the Miami area. The 1980 census revealed that 580,000 Hispanics lived in metropolitan Miami, although not all of them are Cuban. These statistics did not include the 125,000 Mariel refugees of 1980, most of whom also settled in Miami. By the mid-1980s, according to official count, considerably more than 750,000 Hispanics reside in the area, and they comprise over 60 percent of the population of the city of Miami and over 40 percent of the population of Metro-Dade County.[7]

The Miami-area population is highly segregated residentially by race and ethnicity. Several sociological studies, for example, have demonstrated that of more than one hundred large American cities, Miami had the highest degree of residential segregation by race in 1940, 1950, and 1960.[8] Most of Miami's blacks are concentrated in two large ghettos, Liberty City and Overtown, while others reside in half a dozen smaller black neighborhoods scattered throughout the metropolitan area.[9] Miami's new black immigrants—the Haitians—are also highly segregated residentially. At least 60,000 Haitians, but perhaps as many as 100,000, almost all of whom have arrived in Miami in the last decade, are concentrated in eight census tracts on the northern fringe of the city. About 40 percent Haitian in 1984, the area is now called "Little Haiti."[10]

The Cubans and other Hispanic groups are highly concentrated residentially as well.[11] Miami's "Little Havana" is well known as an area of Cuban settlement, but the Cubans have pushed out into other sections of the metropolitan area. Hialeah, Dade County's second largest city with over 150,000 people, is now more than 85 percent Hispanic. Sweetwater, a small municipality west of Miami, is well over 80 percent Hispanic (in 1986), although not all of the Hispanics there are Cuban. Some 40,000 or more Nicaraguan exiles from the Sandinista Revolution currently reside in Sweetwater and adjacent Fontainebleau Park, earning this section of the Miami metropolitan area the appellation "Little Managua."[12] Of the non-Hispanic population, Jews are significant in numbers. Miami's Jews comprise the fifth largest Jewish community of any U.S. metropolitan area. Long heavily concentrated in Miami Beach, the Jews now reside as well in the densely populated condominium districts of North Miami and North Miami Beach.[13]

Two decades of demographic revolution have created a high degree of residential segregation in the Miami metropolitan area. As one social scientist put it in 1979, "the Latin American community of Miami has grown so rapidly in population that it has dramatically affected the residential space of other groups within the city." Not only has neighborhood heterogeneity in Miami been reduced substantially since 1950, but, according to sociologist Morton D. Winsberg, Miami will almost certainly be more ethnically segregated by 1990.[14] Needless to say, a considerable degree of ethnic and racial tension and occasionally open conflict has accompanied the dramatic transformation of Miami's residential space.

Local government in the area is divided between Metro-Dade County—a powerful metropolitan government created in 1957—and twenty-seven separate municipalities, including the city of Miami. The municipalities control police and fire protection, alcohol and taxi regulation, and zoning, while all other governmental powers and services are provided by Metro, as the county government is called. Metro is run on the commission form of government, with nine commissioners elected at large and an appointed manager. Currently, the Metro Commission is composed of seven Anglos, one black, and one Hispanic. The city of Miami also has a commission form of government, with five commissioners elected at large and an appointed city manager. At the present time, one black, one Anglo, and three Cubans make up the Miami City Commission. In Hialeah, which has a strong mayor-council form of government, a long-entrenched Anglo political machine was ousted by Hispanic politicians in 1981.[15]

Thus, three important components of Miami's social and political structure underlie the pattern of recent ethnic politics in the Miami metropolitan area. The tri-ethnic nature of the population, and the heightened sense of this ethnicity, encourages ethnic bloc voting. The high degree of residential segregation not only lends strength to ethnic or racial voting blocs, but intensifies certain kinds of emotional territorial issues such as zoning or public housing location. And, of course, the existing two-tier governmental structure provides the boundaries within which the political game is played out.

Since the 1960s, an increasingly powerful brand of ethnic politics has emerged. There are at least five separate dimensions to this political story. First, a virulent exile politics remains alive in Miami—an exile politics in-tensified by American foreign policy in the Caribbean and more recently in Central America. Second, the growing power of black and Hispanic voters has increasingly dictated electoral outcomes. Third, efforts to alter existing governmental structures, and particularly to shift from at-large to district elections for both Metro and the city of Miami, essentially involve ethnic and racial interests. Fourth, numerous local policy issues such as bilingual-ism have important implications for Miami ethnic groups. And, finally, ad-ministrative politics, especially disputes over dismissals and appointments of such administrative officials as city managers and police chiefs, have come to have an inordinate significance in Miami's new ethnic boiling pot. There may be other sorts of ethnic political controversies, but these five seem to be crucial in understanding the local scene.

When the Cubans first came to Miami in the 1960s, they came as exiles rather than as immigrants. Actually, they were the latest of a long line of Cuban exiles in Florida dating back to the nineteenth century; in the 1950s Fidel Castro himself was an exile in Miami plotting the overthrow of the Batista regime. Almost universally, the newest exiles hoped to depose Castro and return to their homeland. For many years, Castro and Cuba were more important to Miami's newcomers than local political issues. Dozens of militant exile organizations quickly formed, although the Bay of Pigs fiasco in 1961 deflated much Cuban exile activism. By the late 1960s, the hope of return to the island had fizzled for most Cuban exiles. As they began to view their new home as permanent, they put down roots and began the citizenship process. One of the more interesting patterns of political change in Cuban Miami is the at first gradual and later more dramatic shift from exile politics to ethnic politics.[16]

Yet exile politics in Miami has not completely died out. Some militant exile organizations remain active in Miami and in other Cuban-American communities.[17] The Cuban-American National Foundation, a national lobby group based in Washington, took the lead in promoting Radio Martí, the Miami radio station that broadcasts anti-Castro propaganda to Cuba.[18] The Miami City Commission regularly issues its own anticommunist pronouncements. In 1984, for example, Miami Mayor Maurice Ferre refused to meet with a trade envoy from the People's Republic of China, who had been courted by state officials in Tallahassee. The Miami City Commission sought to ban communist countries from participating in a recent Miss Universe contest, suggesting that a contestant from the U.S. Naval base at Guantanamo Bay might represent a "free" Cuba. Miami is probably the only city in America with its own foreign policy. Miami, Hialeah, and Sweetwater have severed sister-city relationships with cities in Nicaragua. Miami-area politicians have quickly come to recognize that a vocal anti-Castro stance is just good politics. Political candidates who are perceived as "soft" on communism stand little chance in the vortex of Miami politics.[19]

While exile politics is less powerful among the Cubans than it was a decade ago, it remains strong among two more recent groups in Miami. For instance, a number of Haitian exile groups organized in Miami with the avowed aim of toppling the Duvalier regime in Haiti. One such group, the Haitian National People's Party headed by Bernard Sansaricq, actually conducted an ill-fated invasion of Haiti in 1982. There is little evidence, however, that Miami Haitians had any influence on the events leading to Jean Claude ("Baby Doc") Duvalier's flight from the country early in 1986.[20] For many years, the Haitian consul in Miami was widely believed to be an agent of the dreaded *tontons macoutes*—the Haitian secret police. Mysterious bombings and fires in Little Haiti were thought to be aimed at silencing outspoken opponents of Baby Doc. Local Haitian leaders regularly blasted American government aid to the Duvalier regime.[21] Miami Haitians followed the Haitian Revolution with intense interest. There was jubilation in the streets when it became clear that Duvalier had fled to France, and some Miami Haitian leaders have returned to Haiti. Old-country issues remain important in Little Haiti at this early stage, but the growing Haitian population in Miami may increase interest in local issues. There are already at least 4,500 Haitian voters in Miami, and there could be as many as 10,000 by 1988. A shift to ethnic politics for these new Caribbean immigrants may not be far off.[22]

Exile politics in Miami has received a new impetus with the arrival of at least 40,000 Nicaraguan exiles since 1979. The new exiles—called Nicas in Miami—are militantly opposed to the Sandinista regime in Nicaragua. Contra (anti-Sandinista) leadership has come to be headquartered in Miami, and some of the private support for the Contra army in Central America is raised or funneled through Nicaraguan and Cuban exile groups in Miami. As one writer noted in 1982, "this city of exiles has become a nerve center of Nicaraguan counterinsurgency"—an observation that has an even greater degree of accuracy in 1987. Among the notables seated on the podium at a recent Nica rally were three state representatives, two Miami-area mayors, and a Metro-Dade County commissioner—all of which suggests the important link between exile politics and ethnic politics. Street confrontations between pro- and anti-Contra groups early in 1986 suggest the outlines of future controversy.[23]

There's more. Miami has become an acknowledged center of international conspiracy and intrigue. As one knowledgeable observer put it in a recent *New York Times* interview: "There are 30 nations in the Caribbean basin, and I think all of them use Miami as a bank to keep their money or a place to obtain gringo expertise to stage political campaigns or military coups." Panamanian exiles in Miami celebrated the news that General Omar Torrijos died in a plane crash in 1981. In 1984 eight Honduran exiles were arrested in Miami for plotting the assassination of their country's president. Thousands of Jamaican exiles returned home from Miami after Edward Seaga defeated socialist Michael Manley in 1980 elections; Miami had become a virtual "suburb" of Kingston in the 1970s, one writer has suggested. During elections in Colombia, candidates take their campaigns to Miami, where an estimated 50,000 or more Colombians reside. And so it goes, among these groups as well as among thousands of Venezuelans, Chileans, Peruvians, Ecuadorians, Argentinians, Puerto Ricans, and other Latins who have made Miami at least a temporary home. The 1980 census reported 174,000 non-Cuban Hispanics in Dade County, and even immigration officials admit to tens of thousands of illegal and uncounted aliens as well—perhaps as many as 200,000 according to one estimate.[24]

Exile politics tends to heighten the sense of national origin and ethnic identification, particularly among large and residentially compact groups such as Cubans, Nicaraguans, and Haitians. But the longer the group remains in the United States, the less compelling is the case for exile politics, especially among the second and later generations. As with the Cubans, the achievement of economic success and citizenship in the United States is often accompanied by a gradual shift in political orientation—a shift from exile politics to ethnic politics.[25]

Ethnicity in the Miami area is clearly reflected in changing patterns of electoral politics. Traditionally, the nonpartisan municipal governments in the Miami metropolitan area were controlled by WASP businessmen and professional elites. In the 1920s the five members of the Miami City Commission were the city's leading bankers. With the exception of Miami Beach, where Jewish mayors were elected in the 1940s, things did not change much over the next thirty years. In the 1960s, as a result of the civil rights movement and voter registration drives in the black community, black Miamians first became a force in city politics. Since 1966 one of the five seats on the Miami City Commission has been filled by a black commissioner. Since 1968, one or more blacks have represented Dade County in the state legislature. Since the 1970s, the Metro Commission has had one black seat. Yet black political power in Miami has been stifled both by the at-large electoral system and by the growing political clout of the Cuban and other Hispanics. Indeed, the political hostility between blacks and Cubans reflects a large conflict dating to the beginning of the Cuban migration—a conflict stemming primarily from competition for jobs and residential space.[26]

The rising power of the Latin vote became apparent in the early 1970s. Maurice Ferre, of Puerto Rican background, was elected to the Miami City Commission in the mid-1960s, then elected mayor in 1973, and reelected five times. Voters also sent the first Cuban politician to the commission in 1973 as a Cuban-American voting bloc began to emerge in Miami.[27] By 1985 Cuban voters clearly had become dominant, as Ferre was ousted by Cuban-born Xavier Suarez. As 1986 began, Hispanics totaled 53 percent of Miami's registered voters, controlled the city commission, held all of the city's major administrative positions except police chief (an office held by a recent black appointee), and filled a growing portion of city jobs.[28] The at-large election system has prevented similar Hispanic inroads at the Metro level, where only one Hispanic has achieved a commission seat.[29]

At the level of partisan politics, the Cubans have dramatically altered the political landscape. Traditionally, Florida was an integral part of the one-party Democratic South. But the Miami Cubans blamed President John F. Kennedy and the Democrats for the failure of the Bay of Pigs invasion. The Republican party has been the beneficiary. Miami's Cubans have strongly supported Republican presidential candidates since the 1968 election. Ronald Reagan received heavy Hispanic support in Miami in 1980 and 1984.[30] In September 1984 after a mass naturalization ceremony in the Orange Bowl, election officials registered over 3,000 new voters; 88 percent of them registered as Republicans and only 10 percent as Democrats.[31] The trend is clear. Increasing numbers of Hispanics are becoming citizens and voters; they register and vote heavily for Republican state and national candidates. At the municipal level, Cubans and other Hispanics will become more powerful politically as time goes on. As numerous observers have noted, Miami-area politics has become "Cubanized" or "Latinized."[32]

It should be noted, however, that Cubans are not always united on political issues and candidates. Cuban politics in Miami has been very fragmented at times, with numerous factions and groups organized around old-country issues or loyalties. Occasionally these internal squabbles result in a level of political violence not customary in the United States, as when a mayoral candidate was machine gunned in front of his Little Havana home in

1981. Nevertheless, Cubans tend to turn out on election day in larger proportions than blacks or Anglos, and they are more likely to vote along ethnic lines against white or black candidates. Ethnic voting, in short, has become commonplace in Miami, dictating political outcomes throughout the metropolitan area.[33]

Ethnic politics is also reflected in long-standing and ongoing battles over the structure of local government in the Miami metropolitan area. Because Metro commissioners are elected at-large, the power of black and Hispanic voting blocs has been diluted considerably, leaving the Metro Commission essentially an Anglo preserve. When Metro was first created in 1957, opposition to the at-large system came largely from smaller municipalities. The civil rights movement and massive Hispanic migration altered the battle lines of metropolitan politics by the late 1960s and 1970s. Black and Hispanic groups have been pushing for a district election system. A charter review commission recommended scrapping the at-large system in 1971, but a county referendum rejected the idea. Ethnic politics was somewhat diffuse in 1971, when blacks were just beginning to participate and Cubans were just becoming citizens. Another charter review commission examined the at-large issue in 1982, but recommended against any change in the election system despite intense ethnic lobbying. The Anglos on the Metro Commission were simply not ready to yield political power to Miami's emerging ethnic groups.[34]

The link between ethnicity and governmental structure also has come to the fore in the city of Miami, which also has an at-large election system. Prior to his electoral defeat in 1985, Miami Mayor Maurice Ferre had been pushing charter revisions that would introduce the strong-mayor system and district elections. Not especially popular in Little Havana, Ferre had long been linked to Miami's downtown Anglo power elite. Ferre feared that the rising proportion of Cuban voters would soon lead to an all-Cuban city commission. The district system, Ferre argued, would maintain representation on the city commission for Miami's blacks and Anglos.[35] The at-large election system works against Hispanics at the Metro level, but works in their favor in Miami where they are a majority of the population. Ironically, the traditional white power elite opposes district elections for Dade County as yielding too much power to black and Hispanic minorities, but sees the same sort of districting as a means of retaining some power in the city of Miami.

The latest twist in this internecine struggle over governmental structure came in 1984 with a new report on Dade County government sponsored by a panel composed mostly of downtown businessmen. Written by University of Miami business professor David B. Hertz, the new report urged the strong-mayor system for Metro, a combination of district and at-large seats for the Metro Commission, and the possible merger of Miami and 26 other municipalities with Metro, thus creating a single metropolitan government.

Ethnic spokesmen quickly concluded that the true purpose of the new plan was to dilute the growing Hispanic power base in Miami. Even with some district seats for Hispanics and blacks, the implementation of the Hertz plan most likely would put the old Anglo power structure back in control. After a brief flurry of debate, the Hertz plan temporarily disappeared from sight, only to reappear early in 1986 in the form of recommendations from a new citizens' committee for Metro charter reform.[36]

New dimensions to the battle over governmental structure emerged in 1986. The *Miami Herald*, long a supporter of the existing Metro arrangement, has recently shifted its position and now advocates the opening up of Metro representation with new district seats grafted onto the current at-large system. In a barrage of editorials and columns in the spring of 1986, the *Herald* also announced support of Metro charter revisions that would substitute a strong-mayor system for the existing weak-mayor, county-manager system. The Metro Commission has long opposed such charter changes, but may not be able to hold off much longer against mounting pressure for change. Such charter revisions as proposed by the *Miami Herald* and others, once implemented, would almost certainly alter substantially the ethnic balance of power on the Metro Commission.[37]

Closely linked to these structural issues is the movement to create a new municipality for Miami's sprawling black ghetto. Much of the Liberty City area lies in unincorporated Dade County and is thus serviced by Metro. Liberty City blacks have long and unsuccessfully complained about bad housing, police brutality, inadequate schools and recreational facilities, and poor transit and other municipal services in the ghetto.[38] One black member serves on the Metro Commission, but blacks clearly have insufficient clout at the Metro level to obtain much in the way of better services.

As a result, some Liberty City blacks have been seeking to create through incorporation a new fifteen square mile municipality with a population of just over 100,000. Black supporters of the plan view this so-called New City as a means of acquiring local political power, a community controlled police force, and a higher level of services. In the wake of the 1980 Liberty City riot, a local black pressure group, the New City Political Action Committee, pushed the idea. But in September 1981 the Metro Commission voted against submitting the New City plan to the voters in a referendum. In 1984 black leaders revived the New City plan, again unsuccessfully.[39] The New City battle represented the new style of ethnic politics in Miami. Excluded from Metro decisionmaking, blacks sought decentralized local government for the Liberty City community. The Anglo power structure, which continues to dominate Metro through at-large elections, resisted the black localist challenge to metropolitan government.

Thus, beyond electoral politics, issues of governmental structure have come to be invested with a tremendous degree of ethnic meaning. In ethnically homogeneous metropolitan areas, these sorts of structural controversies might be seen in economic or class terms, but in Miami virtually every political issue is perceived as an ethnic issue.

Ethnicity also has become an important ingredient in the making of public policy in the Miami metropolitan area. The ongoing controversy over bilingualism provides a case in point. In 1973, reflecting the demographic changes in south Florida, the Metro Commission made Dade County officially bilingual. As a result, most Metro agencies hired Hispanics to serve Spanish-speaking residents. Official documents were published in English and Spanish, and informational signs were made bilingual. These moves paralleled the introduction of some bilingual programs in the Dade County school system, which required English-speaking elementary children to study Spanish.[40]

Anglo opposition to bilingualism boiled to the surface in 1980, during the Mariel boatlift. An Anglo group named Citizens of Dade United used the petition process to force a county referendum on a proposed antibilingualism ordinance. Ironically, the petition drive was led by a multilingual Russian Jewish immigrant to the United States who said she "didn't feel like an American anymore" in Dade County. The key section of the ordinance proposed that "the expenditure of county funds for the purpose of utilizing any language other than English, or promoting any culture other than that of the United States is prohibited. All county government meetings, hearings, and publications shall be in the English language only." Various Hispanic groups, led by the newly organized Spanish-American League Against Discrimination, fought the proposed antibilingualism ordinance, and the newspapers editorialized against it. Nevertheless, a substantial majority of Dade County voters approved the ordinance in November 1980 in a highly charged election. The *Miami Herald* called it an "ethnic-line vote"—71 percent of the Anglo voters favored the measure, while 80 percent of the Hispanic voters opposed it. Observers noted at the time that the bilingualism issue reflected a new sort of ethnic polarization in Miami, one no doubt intensified by the enormous influx of new Cubans earlier in the year.[41]

But this was not the end of the language controversy. In some Miami-area municipalities, the inability of political candidates to speak English has become a campaign issue. One large U.S. corporation stirred up a hornet's nest by prohibiting Hispanic employees in Miami from speaking Spanish at work.[42] Other firms refuse to hire workers who cannot speak Spanish. Hispanic politicians keep pushing for repeal of the antibilingualism ordinance or at least reform to permit the use of Spanish for medical emergencies and for tourism promotion. The issue heated up in 1984, when the Metro Commission amended the ordinance for such purposes. Militant Anglos jumped on the bandwagon of U.S. English, the Washington lobby pushing a constitutional amendment to make English the official language of the United States. The Florida English Campaign, an affiliated group seeking a state constitutional amendment for the same purpose, has strong support among Anglos in Miami. Citizens of Dade United, which initiated the antibilingual issue in Miami, is threatening to mount a new campaign against the Metro Commission. Hispanic community leaders, by contrast, have formed a new organization called English Plus to promote bilingualism in the area.[43]

The language issue is so emotional in Miami because the Cubans and other Hispanics have shown little inclination to abandon their native Spanish. Language scholars have noted that Spanish has been the most persistent of all foreign languages across several generations in the United States.[44] This certainly seems to be true for Miami. The 1980 census demonstrated that about 64 percent of Miami's population above the age of five speak a language other than English at home. More than half of those using other languages in the home were also fluent in English, so Spanish was clearly the language of choice for those families.[45]

Independent research studies have reinforced the census data on language. A 1980 study of Cuban households by the Cuban National Planning Council reported that 92 percent of respondents in Miami spoke only Spanish at home, and 57 percent of Cubans spoke only Spanish or mostly Spanish at work. A Dade County study in 1980 claimed that less than one percent of Cuban children in Miami "used English as the first language between parents and children." Another study in 1983 of 600 Latin families revealed that only Spanish was used in 89.2 percent of Latin homes; 2.6 percent used English and 8.2 percent used both languages. These studies have demonstrated that Spanish remains dominant among Miami Cubans, and that it probably has been strengthened by the recent Mariel refugee influx.[46]

Language is not the only controversial ethnic policy issue. Federal immigration policy has also stirred ugly ethnic passions. Blacks and Anglos alike criticized the federal inaction that permitted the 1980 Mariel boatlift, and then failed to pay for the costs of refugee resettlement in south Florida. Tensions rose in late 1984, when the Immigration and Naturalization Service (INS) announced that the Mariel Cubans would be permitted to seek residency status. This decision, along with an agreement with Cuba normalizing immigration, ultimately would have permitted an additional 300,000 Cubans to join relatives in Florida. Still complaining about job competition, black leaders were outraged. Non-Hispanic whites were worried, too. A great debate began on the radio talk shows, whose hosts organized a new ethnic outfit, Save Our South Florida (SOS), to lobby against the INS immigration decision. As one radio man put it, "The idea that these people are being assimilated is ridiculous. They are absorbing us, and not the other way around." Challenging this position were the Hispanic radio talk shows, which militantly argued their own side of the issue. But the emerging controversy was quickly extinguished. The start-up of Radio Martí led Cuba to abrogate the immigration pact, putting off the next big wave of Cuban immigration to some indefinite future time. By the summer of 1986, however, change was in the wind once again, as the start of informal negotiations between the United States and Cuba suggested that the immigration agreement might soon be reinstated.[47]

There is an undeniable political dimension to these debates over immigration policy. Florida Democrats accused the Reagan administration and the INS of speeding the naturalization of the Cubans as a means of boosting the Republican party in the state. The INS denied charges of politicization of immigration policy, but Republican leaders readily admitted the newly naturalized Cubans would dramatically increase their political power in Florida. When 14,200 immigrants, mostly Cubans, became citizens on July 4, 1986 at a massive naturalization ceremony in Miami's Orange Bowl, the Dade County Republican party surely was delighted.[48]

These controversies over bilingualism and immigration only begin to suggest how public policy issues have generated ethnic tension in Miami. Governmental decisionmaking on many other issues also has raised the level of ethnic political controversy in the metropolitan area. In 1981 white community organizations protested the location of low-cost public housing in their upscale Kendall neighborhood, forcing the Metro Commission to abandon the project; blacks were outraged. In 1983 in a move aimed at Mariel refugees, the Miami Beach City Commission passed an ordinance requiring refugees and their sponsors to register with the police; now Hispanics were outraged, and the measure was soon rescinded. In 1985 middle-class blacks organized public protest and took legal action to prevent the construction of a new sports stadium in north Dade County, which, they claimed, would destroy their neighborhood. White business leaders and politicians were annoyed that the blacks would not go along with the new sports plan. All of these public policy issues, and numerous others, generally pit Miami's ethnic and racial groups against one another, and the battles are usually fought out in the public arena.[49]

In the past decade, ethnic politics also has intruded into governmental administration, particularly in the appointment and dismissal of high-level officials. A classic case recently ran its course in the city of Miami. In October 1984, the Miami City Commission fired black city manager Howard Gary, who had been enormously popular in the black community. Mayor Ferre, who had previously supported Gary and had depended heavily on black electoral support, joined two Cuban commissioners in voting for the manager's ouster. Tensions rose in the black community, touching off fears of a new ghetto riot. Black leaders tempered these hostilities and channeled black outrage into a movement to recall Mayor Ferre. Gary would not go quietly and said he might run for mayor himself.[50]

Meanwhile, various ethnic blocs began positioning themselves for the appointment of the new manager. The crisis peaked in March 1985. On March 8, the City Commission went through thirty-five ballots without successfully choosing a new manager, the five commissioners remaining divided among two Cuban candidates and former city manager Gary. On March 11, the black campaign to recall Ferre failed when the county elections supervisor invalidated several thousand petition signatures. On March 12, on the thirty-sixth ballot, the City Commission chose Cuban-born Sergio Pereira as Miami's new city manager when black commissioner Miller Dawkins broke the deadlock by shifting his vote from Gary to Pereira. In a neat bit of ethnic symbolism not unnoticed in Miami, Dawkins wore a Cuban *guayabera* shirt rather than a suit and tie on the day of the decisive ballot. Dawkins needed Cuban votes to get reelected to the City Commission. And how about this for ethnic symbolism: After his selection, new city manager Pereira read an acceptance speech in English, gave it again in Spanish, and then posed for photographers chomping on a big Cuban cigar.[51]

The outcome of the 1985 city manager controversy, followed quickly by the election of Xavier Suarez as Miami's mayor, suggested the completion of a decisive power shift in the city of Miami. When Pereira resigned within a year to become Metro manager, he was replaced as city manager by another Cuban, but it took only one ballot by the Miami City Commission. The rising proportion of Hispanic voters has put the Cubans firmly in control. The city's rapidly changing demography will strengthen the Hispanic vote even further while proportionately diminishing the Anglo and black vote. A new Cuban-American power structure is emerging—one that worked behind the scenes, for instance, to resolve the city manager standoff to its own liking. The old downtown business elite is concentrating its efforts on new metropolitan government schemes, such as proposed in the Hertz report, to restore eroding political power. Such are the vagaries of ethnic politics in contemporary Miami.

It is my argument, then, that ethnicity is alive and well in Miami. The arrival of the Cubans and other exile and refugee groups since 1960 has dramatically altered the social and political demography of the Miami metropolitan area. Over twenty-five years the Cubans have adjusted rapidly; they have been successful economically—more so than any other Hispanic group in the United States.[52] The second generation, in particular, has internalized much of the mainstream American culture. They have, in short, been acculturated. But it would be difficult to argue that they have been fully assimilated.[53]

Cubans and other ethnic groups have been thrown together in Miami in a struggle for jobs, residential space, and political power. For the Cubans, like other immigrant groups before them, nationality has been the key variable in determining political attitudes and political behavior. Moreover, as sociologist Alejandro Portes has suggested, when ethnic minorities begin competing directly with other groups, the "awareness of racial and cultural differences will be heightened and form the basis for mobilization."[54] Active participation in the political system has provided one means for achieving group goals, while the participation itself has stimulated the sense of ethnic identification and political power. What the future holds for Miami, only time will tell. But it seems certain that ethnicity will dominate the political landscape in the Miami metropolitan area for some time to come.

NOTES

1. Oscar Handlin, "The Immigrant and American Politics," in David F. Bowers, ed., *Foreign Influences in American Life* (Princeton, N.J., 1944), pp. 84-98; Oscar Handlin, *The Uprooted* (Boston, 1951), pp.201-26; W. Lloyd Warner and Leo Srole, *The Social Systems of American Ethnic Groups* (New Haven, 1945), pp.283-84; Edward R. Kantowicz, *Polish-American Politics in Chicago, 1888-1940* (Chicago, 1975), p.223.

2. Nathan Glazer and Daniel Patrick Moynihan, *Beyond the Melting Pot* (Cambridge, Mass., 1963); Michael Novak, *The Rise of the Unmeltable Ethnics* (New York, 1972); Mark R. Levy and Michael S. Kramer, *The Ethnic Factor: How America's Minorities Decide Elections* (New York, 1973); Richard Krickus, *Pursuing the American Dream: White Ethnics and the New Populism* (New York, 1976); and David R. Colburn and George E. Pozzetta, eds., *America and the New Ethnicity* (Port Washington, N.Y., 1979).

3. Raymond E. Wolfinger, "The Development and Persistence of Ethnic Voting," *American Political Science Review* 59 (December 1965), 896; Andrew M. Greeley, *Ethnicity in the United States: A Preliminary Reconnaissance* (New York, 1974), p.138. See also Michael Parenti, "Ethnic Politics and the Persistence of Ethnic Identification," *American Political Science Review* 61 (September 1967), 717-26; Michael Parenti, "Immigration and Political Life," in Frederic Cople Jaher, ed., *The Age of Industrialism in America: Essays in Social Structure and Cultural Values* (New York, 1968), pp.79-99; Robert P. Swierenga, "Ethnocultural Political Analysis: A New Approach to American Ethnic Studies," *Journal of American Studies* 5 (April 1971), 59-79.

4. Lawrence H. Fuchs, ed., *American Ethnic Politics* (New York, 1968), p.164. See also Lawrence H. Fuchs, *The Political Behavior of American Jews* (Glencoe, Ill., 1956). For a useful, if uneven, collection of essays on the subject, see Joseph S. Roucek and Bernard Eisenberg, eds., *America's Ethnic Politics* (Westport, 1982).

5. On these points, see Raymond A. Mohl, "Miami: The Ethnic Cauldron," in Richard M. Bernard and Bradley R. Rice, eds., *Sunbelt Cities: Politics and Growth Since World War II* (Austin, 1983), pp.58-99. On the importance of air conditioning, see Raymond Arsenault, "The End of the Long Hot Summer: The Air Conditioner and Southern Culture," *Journal of Southern History* 50 (November 1984), 597-628. On the emergence of Miami as the "capital" of the Caribbean basin, see Joel Garreau, *The Nine Nations of North America* (Boston, 1981), pp.167-206.

6. Charles Garofalo, "Black-White Occupational Distribution in Miami During World War I," *Prologue* 5 (Summer 1973), 98-101; Raymond A. Mohl, "Black Immigrants: Bahamians in Early Twentieth-Century Miami," *Florida Historical Quarterly* 65 (January 1987), 271-97; Paul S. George, "Colored Town: Miami's Black Community, 1896-1930," *Florida Historical Quarterly* 56 (April 1978), 432-47; Raymond A. Mohl, "Race, Ethnicity, and Urban Politics in the Miami Metropolitan Area," *Florida Environmental and Urban Issues* 9 (April 1982), 1-6, 23-25; Raymond A. Mohl, "Mi-

ami: American Gateway," in Gail F. Stern, ed., *Freedom's Doors: Immigrant Ports of Entry to the United States* (Philadelphia, 1986), pp.70-71.

7. Sergio Diaz-Briquets and Lisandro Perez, "Cuba: The Demography of Revolution," *Population Bulletin* 36 (April 1981), 25-28; Thomas D. Boswell, "The Migration and Distribution of Cubans and Puerto Ricans Living in the United States," *Journal of Geography* 83 (March-April 1984), 65-72; U.S. Bureau of the Census, *1980 Census of Population.* Vol. 1, *Characteristics of the Population*; PC80-1-C11; *Florida* (Washington, D.C., 1983), pp.11-49; *Miami Herald* (March 18, July 3, 1986).

8. Donald O. Cowgill, "Trends in Residential Segregation of Non-Whites in American Cities, 1940-1950," *American Sociological Review* 21 (February 1956), 43-47; Karl E. Taeuber and Alma F. Taeuber, *Negroes in Cities: Residential Segregation and Neighborhood Change* (Chicago, 1965), pp.40-41; Annemette Sorenson et al., "Indexes of Racial Residential Segregation for 109 Cities in the United States, 1940-1970," *Sociological Focus* 8 (1975), 125-42.

9. Reinhold P. Wolff and David K. Gillogly, *Negro Housing in the Miami Area: Effects of the Postwar Building Boom* (Coral Gables, 1951); Harold M. Rose, "Metropolitan Miami's Changing Negro Population, 1950-1960," *Economic Geography* 40 (July 1964), 221-38.

10. Robert A. Ladner et al., *Demography, Social Status, Housing and Social Needs of the Haitian Population of Edison-Little River* (Miami, 1983), pp.1-8; Alex Stepick, *The Business Community of Little Haiti* (Miami, 1984), p.8; Stewart Power, "The Struggle to Regain Paradise Lost," *U.S. News and World Report* 90 (February 24, 1986), 22.

11. Morton D. Winsberg, "Housing Segregation of a Predominantly Middle Class Population: Residential Patterns Developed by the Cuban Immigration into Miami, 1950-74," *American Journal of Economics and Sociology* 38 (October 1979), 403-18; Morton D. Winsberg, "Ethnic Competition for Residential Space in Miami, Florida, 1970-80," *American Journal of Economics and Sociology* 42 (July 1983), 305-14; B.E. Aguirre et al., "The Residential Patterning of Latin American and Other Ethnic Populations in Metropolitan Miami," *Latin American Research Review* 15, no. 2 (1980), 35-63; Rosemary Santana Cooney and Maria Alina Contreras, "Residence Patterns of Social Register Cubans: A Study of Miami, San Juan, and New York SMSAs," *Cuban Studies* 8 (July 1978), 33-49.

12. *Miami Herald*, (January 17, February 14, November 1, 1982; July 19, 1984; December 23, 1985); *Miami News* (July 19, August 22, 1984; June 21, 1986); *USA Today* (September 10, 1984).

13. Winsberg, "Housing Segregation," 406, 415; Winsberg, "Ethnic Competition," 306-7; *Miami Herald* (November 4, 1984).

14. Winsberg, "Housing Segregation," 415; Winsberg, "Ethnic Competition," 305, 313-14.

15. Reinhold P. Wolff, *Miami Metro: The Road to Urban Unity* (Coral Gables, 1960); Edward Sofen, *The Miami Metropolitan Experiment* (rev. ed., New York, 1966); Raymond A. Mohl, "Miami's Metropolitan Government: Retrospect and Prospect," *Florida Historical Quarterly* 63 (July 1984), 24-50.

16. William C. Baggs, "The Other Miami—City of Intrigue," *New York Times Magazine* (March 13, 1960), 25, 84-87; Tad Szulc, "*Guerra!*—Still the Word in Miami," *New York Times Magazine* (July 5, 1964), 9, 14-15; Al Burt, "Cuban Exiles: The Mirage of Havana," *The Nation* 200 (January 25, 1965), 76-79; Horace Sutton,

"The Curious Intrigues of Cuban Miami," *Saturday Review* (September 11, 1973), 24-31; Max Azicri, "The Politics of Exile: Trends and Dynamics of Political Change among Cuban-Americans," *Cuban Studies* 11-12 (July 1981-January 1982), 55-73. On the Bay of Pigs invasion, see Haynes Johnson, *The Bay of Pigs: The Leaders' Story of Brigade 2506* (New York, 1964); and Peter Wyden, *Bay of Pigs: The Untold Story* (New York, 1979).

17. Andrew St. George, "Hit and Run to Cuba with Alpha 66," *Life* (November 16, 1962), 55-58; Jeff Stein, "An Army in Exile," *New York* 12 (September 10, 1979), 42-49; Jeff Stein, "Face to Face with Omega 7," *Cubatimes* 1 (Spring 1980), 3-12; Dade County, Florida, *Needs Assessment Study: Terrorism in Dade County, Florida* (Miami, 1979); Lourdes Arguelles, "Cuban Miami: The Roots, Development, and Everyday Life of an Emigré Enclave in the U.S. National Security State," *Contemporary Marxism* 5 (Summer 1982), 27-43.

18. Thomas D. Boswell and James R. Curtis, *The Cuban-American Experience: Culture, Images, and Perspectives* (Totowa, N.J., 1983), p.172.

19. *Miami News* (August 1, 8, 17, December 20, 1984); *Miami Herald*, (May 22, August 18, December 12, 1984).

20. Anthony Summers, " 'A Hope and a Doom': Profile of an Invasion," *Miami Magazine* 33 (April 1982), 70-75, 139-44; Jake C. Miller, *The Plight of Haitian Refugees* (New York, 1984), pp.208-15; *Miami News* (March 19, July 10, 1982); *Miami Herald* (March 6, 1983, June 1, 1984).

21. *Miami Herald*, (November 1, 1982; April 12, 15, 30, May 17, June 4, August 4, 1984); *Miami Times* (December 2, 1982; May 24, 1984).

22. *Miami Times* (February 11, 1982); *Miami Herald* (January 31, 1984); *Miami News* (October 22, 1985, February 1, 7, March 7, 1986); *New York Times* (February 8, 1986).

23. *Miami Herald* (November 26, 1982, July 19, 1984, March 16, 1986); *Miami News* (December 7, 1982, July 19, 1984, April 27, 1985).

24. *Miami Herald* (August 4, 1981, July 24, 1983, November 2, 3, 1984, May 18, 24, 1986); *Miami News* (July 17, 1985); *New York Times* (December 29, 1984); Kari Polanyi-Levitt, *Jamaica: Lessons from the Manley Years* (Kingston, Jamaica, 1984), p.8; Powell, "The Struggle to Regain Paradise Lost," 22; John Dorschner, "Welcome to Casablanca," *Miami Herald, Tropic Magazine* (June 15, 1986), 12-24.

25. Alejandro Portes, "The Rise of Ethnicity: Determinants of Ethnic Perceptions Among Cuban Exiles in Miami," *American Sociological Review* 49 (June 1984), 383-97.

26. Mohl, "Miami: The Ethnic Cauldron," 82-83. On the conflict between blacks and Cubans, see Allan Morrison, "Miami's Cuban Refugee Crisis," *Ebony* 18 (June 1963), 96-104; Neil Maxwell, "Unwelcome Guests," *Wall Street Journal* (May 6, 1963; Anthony Ramirez, "Cubans and Blacks in Miami," ibid. (May 29, 1980); Larry Mahoney, "The Cubans and the Blacks," *Miami Mensual* 5 (February 1985), 24-30, 90-94; *Miami News* (May 29, 1986).

27. Paul S. Salter and Robert C. Mings, "The Projected Impact of Cuban Settlement on Voting Patterns in Metropolitan Miami, Florida," *Professional Geographer* 24 (May 1972), 123-31; Linda Lanier, "Miami's Cubans—Getting a Taste for Politics," *U.S. News and World Report* 80 (April 5, 1976), 29; "Hispanics Make Their Move," ibid. 91 (August 14, 1981), 60-64; *Miami Herald* (April 21, 1972); *New York Times* (July 8, 1972, April 18, November 7, 18, 1973).

28. *Miami News* (May 5, June 19, July 13, August 29, 1981, September 6,

November 24, 1984; June 23, 1981, January 18, 1985); Sylvan Meyer, "Cuban Power: Cracking the Anglo Structure," *Miami Magazine* 28 (August 1977), 22-27, 47; Sonia L. Nazario, "Yanqui Si: After a Long Holdout, Cubans in Miami Take a Role in U.S. Politics," *Wall Street Journal* (June 7, 1983); Kathy A. Darasz, "Cuban Refugees in Miami: Patterns of Economic and Political Adjustment" (M.A. thesis, Florida Atlantic University, 1982), pp. 70-113.

29. *Miami News* (August 18, September 3, 1981).

30. Benigno E. Aguirre, "Ethnic Newspapers and Politics: *Diario Las Americas* and the Watergate Affair," *Ethnic Groups* 2 (1979), 155-65; Dan Millott, "Cuban Thrust to the GOP," *New Florida* 1 (September 1981), 70-71; Bob Greenberg, "Cuban-American Voters Surveyed," *Cubatimes* 5 (January/February 1985), 10-11; *Miami Herald* (November 5, 1980, November 8, 1984); Christopher L. Warren, "Hispanics," in Manning J. Dauer, ed., *Florida's Politics and Government* (2nd ed., Gainesville, Fla., 1984), pp.321-30; Max Azicri, "Cultural and Political Change Among Cuban-Americans (1958-1982), *Revista/Review Interamericana* 12 (Summer 1982), 200-20.

31. *Miami News* (September 18, 1984).

32. Herbert Burkholz, "The Latinization of Miami," *New York Times Magazine* (September 21, 1980), 45-46, 84-88; *Miami Herald* (July 13, 1981); Thomas B. Morgan, "The Latinization of America," *Esquire* 99 (May 1983), 47-56; Jim Minter, "GOP's Latin Clout in Dade Has State Democrats Worried," *South Florida Business Journal* (October 8, 1984), 13; Sylvan Meyer, "The Hispanic Shift," *Miami Magazine* 9 (February 1985), 12-15; *Miami News* (June 18, 1986).

33. *New York Times* (November 18, 1973); *Miami Herald* (May 5, August 29, 1981); *Miami News* (April 24, 25, 26, 1981); *Diario Las Americas* (Miami) (April 25, 26, 1981).

34. Raymond A. Mohl, "Miami Metro, Charter Revisions, and the Politics of the Eighties," *Florida Environmental and Urban Issues* 10 (October 1982), 9-13, 21-23.

35. *Miami Herald* (May 9, 20, June 10, 1982); *Miami News* (May 19, 20, July 20, 22, 24, 1982, August 1, 6, 10, 1984).

36. David B. Hertz, *Governing Dade County: A Study of Alternative Structures* (Miami, 1984); *Miami News* (December 8, 10, 1984, January 21, 1985, April 17, 1986).

37. *Miami Herald* (March 29, April 4, May 9, June 6, 8, 1986).

38. On these points, see National Commission on the Causes and Prevention of Violence, *Miami Report: The Report of the Miami Study Team on Civil Disturbances in Miami, Florida, During the Week of August 5, 1968* (Washington, D.C., 1969); U.S. Commission on Civil Rights, *Confronting Racial Isolation in Miami* (Washington, D.C., 1982); Bruce Porter and Marvin Dunn, *The Miami Riot of 1980: Crossing the Bounds* (Lexington, Mass., 1984).

39. *Miami Times* (July 23, 30, 1981); *Miami Herald* (September 18, 24, 1981, December 11, 1984); *Miami News* (September 21, 22, 24, 25, 1981, December 21, 1984).

40. *New York Times* (April 18, 1973); "Backlash in Miami," *Newsweek* (March 17, 1975), 29-33.

41. *Miami Herald* (August 3, September 30, October 7, 26, November 5, 1980, September 22, 1981); *Diario Las Americas* (July 25, August 10, October 23, November 7, 1980).

42. *Miami Herald* (May 3, 1983, June 10, 1984); *Miami News* (June 9, 1984).

43. *Miami Herald* (December 7, 1983, June 13, September 14, 1984, February 14, March 21, December 5, 1985); *Miami News* (September 18, 1984, February 6, 1985).

44. Joshua A. Fishman, *Language Loyalty in the United States* (The Hague, Netherlands, 1966), pp. 42-47.

45. U.S. Bureau of the Census, *1980 Census of Population.* Vol. 1, *Characteristics of the Population.* PC80-1-C11, *Florida*, pp. 11-15, 161-162; *Miami Herald* (April 22, 1982).

46. Guarione M. Diaz, ed., *Evaluation and Identification of Policy Issues in the Cuban Community* (Miami, 1981), p. 48; Aida Tomas Levitan, *Hispanics in Dade County: Their Characteristics and Needs* (Miami, 1980), p. 29; *Miami Herald* (April 29, 1983, February 27, 1984).

47. *Miami Herald* (January 13, November 20, December 2, 6, 9, 14, 15, 16, 1984, July 4, 7, 1986); *Miami News* (December 6, 11, 1984, July 3, 1986).

48. Carla Anne Robbins, "South Florida's Melting Pot Is About to Boil," *Business Week* (February 4, 1985), 86-87; *Miami Herald* (July 3, 1986).

49. *Miami Herald* (July 15, 19, December 2, 1981); *Miami News* (July 22, 23, 1981, September 22, October 6, 1983); *Miami Times* (July 23, 30, 1981, December 13, 1984); *New York Times* (March 3, 1985).

50. *Miami News* (October 26, November 17, December 4, 1984); *Miami Herald* (October 26, 27, 28, 30, November 3, 27, December 4, 1984, January 28, 1985); *Miami Times* (November 8, December 27, 1984, January 3, 1985).

51. *Miami Herald* (March 9, 12, 13, 15, 1985); *Miami Times* (March 21, 1985).

52. A. J. Jaffe et al., *The Changing Demography of Spanish Americans* (New York, 1980), pp.254-67; Alejandro Portes and Robert L. Bach, "Immigrant Earnings: Cuban and Mexican Immigrants in the United States," *International Migration Review* 14 (Fall 1980), 315-41; Kenneth L. Wilson and W. Allen Martin, "Ethnic Enclaves: A Comparison of the Cuban and Black Economies in Miami," *American Journal of Sociology* 88 (July 1982), 135-60; Lisandro Perez, "Immigrant Economic Adjustment and Family Organization: The Cuban Success Story Reexamined," *International Migration Review* 20 (Spring 1986), 4-20. For two recent books on the economic adjustment of the Cubans, see Alejandro Portes and Robert L. Bach, *Latin Journey: Cuban and Mexican Immigrants in the United States* (Berkeley, Calif., 1985); and Silvia Pedraza-Bailey, *Political and Economic Migrants in America: Cubans and Mexicans* (Austin, 1985).

53. Roberto F. Fleitas, "Adjustment without Assimilation: The Cubans in the United States, 1959-1976" (M.A. thesis, University of Miami, 1976); Raymond A. Mohl, "An Ethnic 'Boiling Pot': Cubans and Haitians in Miami," *Journal of Ethnic Studies* 13 (Summer 1985), 51-74; Raymond A. Mohl, "The New Caribbean Immigration," *Journal of American Ethnic History* 5 (Spring 1986), 64-71; Joan Moore and Harry Pachon, *Hispanics in the United States* (Englewood Cliffs, N.J., 1985), p. 46.

54. John T. Butterwick, "A Dimensional Comparison of the Political Cultures of Cuban and American Community College Students in the Miami Area" (Ph.D. dissertation, University of Miami, 1973); Portes, "The Rise of Ethnicity," 385. See also Alejandro Portes et al., "Assimilation or Consciousness: Perceptions of U.S. Society Among Recent Latin American Immigrants to the United States," *Social Forces* 59 (September 1980), 200-24.

9

From Dixie to Dreamland: Demographic and Cultural Change in Florida, 1880-1980

Raymond Arsenault and Gary R. Mormino

"Afterlife for Ohio, surrogate for Cuba, landing strip for Colombia, laundromat for the mob, beach for Brooklyn," was the opening quip of a recent article on Florida in *Rolling Stone* magazine.[1] In the iconography of popular culture, Florida has leaped into the American consciousness: a Miami beleaguered by race riots, right-wing commandoes, and Latin drug dealers; an almost endless array of condos inhabited by geritol-swigging octogenarians; a chain of gaudy tourist meccas connected by interstate highways. For some, "Florida" still evokes pleasant images of a tropical paradise, but for many others the Sunshine State has become a wasteland of violence and cultural sterility.

Florida is, of course, much more complicated than these stereotypes suggest. Beneath the veneer of Sunbelt and "Miami Vice" caricatures is a complex social reality that reflects more than four centuries of historical development. Florida has passed from New Spain to Old South to New South to an emerging Sunbelt, and in the process has picked up more than its share of cultural complexity. This chapter explores the last century of Florida's past, focusing on three critical dates: 1880, 1930, and 1980. Using these chronological signposts we hope to illuminate the dominant demographic and cultural characteristics of modern Florida: the powerful legacy of slavery and racial exploitation, the continuing influence of transplanted Caribbean cultures, the increasing significance of Floridians born in other countries or other states, the surprisingly recent "aging" of the state's population, the belated but imposing arrival of urbanization, and the consequences of uneven and unplanned growth. By tracing the outlines of Florida's social history, we can better understand not only where the state has been but also where it is going.

Admitted to the Union in 1845, Florida embraced the Confederate cause in 1861 and later suffered the consequences of naval blockade, military defeat, and civil reconstruction. If Florida was spared the physical ravages of Sherman and Grant, it was probably because it had little worth destroying. Once the poor stepchild of the Old South, the state became an underpopulated, impoverished adolescent in the New South. Editors in Pensacola and Jacksonville may have listened to Henry Grady's optimistic projections of a New South modernized with Yankee efficiency, but the rhetoric did not sweeten the bitter reality of the 1880s. The paucity of people shocked visitors to the state, just as it had for decades. While most areas of the United States received record numbers of new immigrants from the 1840s onward, Florida languished. During the period 1840-1880, Alabama's population rose from 590,756 to 1,262,505, and Georgia's soared from 691,392 to 1,542,180. But in Florida the forty-year gain was barely 200,000, from 54,477 in 1840 to 269,493 in 1880. Despite being the second largest (58,600 square miles) state east of the Mississippi River, Florida ranked thirty-fourth out of thirty-seven states in population in 1880. Only Oregon, Nevada, and Delaware had fewer inhabitants. Indeed, the population of Florida was smaller than that of the city of Baltimore.[2]

Table 9.1
Population, 1830-1980

| Year | Population | | % Increase Over Preceding Census | |
	Florida	U.S.	Florida	U.S.
1830	34,370	12,866,020	----	33.5
1840	54,477	17,069,453	56.9	32.7
1850	87,445	23,191,876	60.5	35.9
1860	140,424	31,443,321	60.6	35.6
1870	187,748	39,818,449	33.7	26.6
1880	269,493	50,155,783	43.5	26.0
1890	391,422	62,947,714	45.2	25.5
1900	528,542	75,994,575	35.0	20.7
1910	752,619	91,972,266	42.4	21.0
1920	968,470	105,710,620	28.7	14.9
1930	1,468,211	122,775,046	51.6	16.1
1940	1,897,414	131,669,275	29.2	7.2
1950	2,771,305	150,697,361	46.1	14.5
1960	4,951,560	179,323,175	78.7	18.5
1970	6,789,443	203,302,031	37.1	13.4
1980	9,746,324	226,504,825	43.6	11.4

Sources: *Statistical Abstract of the United States 1981*, p. 5; Donald B. and Wynelle S. Dodd, *Historical Statistics of the South 1790-1970* (University of Alabama, 1973), 14-15.

Had Frederick Jackson Turner turned his eyes southward rather than westward in the 1880s, he would have discovered a state still in the throes of the frontier. Vast amounts of Florida lay unsettled, and one had to travel to the Rocky Mountain territories to find density rates lower than Florida's. If we accept the federal census's definition that areas with less than two inhabitants per square mile belonged to the frontier, then most of south and central Florida, a vast region covering three-quarters of the state, was frontier in 1880. As shown in Table 9.2, Florida's population density (4.9 per square mile) was well below the average for the nation (16.9) and the South Atlantic region (28.3). In fact, it was the only state east of the Mississippi with a population density of less than twenty-one inhabitants per square mile. "From what I have observed," a visitor told Harriet Beecher Stowe in 1872, "I should think Florida was nine-tenths water, and the other tenth swamp." Senator John Holmes of Maine declared that Florida was so worthless that it would not be much of "a loss to the United States were the whole peninsula of Florida to sink into the Gulf of Mexico."[3]

Table 9.2
Population per Square Mile, 1830-1980

Year	Florida	U.S.	South[a] Atlantic
1830	0.6	7.4	13.6
1840	1.0	9.8	14.6
1850	1.6	7.9	17.4
1860	2.6	10.6	20.0
1870	3.4	13.4	21.8
1880	4.9	16.9	28.3
1890	7.1	21.2	33.0
1900	9.6	25.6	38.9
1910	13.7	31.0	45.3
1920	17.7	35.6	52.0
1930	27.1	41.2	58.8
1940	35.0	44.2	66.4
1950	51.1	50.7	79.0
1960	91.5	50.6	97.1
1970	125.5	57.4	114.9
1980	180.0	63.9	138.4

Sources: Historical Statistics of the United States: From Colonial Times to 1970, pp. 26, 28; Statistical Abstract of the United States 1982-83, pp. 6, 11; Twelfth Census of the U.S.: 1900, Vol. 1, Population, Part 1, p. xxxiii; U.S. Bureau of the Census, Census of Population: 1960, Vol. 1, Characteristics of the Population, Part A, Number of Inhabitants, pp. 1-20.

[a] The South Atlantic region includes Delaware, District of Columbia, Florida, Georgia, Maryland, North Carolina, South Carolina, Virginia, and West Virginia.

Despite its frontier status, Gilded Age Florida possessed a distinctively southern flavor. This is not surprising since a large majority of the state's population lived within a two-day ride of the Georgia and Alabama border. As Table 9.4 demonstrates, 76.6 percent of the population resided in the northern tier of counties, compared with only 19.2 percent in the central region and a mere 4.2 percent in the south. Like most southern states, Florida was predominantly rural (90.0 percent in 1880), depended almost

Table 9.3
Percent Urban, 1830–1980[a]

Year	Florida	U.S.	South[b]	South[c] Atlantic
1830	0.0	8.8	5.3	6.2
1840	0.0	10.8	6.7	7.7
1850	0.0	15.3	8.3	9.8
1860	4.1	19.8	9.6	11.5
1870	8.1	25.7	12.2	14.4
1880	10.0	28.2	12.2	14.9
1890	19.8	35.1	16.3	19.5
1900	20.3	39.7	18.0	21.4
1910	29.1	45.7	22.5	25.4
1920	36.5	51.2	28.1	31.0
1930	51.7	56.2	34.1	36.1
1940	55.1	56.5	36.7	38.8
1950	65.5	64.0	48.6	49.1
1960	74.0	69.9	58.5	57.2
1970	80.5	73.5	64.6	63.7
1980	84.3	73.7	66.9	67.1

Sources: Statistical Abstract of the United States 1981, pp. 10–12; *Statistical Abstract of the United States 1982–83*, pp. 20–21; *1983 Florida Statistical Abstract*, p. 3; Donald B. and Wynelle S. Dodd, *Historical Statistics of the South 1790–1970*, pp. 14–15; *Twelfth Census of the U.S.: 1900*, Vol. 1, *Population*, Part 1, p. lxxxiii; U.S. Bureau of the Census, *Census of Population: 1960*, Vol. 1, *Characteristics of the Population*, Part A, *Number of Inhabitants*, pp. 1-29-1-37; U.S. Bureau of the Census, *1970 Census of Population*, Vol. 1, *Characteristics of the Population*, Part 1, Section 1, Table 18.

[a]For the censuses from 1830 to 1940, percent urban represents the population living in communities of 2,500 or larger. Beginning with the 1950 census, the definition of percent urban was adjusted to include the population in certain "urban fringe" areas that did not fall within the boundaries of incorporated communities of 2,500 or more.
[b]Includes the seventeen states in the South Atlantic, East South Central, and West South Central census divisions. The states are Alabama, Arkansas, Delaware, District of Columbia, Florida, Georgia, Kentucky, Louisiana, Maryland, Mississippi, North Carolina, Oklahoma, South Carolina, Tennessee, Texas, Virginia, and West Virginia.
[c]The South Atlantic region includes Delaware, District of Columbia, Florida, Georgia, Maryland, North Carolina, South Carolina, Virginia, and West Virginia.

entirely on agriculture and extractive industries, had a high percentage (47.1 percent) of blacks and a rigid color line, and boasted a relatively young population. This was obviously a Florida that bore little resemblance to the Florida of today. The state that would later gain fame as a retirement haven—earning the nickname "God's Waiting Room"—had a median age of eighteen in 1880 (compared with 34.7 in 1980). Most striking, a century ago only 2.3 percent of Florida's population was sixty-five years old or older; the comparable figure for 1980 is 17.3 percent (see Table 9.8). The state that would eventually become one of the most urbanized (84.3 percent of Florida's population was classified as urban in 1980) areas in the nation was almost devoid of urban culture in 1880. The vast majority of Florida

Table 9.4
Regional Distribution of Florida Population, 1830-1980[a]

| | % of State Population Living In: | | |
Year	North Florida	Central Florida	South Florida
1830	96.4	2.1	1.5
1840	96.9	1.0	2.1
1850	87.9	8.7	3.4
1860	84.1	13.8	2.1
1870	79.8	17.1	3.1
1880	76.6	19.2	4.2
1890	67.0	27.6	5.4
1900	66.2	28.9	4.9
1910	60.9	32.6	6.5
1920	43.7	35.6	10.7
1930	41.4	40.4	18.3
1940	38.2	37.9	23.9
1950	34.3	37.0	28.7
1960	26.3	39.5	34.2
1970	22.7	39.7	37.6
1980	19.8	41.1	39.1

Sources: T. Stanton Dietrich, *The Urbanization of Florida's Population: An Historical Perspective of County Growth 1830-1970* (Gainesville, 1978), pp. 33, 58-77; *St. Petersburg Times,* November 7, 1982.

[a] Central Florida represents the area presently occupied by Brevard, Citrus, DeSoto, Hardee, Hernando, Highlands, Hillsborough, Indian River, Lake, Levy Manatee, Marion, Okeechobee, Orange, Osceola, Pasco, Pinellas, Polk, Sarasota, Seminole, Sumter, and Volusia Counties. South Florida represents the area presently occupied by Charlotte, Broward, Collier, Dade, Glades, Hendry, Lee, Martin, Monroe, Palm Beach, and St. Lucie Counties. North Florida constitutes the remainder of the state.

families, black or white, lived off the land, either by farming, husbandry, or the production of lumber and naval stores.

Key West was the largest city in the state in 1880, yet it had only 9,890 citizens. Jacksonville was second with a population of 7,765, and Pensacola was third with 6,845. No other Florida community had passed the 3,000 mark. Part of the blame can be attributed to the annual scourge of yellow fever, but the shortage of railroads and the primitive condition of the local economy, especially inland, were undoubtedly the most fundamental limiting factors. Except for the capital city of Tallahassee, which owed its existence to politics, Florida's "cities" were all seaports. And Tallahassee, with a population of 2,494 in 1880, was far and away the nation's smallest state capital. Even the most isolated of capital cities, Carson City, Nevada, could claim 4,229 inhabitants.[4]

Key West's wharves were loaded with fish, cigars, and, on occasion, guns.

Table 9.5
Percent Foreign-Born, 1880–1980

Year	Florida	U.S.	South[a] Atlantic
1880	3.8	13.3	
1890	5.9	14.8	2.4
1900	4.5	13.6	2.1
1910	5.4	14.7	2.5
1920	5.6	13.2	2.4
1930	4.0	11.6	2.0
1940	4.1	8.8	
1950	5.1	6.9	
1960	5.5	5.4	2.1
1970	8.0	4.7	
1980	10.9	5.4	

Sources: Irene and Conrad Taeuber, *People of the United States in the 20th Century* (Washington, 1971), p. 680; *Statistical Abstract of the United States 1982-83,* pp. 36–37; *St. Petersburg Times,* November 7, 1982; *Compendium of the 9th Census of the U.S.: 1870,* p. 376; *Eighth Census of the U.S.: 1860, Population,* p. xxxi; *Twelfth Census of the U.S.: 1900,* Vol. 1, *Population,* Part 1, p. ciii; U.S. Bureau of the Census, *Thirteenth Census of the U.S.: 1910, Abstract with Supplement for Florida,* p. 585; *Thirteenth Census of the U.S.: 1910, Population,* Vol. 1, p. 135; U.S. Bureau of the Census, *Fourteenth Census of the United States: 1920,* Vol. 3, *Population,* p. 19; U.S. Bureau of the Census, *1950 Census of Population,* Vol. 2, Part 10, *Florida,* Table 54; U.S. Bureau of the Census, *1960 Census of Population, Subject Reports,* Vol. 2, Part 1, p. 4; U.S. Bureau of the Census, *1970 Census of Population, Subject Reports,* 2A, Table 5.

[a] The South Atlantic region includes Delaware, District of Columbia, Florida, Georgia, Maryland, North Carolina, South Carolina, Virginia, and West Virginia.

And the harbors of Jacksonville and Pensacola bustled with shipments of yellow pine, red snapper, naval stores, cotton, and citrus. But there was little excitement elsewhere. Phosphate, which would later benefit Tampa, was not discovered until 1883. Cedar Keys, which boomed for a time as the world's supplier of cedar for the pencil industry, would soon slump into oblivion, its forests denuded of cedar, its population thinned by yellow fever, and its harbor smashed by hurricanes. Even the fabled St. Augustine rested in antique splendor, its 2,293 residents barely surpassing the population of a century earlier.[5]

Table 9.6
Percent Nonwhite, 1830-1980[b]

Year	Florida	U.S.	South[a]
1830	47.0	18.1	37.9
1840	48.7	16.8	38.0
1850	46.0	15.7	37.3
1860	44.6	14.4	36.8
1870	48.8	12.9	36.0
1880	47.1	13.5	36.1
1890	42.5	12.5	34.1
1900	43.7	12.1	32.6
1910	41.1	11.1	30.1
1920	34.1	10.3	27.2
1930	29.5	10.2	26.9
1940	27.0	10.2	24.0
1950	21.8	10.5	21.9
1960	17.9	11.4	20.9
1970	15.8	12.5	19.7
1980	16.0	16.8	21.8

Sources: Historical Statistics of the United States: From Colonial Times to 1970, p. 22; Donald Bogue, The Population of the United States, p. 124; Negro Population in the United States 1790-1915, p. 51; Negroes in the United States 1920-1932, p. 15; County and City Data Book 1956, p. 2; Statistical Abstract of the United States 1942, p. 21; Statistical Abstract of the United States 1962, p. 26; Statistical Abstract of the United States 1981, p. 32; T. Stanton Dietrich, The Urbanization of Florida's Population: An Historical Perspective of County Growth 1830-1970 (Gainesville, 1978), p. 3; Donald B. and Wynelle S. Dodd, Historical Statistics of the South 1790-1970, pp. 14-15.

[a] Includes the seventeen states in the South Atlantic, East South Central, and West South Central census divisions. The states are Alabama, Arkansas, Delaware, District of Columbia, Florida, Georgia, Kentucky, Louisiana, Maryland, Mississippi, North Carolina, Oklahoma, South Carolina, Tennessee, Texas, Virginia, and West Virginia.
[b] The nonwhite category includes blacks, American Indians, Chinese, Japanese, Asian Indians, Filipinos, Koreans, Vietnamese, people classified as belonging to "other races," and most but not all people of Spanish origin.

Tourists would eventually prompt St. Augustine's growth. But tourists were a rare sight in Florida in 1880. The tourist industry was then in its infancy, and most of the communities that would later attract hordes of vacationers were still small villages. Some, of course, did not exist at all. Daytona, the future destination of collegiate sun seekers, had a population of 321 in 1880. Ft. Lauderdale, Miami Beach, and other "Gold Coast" communities were not even incorporated as towns until after the turn of the century, and some still lay in the ocean and swamp muck awaiting the miracle of landfill. Dade County, with an area larger than the state of Delaware, had a total population of 224. Florida's lower Gulf Coast was only slightly less desolate. St. Petersburg was a tiny hamlet known as Paul's Landing and would not be incorporated until 1892. Sarasota, as yet undisturbed by John Ringling and Mrs. Potter Palmer, was a village of 177 people. Only Tampa, with a population of 720, gave even a hint of urbanization, yet even here the

Table 9.7
Median Age of the Population, 1880–1980

Year	Florida	U.S.	South[a]	South[b] Atlantic
1880	18.0	20.9		
1890		22.0	18.8	
1900	20.4	22.9		
1910		24.1	20.7	
1920		25.3	21.7	
1930	25.8	26.5	23.1	
1940	28.9	29.0	25.7	25.5
1950	30.9	30.2	27.2	27.3
1960	31.2	29.5		27.5
1970	32.3	28.1	27.3	27.7
1980	34.7	30.0		30.7

Sources: Historical Statistics of the United States: Colonial Times to 1970, p. 19; The Florida Almanac 1983–84, p. 106; Donald Bogue, The Population of the United States, pp. 95, 109, 116; Statistical Abstract of the United States, 1942, p. 25; Statistical Abstract of the United States, 1962, p. 27; Statistical Abstract of the United States, 1982–83, pp. 25, 28–29; U.S. Bureau of the Census, 1970 Census of Population, Vol. 1, Characteristics of the Population, Part 1, Section 1, Table 63.

[a] Includes the seventeen States in the South Atlantic, East South Central, and West South Central census divisions. The states are Alabama, Arkansas, Delaware, District of Columbia, Florida, Georgia, Kentucky, Louisiana, Maryland, Mississippi, North Carolina, Oklahoma, South Carolina, Tennessee, Texas, Virginia, and West Virginia.
[b] The South Atlantic region includes Delaware, District of Columbia, Florida, Georgia, Maryland, North Carolina, South Carolina, Virginia, and West Virginia.

population was in decline, down 10 percent since 1870. As one visitor to the city put it, "Your morning slumbers will not be interrupted here by the hammers of rude workmen." Of course, the state's vast interior was even more rustic than the coastal areas. The "long frontier" stretched from Ocala to the Everglades, punctuated only by an occasional trading village such as Orlando (population 1,000) or Ocala (803). Isolated and undeveloped, the interior was still encased in thick palmetto scrublands, trackless pine forests, and impenetrable sawgrass.[6]

Key West was the great aberration in Florida in 1880. The nation's southernmost city was literally and figuratively an island in the deepest South: an urban enclave in an agrarian frontier and an ethnic oasis in

Table 9.8
Percent 65 Years Old and Over, 1880–1980

Year	Florida	U.S.	South[a]	South[b] Atlantic
1880	2.3	3.4		
1890	2.5	3.9	3.1	3.4
1900	2.6	4.1		3.5
1910	2.9	4.3	3.4	3.6
1920	4.2	4.7	3.8	4.0
1930	4.8	5.4	4.2	4.4
1940	6.9	6.8	5.5	5.4
1950	8.5	8.2	6.9	6.6
1960	11.2	9.1		8.1
1970	14.6	9.9	9.6	9.6
1980	17.3	11.4		12.0

Sources: Irene and Conrad Taeuber, *People of the United States in the 20th Century,* pp. 142, 975; *1983 Florida Statistical Abstract,* pp. 21, 30; Donald Bogue, *The Population of the United States,* pp. 96, 112–113; *Statistical Abstract of the United States, 1933,* p. 38; *Statistical Abstract of the United States, 1942,* pp. 5, 15; *Statistical Abstract of the United States, 1962,* p. 19; *Twelfth Census of the U.S.: 1900,* Vol. 2, *Population,* Part 2, p. liii; U.S. Bureau of the Census, *Thirteenth Census of the U.S.: 1910, Abstract With Supplement for Florida,* p. 586; *Thirteenth Census of the U.S.: 1910,* Vol. 1, *Population,* p. 331 U.S. Bureau of the Census, *1950 Census of Population,* Vol. 2, Part 10, *Florida,* Table 16; U.S. Bureau of the Census, *1970 Census of the Population,* Vol. 1, *Characteristics of the Population,* Part 1, Section 1, Table 59.

[a] Includes the seventeen States in the South Atlantic, East South Central, and West South Central census divisions. The states are Alabama, Arkansas, Delaware, District of Columbia, Florida, Georgia, Kentucky, Louisiana, Maryland, Mississippi, North Carolina, Oklahoma, South Carolina, Tennessee, Texas, Virginia, and West Virginia.
[b] The South Atlantic region includes Delaware, District of Columbia, Florida, Georgia, Maryland, North Carolina, South Carolina, Virginia, and West Virginia.

a state dominated by native-born whites and blacks. The reasons behind the city's rise to prominence were its status as a military town (the first federal lighthouse was built in 1825, and Fort Taylor was begun in 1844), a line of treacherous reefs that benefited generations of salvagers, the Cuban revolution, and cigars. Beginning in 1868, Cuba's "Ten Years War" drove 6,000 Cubans into asylum in the United States, chiefly in New York and Florida. Many of these Cuban emigrés were cigar workers, and by 1880 a thriving cigar industry had taken hold in Key West. The city also claimed the bulk of the state's 2,793 West Indians, most of whom belonged to the "Conch" community. Descended from English cockneys, by way of the Bahamas, the Conchs dominated the local sponge industry and did more than their share of ship salvaging.[7]

Florida, it is often said, is where everyone is from somewhere else. This was not the case in 1880, when 64.4 percent (see Table 9.9) of Florida's residents had been born in the state. The proportion of native Floridians would never again be this high. Interestingly, black Floridians (71 percent) were more likely to have been born in the state than whites (63 percent). Despite the intrusions of war and Reconstruction, the racial blend of the state's population, which was 47.1 percent nonwhite, was virtually the same

Table 9.9
Percent Born in State of Residence, 1880-1980[a]

Year	Florida	U.S.
1880	64.4	67.6
1890	————	67.5
1900	64.9	68.6
1910	61.5	66.9
1920	57.8	67.2
1930	50.4	67.3
1940	49.5	70.3
1950	43.5	68.4
1960	36.0	66.6
1970	34.2	64.6
1980	31.2	64.0

Sources: Irene and Conrad Taeuber, People of the United States in the 20th Century, pp. 680–681; Historical Statistics of the United States: Colonial Times to 1970, p. 89; Twelfth Census of the United States: 1900, Vol. 1, Population, Part 1, pp. cxxv, cxlvii; U.S. Bureau of the Census, 1960 Census of Population, Subject Reports, 2A, Table 10; U.S. Bureau of the Census, 1970 Census of Population, Subject Reports, 2, Table 5; St. Petersburg Times, November 7, 1982.

[a] Percent of total population, including the foreign-born.

Table 9.10
Nativity of Florida's Foreign-Born Population, 1880-1980

Country of Birth	1880	1930	1980
Cuba	2,170	6,287	366,057
Canada	446	8,260	70,603
Germany	978	5,454	53,376
England and Wales	897	7,373	35,149
U.S.S.R.	32	2,180	34,859
Italy	77	5,262	29,185
Poland	26	945	26,730
Jamaica	----	----	25,387
Mexico	44	215	13,704
Austria	49	825	11,576
Scotland	236	1,797	11,551
Hungary	8	652	11,048
Philippines	----	----	10,258
France	221	902	8,495
Greece	7	1,552	7,719
Ireland	652	1,309	7,338
Dominican Republic	----	----	7,139
Czechoslovakia	----	638	6,665
Vietnam	----	----	6,347
Sweden	231	2,145	6,054
Netherlands	19	476	5,467
Japan	----	----	4,724
Korea	----	----	4,322
India	----	----	4,278
China	----	----	4,003
Yugoslavia	----	160	3,819
Portugal	41	122	1,690
Northern Ireland	----	534	1,348
Spain	91	4,125	----
Norway	79	859	----
Denmark	259	921	----
Belgium	13	217	----
Switzerland	43	500	----
Finland	----	333	----
Romania	----	645	----
Other Europe	29	254	39,268
Other Asia	24	1,318	21,959
South America	----	----	61,340
North Africa	----	----	3,109
Other Africa	----	----	5,361
Other West Indies	----	----	37,657
Central America	----	----	26,908
Other America	2,830	2,524	----
All Other Countries or Country Not Reported	427	384	81,214
TOTAL FOREIGN BORN	9,909	59,178	1,058,732

Sources: Tenth Census of the United States: 1880 Statistics of the Population of the U.S., Tables VI, X, XII, XXV; *Fifteenth Census of the United States: 1980, Population*, Vol. 3, Part 1, Table 52; *1980 Census of Population: General Social and Economic Characteristics*, Vol. 1, Part 2, *Florida*, Table 61.

as it had been in 1830 (see Table 9.6). Many blacks simply had exchanged racial bondage for economic servitude, thanks to the crop-lien system and the peonage-like conditions that existed in lumber and turpentine camps. Though most blacks remained tied to the land, several thousand abandoned the world of sharecropping and migrated to cities such as Jacksonville and Pensacola, where they comprised roughly half of the population in 1880.[8]

The black community was far and away the state's largest ethnic minority in 1880. Like most of the South, Florida received relatively few European and Asian immigrants in the late nineteenth century. Considering the alternatives available in the urban Northeast, the opportunities for homesteading in the West and the Midwest, and the inevitable competition in the South with poor native whites and blacks, immigrants had good reasons to avoid the region. In relative terms, Florida's proportion of foreign born (3.8 percent in 1880) was higher than the southern average (approximately 2 percent). But in absolute terms, only North Carolina (3,742), South Carolina (7,686), Mississippi (9,209), and Alabama (9,734) contained fewer foreign born than Florida (9,909) in 1880. By contrast, Minnesota's foreign born numbered more than 400,000 and comprised 52 percent of the state's population. In the nation as a whole, the foreign-born component was 13.3 percent, a figure that would rise to 14.8 percent by 1890.[9]

Even the Irish, who migrated to the South in relatively large numbers (Louisiana had 13,421 Irish-born citizens in 1880, while Kentucky had 18,256), avoided Florida. The number of Irish-born Floridians (652) was almost negligible, and even second-generation Irish Americans were rare. Only 3,400 Floridians could claim an Irish-born mother or father, a figure only slightly higher than that of territorial New Mexico.[10]

Florida's German community was also extremely small. Germans constituted the largest foreign-born group in the South in 1880—Louisiana alone boasted 17,475 Germans—but very few (978) lived in Florida. In fact, only North Carolina (950) attracted fewer German-born settlers. Florida's Jewish population was correspondingly sparse. Although several thousand German and eastern European Jews migrated to southern cities in the mid- and late-nineteenth century, very few made their way to Florida. One notable exception was Herman Glogowski, who left Germany in the 1870s to settle in Tampa where he managed a dry goods store and served as mayor from 1886 to 1894. For the most part, Florida's primitive economy offered few opportunities for German merchants or craftsmen. Perhaps most telling, the entire state could claim only one professional brewer in 1880, a sure sign of German absence.[11]

In 1880 "new" immigrants from southern and eastern Europe had yet to arrive in the United States in large numbers. So it is not surprising that the Italian, Polish, and Russian communities were almost nonexistent in Florida. The state's Italian-American population numbered 77, while the Polish-American population was 26. Florida's ethnic diversity, insofar as it existed in 1880, lay in the state's Cuban and West Indian populations. Only New York had attracted more Cuban migrants than Florida, and no state had more West Indians than the colony in Key West. Ironically, Tampa and Miami, the future bailiwicks of Florida's Cubans, contained a grand total of three such immigrants in 1880. The "new" immigration also bypassed north Florida, where even the port cities of Jacksonville and Pensacola were more than 90 percent native born. Indeed, the only city in Florida to attract a sizable number of immigrants of any kind was Key West; there alone the foreign-born population (54 percent) was in the majority. Without Key West's large immigrant community, Florida's foreign-born population would have been reduced to 1.7 percent, a figure roughly equivalent to that of Arkansas.[12]

The federal census of 1880 gives us a last glimpse of pioneer Florida. The state was on the threshold of change, as land speculators, financiers, railroad developers, and even a few manufacturers were poised to capitalize on Florida's undeveloped potential. For better or worse, entrepreneurs such as Hamilton Disston, William Chipley, Henry Flagler, Henry Plant, and Vicente Martínez Ybor would soon usher in the rudiments of modern development. Yet despite their best efforts, these men could not change Florida overnight. The state would remain underpopulated and relatively undeveloped well into the twentieth century. Native-born farm families would remain in the majority, and an agrarian ethos, symbolized by a county-unit system that mandated one state senator per county regardless of population, would continue to dominate the state for decades to come.

The pace of change may have seemed painfully slow to impatient developers, but by the 1930s they clearly had the upper hand, even though the real estate bust of 1926 and the stock market crash of 1929 had deflated their prospects. During the half century since 1880, Florida had witnessed profound changes in the character and composition of its population and culture. If the state was not yet the Sunbelt magnet of the 1980s, neither was it the marginal frontier of the 1880s. The Florida of 1930 was a state in mid-passage: though still underpopulated, it was no longer an empty quarter; though still predominantly rural, it was urbanizing rapidly; though its population was still overwhelmingly native born, Florida now included a notable leaven of immigrant ethnicity; and though still identifiably southern, the state was in the process of taking on a regional character of its own.

With the census of 1930, Florida's population officially passed the long-awaited one million mark. Nevertheless, with 1,448,211 inhabitants, Florida still ranked last among southern states. Even Arkansas, with its remote Ozark backcountry, was approaching a population of two million in 1930. Moreover, with 26.7 persons per square mile, Florida remained the least densely populated state east of the Mississippi. Nearby Georgia, by contrast, had 49.5 persons per square mile. If the census had been taken in 1925, before the collapse of the real estate boom and before many discouraged settlers had left the state, Florida's population figures might have been more encouraging. But no amount of boosterism could hide the fact that the state remained seriously underpopulated.[13]

On the other side of the ledger, Florida's long-term demographic trends looked very favorable in 1930. Even with the bust, Florida's decennial growth rate for the 1920s was an impressive 51.7 percent, nearly twice the rate of the previous decade. Although Florida had the lowest annual birth rate in the South in 1930—18.2 live births per 1,000 women of child-bearing age—the pace of in-migration more than picked up the slack. The proportion of Floridians born in the state (50.4 percent) had declined dramatically since the turn of the century, when in-state nativity had reached an all-time high of 64.9 percent. In 1930 the authentic Florida "cracker" was not yet an endangered species, but the in-state nativity rate was already well below the national average of 67.3 percent.[14]

Some early twentieth-century migrants to Florida were retirees, and the image of Florida as a retirement haven was beginning to catch on. Nevertheless, the state's "senior citizen" component remained small by the standards of the post–Social Security Act era. Although both the median age (25.8 in 1930) and the proportion sixty-five years old or older (4.8 percent in 1930) had risen significantly since the nineteenth century, Florida's age profile remained relatively young. In the nation as a whole in 1930, the median age was 26.5, and the proportion sixty-five years old and older was 5.4 percent. Florida's population was already the oldest in the South, but nationally the state did not yet stand out as a geriatric center. This was true even though tourists who visited the recently settled areas of central and south Florida often came away with an upwardly skewed picture of the state's age profile. At the beginning of the Great Depression, the largest concentrations of elderly citizens lived not in Florida or Arizona, but in New England. Rhode Island, where 12.2 percent of the population was 65 years old or older, led the way, closely followed by Massachusetts (11.0 percent) and New Hampshire (8.9 percent).[15]

The "aging" of Florida's population may have caught the attention of a few demographers in 1930, but there were far more striking demographic trends to consider. Most obvious was that the regional distribution of the state's population was changing rapidly. The traditionally dominant counties of northeastern Florida and the Panhandle, which had accounted for 76.6 percent of the state's population in 1880, now accounted for only 41.4 percent. Even though the population of north Florida had nearly tripled in size since 1880, the region's growth rate had lagged far behind that of central and south Florida. The geographic center of Florida's population had shifted southward to the Ocala area (see Table 9.4), and central Florida now had roughly the same number of inhabitants as north Florida. To the dismay of many north Floridians, who were accustomed to having things their way, this shift had important political and cultural implications. Despite the conservatizing influence of the county-unit system, which tended to mute the effects of population growth, north Florida's control over the legislature was no longer a foregone conclusion. In fact, some central Florida politicians had begun to question the advisability of keeping the state government in Tallahassee, which was growing increasingly remote from the state's major population centers. In south Florida the mood was not quite so aggressive. Although the population of south Florida had increased more than tenfold since 1900, the region still claimed less than a fifth of Florida's population. Moreover, following the bust of 1926, few people had much faith in the region's future. Once the dreamland of real estate tycoons and railroad developers, Dade, Broward, and Palm Beach Counties then seemed destined to return to their natural state. The alligators and the egrets had won after all, or so it seemed.[16]

The southward shift of Florida's population was accompanied by a marked dilution of traditional Dixie culture. Although north Florida remained unmistakably southern, large pockets of central and south Florida maintained only a tenuous connection to southern sectionalism. Cities such as Miami and St. Petersburg, where many citizens had been born and bred in the Northeast or Midwest, were sectional hybrids. Even though many of their citizens, southernborn or otherwise, seemed willing to defend the vaunted "southern way of life," these cities were too heterogeneous to be placed within the cultural boundaries of the Deep South. Not surprisingly, their closest connection to the Deep South lay in the area of race relations. Passionately committed to the Jim Crow system, these cities were every bit as segregated as Jacksonville or Tallahassee. Indeed, in terms of residential segregation, they were more segregated than the older north Florida cities, having had no experience with the "distant intimacy" paternalism of the nineteenth-century South. Of course, by north Florida standards, the black communities of Miami (23 percent black in 1930), St. Petersburg (18 percent black), and Tampa (21 percent black) were relatively small. In north Florida cities the black proportion of the population ranged from a low of 30 percent in Pensacola to a high of 48 percent in Sanford. Tallahassee was 41 percent black, and Jacksonville alone, with a black population approaching 50,000 in 1930, had more blacks than all of south Florida.[17]

Jacksonville's vibrant black neighborhoods were the pride of Florida's urban black population. But the community that spawned James Weldon and Rosamond Johnson was not yet representative of black Florida. In 1930, less than half (44 percent) of the state's black population lived in urban areas. The majority lived in "the other Florida"—in the world of isolated homesteads and dusty crossroads hamlets—the world that Zora Neale Hurston would describe so movingly in *Mules and Men* (1935) and *Dust Tracks on a Road* (1942). Hurston's ethnographic and literary artistry captured a rural black subculture that was barely visible to the citified white mainstream. Despite Hurston's efforts, by the 1930s Florida was beginning to lose much of its biracial character. Part of the change can be traced to the work of lily-white public relations men who hoped to sanitize the state's image. But a more fundamental transformation rooted in demography had also taken its toll. For nearly a century, from the territorial period to World War I, blacks accounted for almost half of the state's population. But this was no longer the case in 1930, when the census revealed that the black proportion of Florida's population had dipped below 30 percent. Beginning with the great migration of 1915, thousands of Florida blacks left the state in search of industrial employment (which had been all but barred to them prior to the expansion of war-related industries in 1914) and a more relaxed racial code. Even with the wartime exodus, the absolute size of Florida's black population increased by 7 percent from 1910 to 1920. Yet during the same period, the white population increased by 44 percent. This pattern has prevailed to the present day. Although Florida's black population has continued to grow, it has been submerged in an increasingly dominant white majority.[18]

The most dramatic demographic trend in early twentieth-century Florida was urbanization. Although the state had been urbanizing for decades, the 1920s proved to be a great watershed for Florida's cities. The prosperous decade following World War I produced a massive boom under the Florida sun. Propelled by lavish public relations campaigns and arrayed in the Mediterranean Revival architecture of Addison Mizner, the Florida boom epitomized the vitality, decadence, and materialism of the Jazz Age. "All of America's gold rushes," observed the journalist Mark Sullivan from the vantage point of the 1930s, "all her oil booms, and all her free-land stampedes dwindled by comparison . . . with the torrent of migration pouring into Florida." And most of the torrent poured into the cities. In 1930, for the first time in the state's history, a majority (51.7 percent) of Floridians lived in urban areas. To the amazement of many long-time residents, the census revealed that less than 20 percent of the state's population lived on farms. Florida now ranked as the most urbanized southern state, with Louisiana (39.7 percent urban) a distant second. And no other state in the region had such a high proportion (33 percent) of its population living in cities over 25,000. If this was not quite "megalopolis," it nonetheless presented a striking contrast with nineteenth-century Florida. In 1880 no Florida community had a population over 10,000, but in 1930 there were fourteen such communities. Indeed, three cities—Jacksonville (129,549), Miami (110,637), and Tampa (101,161)—had passed the 100,000 mark.[19]

The sources of Florida's urban growth varied from city to city. Of the state's three largest cities, only Miami was a district by-product of real estate speculation. Incorporated in 1896, Miami was still a small town on the eve of the boom. Then suddenly, between 1920 and 1923, its population more than doubled, as fast-talking real estate agents and binder boys transformed a sleepy town into the "Magic City." The speculative fever raged until 1926, when the combined forces of a devastating hurricane and a financial panic finally cooled things down.[20]

Jacksonville avoided the highs and lows of the boomtown to the south, but as the economic hub of northeastern Florida and southeastern Georgia, the city developed into a major shipping and railroad center. Despite its expansion, the city retained much of its "old Florida" flavor. Demographically it was still more than 97 percent native born, and politically it was still allied with the agrarian conservatives of the Panhandle.[21]

Tampa, like Jacksonville, was a regional marketing and transportation center. Little more than an overgrown village at the end of Reconstruction, Tampa became the major terminus of Henry Plant's railroad empire in 1883. Almost simultaneously, the discovery of massive phosphate deposits in Bone Valley, east of Tampa, created a new extractive-shipping industry. Even more important, in 1886 the local economy acquired an industrial base when Don Vincente Ybor and Ignacio Haya moved their cigar factories from Key West and New York to Tampa. With the arrival of thousands of Cuban, Spanish, and Italian cigar workers, Tampa's Ybor City replaced Key West as Florida's primary ethnic enclave. The city also became Florida's leading industrial center. By the turn of the century, 111 million cigars a year were rolling off the city's cigar benches. During the 1920s the local cigar industry began to decline, falling victim to protracted strikes, changing consumer tastes, and mechanization. But on the eve of the Great Depression, the city known as "Havana on the Hillsborough" could still claim more than 11,000 cigar workers, most of whom were first- or second-generation immigrants.[22]

The "immigrant world" of Ybor City was an anomaly in early twentieth-century Florida: In most areas of the state the population remained overwhelmingly native born. Yet by 1930 Florida's ethnic profile clearly was moving away from the traditional native-born southern pattern. Both absolutely (59,178) and proportionately (4.0 percent), Florida's foreign-born population far surpassed that of any other southern state. Louisiana, with 24,190 foreign born (1.7 percent), was a distant second. In seven southern states—Alabama, Arkansas, Georgia, Mississippi, North Carolina, South Carolina, and Tennessee—the foreign born comprised less than one half of 1 percent of the population. Thus, in its regional context Florida had become a conspicuous haven for foreigners, even if by national standards it was still something less than an ethnic mosaic.[23]

In 1930, Florida's foreign-born population was almost equally divided between "old" and "new" immigrants. Among the "old" immigrants, the Canadians (8,260), the English and Welsh (7,373), and the Germans (5,454) were the most numerous. But there were also more than a few Swedes (2,145), Scots (1,797), and Irish (1,309). Most of Florida's "old" immigrants lived outside of ethnic colonies, thus reducing their ethnic visibility. Yet there were a few identifiable "old" immigrant communities, most notably in Miami, St. Petersburg, and St. Augustine. The Swedish settlement near Miami, for example, was a tightly knit Lutheran community that reveled in its annual celebration of *Martinaas*, St. Martin's Feast Day. For six months every year, Finns congregated at Lake Worth, constituting one of the largest Finnish colonies in North America. In Pinellas and Dade Counties there were several large clusters of Anglo Canadians, most of whom maintained strong ties to Canadian culture. Although the great French-Canadian migration would not begin until after World War II, the Anglo-Canadian presence in Florida was already substantial, especially during the winter months when seasonal visitors descended upon the state.[24]

Florida's "new" immigrants tended to be more visible than their counterparts from Western Europe. With few exceptions, they chose, or were forced, to live in ethnic enclaves. This tendency to cluster can be attributed, in large part, to an internal commitment to traditional modes of culture. But in many instances, external hostility also played an important role in inhibiting acculturation. To Florida's native-born majority, the languages and cultural mores of Russians, Poles, Czechs, Italians, Spaniards, and other "new" immigrants seemed strange or even shocking. Considering the suspicious, sometimes xenophobic, attitudes endemic in Florida's "cracker" culture—the strident anti-Catholic nativism of Governor Sidney Catts (1916-1920) being the most obvious example—it is not surprising that the "new" immigrants banded together in ethnic colonies. Varying in size from a few families to several thousand people, these ethnic colonies dotted the state. The vast majority of Florida's 5,262 Italians lived and worked in Ybor City; more than a thousand Greeks congregated in the fishing and sponging center of Tarpon Springs; and several hundred Russians clustered in Miami and St. Petersburg. There was a small but vibrant Czech community in Masaryktown, a Polish settlement in Korona, a hybrid community of Sicilian and Greek fishermen in Fernandina and Pensacola, a sprawling Austro-Hungarian farm colony in the Panhandle, and a Japanese settlement in Yamato, in southeast Florida.[25]

The largest and most visible of Florida's "new" immigrant communities were, of course, Hispanic. (The classification of Hispanics as "new" immigrants is necessary but somewhat ironic, considering Spain's four centuries of experience in Florida.) In 1880 a large majority of Florida's Spanish-speaking immigrants had been living in Key West. But by 1930 Key West's Cuban community had dwindled to 655, and the center of Hispanic Florida had long since shifted to Tampa. With nearly 5,000 Cubans and 3,300 Spaniards (plus an even larger number of second- and third-generation Hispanics), Tampa's Ybor City was the largest Cuban/Spanish settlement in the United States. When combined with the local Italian population, Ybor City's Hispanics created an expanded "Latino" community that dwarfed every other immigrant community in the South, with the exception of New Orleans's large Irish-Italian enclave. To most Floridians, Ybor City was pure exotica, a bewildering array of sights and sounds punctuated by foreign dialects and ethnic cuisine—both Caribbean and Mediterranean—as well as traditions of political radicalism and labor militancy that were unimaginable in other parts of the South. Although Ybor City's unique culture was already in decline in 1930, its multicultural cosmopolitanism provided a dramatic preview of Florida's future.[26]

During the half century since 1930, Florida has experienced a firestorm of change. Although much of north Florida has retained the traditional style and pace of the rural South, the rest of the state has changed beyond all recognition. In a few short decades, Florida has witnessed explosive population growth, an unprecedented mass migration of retirees, the development of one of the largest tourist industries in the world, the Cuban exodus and the subsequent "Hispanization" of Miami, a massive infusion of federal funds and military personnel, and the rise and fall of the aerospace industry. What was once a sparsely populated appendage of the Deep South has been transformed into a Sunbelt superpower.

The catalyst for all this change was World War II, which brought hundreds of thousands of servicemen to the state. Men and women from all over the United States came to Florida for military training, and more than a few became enamored with the semitropical climate and relaxed pace of life. After the war, a large number of these veterans relocated in the state. Others went back to resume their careers in their home states, but not without a positive image of Florida living. Of these, many would eventually return to Florida as retirees. During the postwar era, retirement in the Florida sun became a capstone of the American dream, thanks to the Social Security Act and the proliferation of private pension funds. At the same time, Florida became more accessible with the construction of an interstate highway system and the spread of air travel. The state also became much more livable with the advent of air conditioning and pesticides. Following the dual conquest of humidity and mosquitoes, the new Florida became a public relations dream, the embodiment of values that dominated postwar America: leisure, mobility, and affluence. Television also played a key role in the boom, imprinting Florida images in American popular culture. By the 1960s, who had not seen Arthur Godfrey strumming his ukulele in Miami Beach's Fountainbleau Hotel, or Anita Bryant touting the virtues of the sunshine tree, or the "right stuff" emanating from Cape Canaveral? For better or worse, the age of the Sunbelt, with all its glitter and hype, was upon us.[27]

Florida's cultural transformation was ensured by the sheer magnitude of population growth. Between 1930 and 1980, Florida's population increased 564 percent, from less than one and a half million to nearly ten million. During the same period, by contrast, the neighboring states of Alabama and Georgia grew 47 and 88 percent, respectively. No state in the nation matched Florida's rate of increase. And in terms of absolute increase, Florida was surpassed only by the much larger states of California and Texas. In terms of population density, Florida did not reach the national average until

1950. Yet by 1980, the state's population density was nearly three times the national norm.[28]

Few states have ever experienced such sustained growth. Even during the Depression decade of the 1930s, when most of the nation languished demographically, Florida's population increased by 29.2 percent. During the 1940s, the decennial rate of increase rose to 46.1 percent, and in the 1950s to a staggering 78.7 percent. Although the rate of increase declined after 1960, in absolute terms Florida's population growth was greater than ever. The state gained nearly two million people in the 1960s and another three million in the 1970s. By 1987 Florida had passed the twelve million mark to become the fourth most populous state in the nation, behind California, New York, and Texas. And there is no end in sight. As Florida's ecologists and water resource managers grapple with the problem of overcrowding, it is hard to imagine that this is a state that entered the twentieth century with fewer inhabitants than the state of Maine.[29]

Remarkably, Florida's spiraling growth has been accomplished without the aid of a high birth rate. Here, as elsewhere, mass migration has been the key factor behind the Sunbelt phenomenon. Florida, like California, has become a testament to the American passion for geographic and social mobility. Goaded by slick media images and clever real estate promotions, millions have chosen to relocate in the Florida sun. Some have come in search of wealth or status, while others have sought security or perhaps just a little peace and quiet. But whatever their primary motivation, the stream of newcomers has never slackened.[30]

The transplant, to use a popular euphemism, has come to dominate Florida's demography, so much so that in some areas of the state the native-born Florida "cracker" has become an endangered species. In 1980 Florida natives accounted for only 31.2 percent of the state's population. A century earlier the comparable figure was 64.4 percent, and as recently as 1930 more than half of the population was Florida-born. In the nation as a whole in 1980, the in-state nativity level (64.0 percent) was more than twice that of Florida.[31]

Not all of Florida has surrendered to the newcomers. In north Florida native-born Floridians were still in the majority (54.0 percent) in 1980, and in fifteen north Florida and Panhandle counties, natives accounted for more than two thirds of the local population. But once one gets south of Ocala, the "cracker" population thins noticeably, as the barbecue places become rarer and the southern drawl is drowned out by the New Jersey or Ohio twang. The southwestern rim, stretching along the Gulf from Sarasota to Naples, has the highest concentration of transplants. Charlotte County, where only 12 percent of the residents in 1980 were Florida born, is the most extreme example. Charlotte, along with four other counties, claimed fewer than 20 percent of its residents native to the state. But virtually everywhere in south Florida transplants outnumber natives by a ratio of four or five to one. If we factor in the annual influx of tourists, which now exceeds 40 million people, it is little wonder that the native Floridians have gotten lost in the shuffle.[32]

Florida has always been culturally diverse, thanks to its proximity to the Caribbean and to an elongated geography—Pensacola is closer to Chicago than it is to Key West—that has inhibited statewide communication and cultural convergence. But in the Sunbelt era this cultural fragmentation has reached new heights, as Florida has welcomed migrants of every conceivable description and background. In the process, the state has shed most of its early twentieth-century southern parochialism. Unfortunately, it has also lost most of its historical consciousness. From the 1920s onward, and especially since 1950, the variety and pace of change have been too great to allow for an orderly integration of the old and the new. In accommodating itself to the influx of new people and new lifestyles, Florida has become relentlessly present-minded. When strip malls and tract houses are in such urgent demand, the lessons and dictates of the past carry little weight. In the new Florida, where nearly everyone is a displaced person of one kind or another, lack of tradition has become a tradition, and whatever sense of community the state has developed has come not from history or state pride but from a shared experience of transience.

North Florida stands out as a major exception to this jumble. However, the force of its traditionalist dissent has waned considerably in recent years. Today north Florida accounts for less than 20 percent of the state's population, whereas a century ago it accounted for more than 70 percent. For several decades the social and political implications of this demographic shift were blunted by legislative malapportionment. Taking full advantage of a county-unit system that all but disfranchised urban voters, the so-called pork chopper politicians of north Florida routinely overruled the upstart "lamb choppers" of central and south Florida. When the U.S. Supreme Court finally outlawed the county-unit system in 1962 in the *Baker* v. *Carr* case, Florida had one of the most malapportioned legislatures in the nation; although Florida's five most populous counties—Dade, Duval, Hillsborough, Pinellas, and Broward—accounted for more than half of the total population, they were allocated only 14 percent of the state senate seats.

Since *Baker* v. *Carr*, the political stranglehold of the north Florida pork choppers has been broken. This has led to a major partisan realignment, because, more often than not, the transplants of central and south Florida have voted Republican. Florida's Republican party, which barely existed prior to 1960, has become a major element in state and national politics. Yet surprisingly little has changed ideologically. To the dismay of liberal Democrats, reapportionment seems to have had more impact on the style of Florida politics than on its substance. Even though the voters have elected two liberal governors, Reubin Askew and Robert Graham, legislative and congressional/presidential politics in Florida remain profoundly conservative. The Sunbelt Republicans of today are no less willing to vote against school bonds and expanded social services for the poor than were the Dixie Democrats of the pork-chop era.[33]

Florida's renewed political conservatism can be attributed, in part, to the state's unusual age profile. The popularity of liberal Democratic Congressman Claude Pepper notwithstanding, the political balance among Florida's senior citizens has been weighted heavily toward conservative Republicanism. Of course, whatever their political bent, in recent years the elderly have exerted an ever-widening influence on the state's social and cultural life. As recently as 1940, the median age of Floridians was actually lower than the median age of Americans as a whole. But since World War II, the state has been deluged by wave after wave of elderly or middle-aged migrants. By 1980, Florida led the nation in median age (34.7), percentage of population sixty-five years old or older (17.3), and deaths (10.4 per thousand residents). In several south Florida counties, the median age has risen to well over 50. And in Miami Beach the median age was 65.7. Not to be outdone, two St. Petersburg census tracts topped out with median ages over 73. If present trends continue as expected, by the year 2000 more than 20 percent of the state's population will be 65 years old or older, an incredible statistic considering that the comparable figure was 2.3 percent in 1880, and less than 10 percent as late as 1950.[34]

It is little wonder that Florida has become synonymous with old age or that Johnny Carson once quipped that the state has only two groups—"the newly arrived and the nearly dead." As the baby boom era moved into full swing, the boomers' grandparents quietly slipped away to Florida. In 1940, Floridians eligible for Social Security benefits numbered 2,550; in 1984, that figure had exploded to over two million. Early retirement options, an increasing emphasis on "living the good live," a generous Social Security program, and a reasonable expectation of surviving past the age of seventy led millions of Americans to retire in the sun. Not surprisingly, they were greeted by eager developers who peppered the state with rest homes, senior citizen condominium complexes, adult-only mobile home parks, and entire geriatric communities, such as Sun City. The economic fallout from this migration has been considerable, and in some areas a peculiar "mailbox economy" has emerged. In 1982, two million Floridians received a total of $9.7 billion in Social Security benefits. Pinellas County alone, which includes St. Petersburg and Clearwater, accounted for more than $1 billion. In neighboring Pasco County, 19 percent of total household income came from the mailbox economy of pension and Social Security checks. Perhaps most telling, for many years the St. Petersburg area has supported a thriving air freight business that specializes in flying corpses to northern graveyards. Between 1980 and 1982, Pinellas County recorded 13,973 births and 23,245 deaths.[35]

Florida's population has not only aged during the past half century; it has also moved to the city. In 1930 roughly half of the state's population lived in rural areas, but today less than one sixth of the population is rural. An area that a century ago was an agrarian frontier interrupted only by a handful of market towns has been transformed into one of the nation's most urban states. Florida's cities have not only become larger and more numerous; several have evolved into major metropolitan centers. In 1980, Florida boasted eight cities with populations of more than 100,000, and seventeen urban areas that qualified as Standard Metropolitan Statistical Areas (SMSAs). The Miami-Ft. Lauderdale area with a population of 2,643,981 in 1980 was the nation's twelfth largest SMSA, and the Tampa-St. Petersburg SMSA, with a population of 1,613,603, was the twenty-second largest. One way to put these figures into perspective is to recall that the entire state of Florida had less than two million people at the beginning of World War II.[36]

Almost all of Florida's cities have grown significantly in recent years, but some have experienced truly spectacular growth. During the decade of the 1970s, the Fort Myers-Cape Coral and Sarasota SMSAs nearly doubled their populations, and the Miami-Ft. Lauderdale area added more than 750,000 new residents. At this pace, urban growth has often outrun the mental and physical resources of even most conscientious urban planners and politicians. Florida is now dominated by sprawling, low-density (Pinellas County, with a population density of nearly 3,000 per square mile, stands out as an exception) metropolitan areas, whose settlement patterns press ever outward into unincorporated areas. In 1980, half of Miami's metropolitan population lived in unincorporated areas. In Hillsborough County, unincorporated areas accounted for 83 percent of the county's population growth during the 1970s. One symbol of this unplanned and generally unregulated growth is Florida's booming septic tank industry. To the embarrassment of local officials, the Tampa-St. Petersburg area now leads the nation in septic tank use. Of course, strained natural resources and overburdened public facilities have become common facts of life in a state that has indulged in more than its share of ecological brinksmanship.[37]

The racial composition of Florida has also undergone significant change during the last half century. The proportion of nonwhites in the population has fallen steadily from 29.5 percent in 1930 to 21.8 percent in 1950 to 16.0 in 1980. If we eliminate Hispanics (only some of whom are classified as nonwhite), American Indians, Asians, and other similar groups from the nonwhite category, the black proportion of the 1980 population drops to 13.8 percent. The decline has been dramatic in some locales. Charlotte County, a retirement haven along the southwest Gulf Coast, included 19 percent Afro-Americans in its 1920 census; in 1980, that percentage had fallen to below two. Although the absolute number of blacks in the state has increased from 432,000 in 1930 to 1,342,688 in 1980, a massive influx of white Americans and Hispanic Cubans has weakened the blacks' demographic position and diminished their visibility. In any event, culturally and economically the black Florida of the 1930s is all but gone. Since the era of the Great

Depression, a number of factors has shifted blacks from Panhandle farms to cities both inside and outside the state. Agricultural mechanization, along with increasing economic and educational opportunities in the cities, has pulled many Florida blacks away from a bittersweet agrarian heritage. Black family farms still dot the state, but by the 1980s nearly 85 percent of Florida's black population lived in urban areas, the highest percentage in the South.[38]

Among blacks, Florida's reputation on matters of race has never been especially ennobling. Though always on the fringe of the Deep South, the state has had more than its share of racial exploitation and Klanism. During the half century following Reconstruction, Florida's lynching rate was among the highest in the South. And on at least two occasions, at Ocoee in 1920 and Rosewood in 1923, whole communities of blacks were massacred by rampaging whites. Thus, it is not surprising that during the 1940s and 1950s, particularly during the era of "massive resistance" following the 1954 *Brown* decision, some blacks left the state in despair or disgust. However, most Florida blacks stayed, and, beginning with the 1956 Tallahassee bus boycott and the 1963 civil rights struggle in St. Augustine, they were able to bring a measure of desegregation and racial justice to the state. The fruits of the civil rights movement—voting rights, school desegregation, increased economic and social opportunities, and a general decline in racial prejudice—have opened new worlds to Florida blacks, even though many problems remain. Chronic unemployment, residential segregation, a less than color-blind criminal justice system (Florida has more blacks on death row than any other state), the deplorable living conditions of most black migrant laborers, and the special frustrations inherent in Miami's black-Hispanic rivalry continue to plague Florida's black community. But at the very least the spell of Jim Crow has been broken, and only the most myopic of observers would deny that the black minority has an important role to play in Florida's future.[39]

In the state as a whole, the demographic profile has become progressively older, whiter, more urban, and less distinctively southern. But in some areas of Florida these trends have been overshadowed by an even more dramatic development: the emergence of ethnic pluralism and bilingualism on a grand scale. In the 1980s, the foreign-born segment of Florida's population has reached an all-time high, both absolutely (1,058,732 in 1980) and proportionally (11.9 percent). With a million-plus immigrants, Florida now has the fourth largest foreign-born population in the nation. Yet these figures are somewhat deceiving, since Florida's immigrants are heavily concentrated in the greater Miami area. Many Florida communities include pockets of ethnicity: Clearwater claims its Canadians, Lake Worth has its Finns, Tarpon Springs its Greeks, Belle Glade its Jamaicans, and so on. And, of course, despite the decline of the cigar industry, Tampa still has the descendants of the Italians, Spaniards, and Cubans who dominated Ybor City in its heyday. Bob Martinez, Florida's newest governor, represents the first Spanish-American governor in two hundred years. But only in Miami have immigrants created an ethnic "boiling pot," to use the phrase of former Miami Mayor Maurice Ferre. Successive streams of Bahamians, eastern European Jews, Cubans, Haitians, and South and Central Americans have given Miami an international flavor that few American cities can match.

Since World War II, hundreds of thousands of first-, second-, third-, and fourth-generation ethnics have moved from the Rustbelt to Sunbelt Florida. The Jewish diaspora to greater Miami has been well documented. Not so well known is the staggering numbers of other ethnics, such as Italian Americans, who have settled in the state. For instance, metro-Miami, Fort Lauderdale, and St. Petersburg—cities that attracted negligible numbers of Italian immigrants prior to the 1940s—have respective Italian-American populations in 1985 of 56,356, 106,070, and 51,858. There are today more Italian Americans (absolutely) in Fort Lauderdale (10.5 percent of the city's population) than in New Haven, New Orleans, Baltimore, Albany, St. Louis, Syracuse, or Youngstown.[40]

A half century ago Miami was a small resort city with a WASPish mentality, its predominantly native-born population leavened only by small communities of Cubans and Panamanians and a somewhat larger community of Bahamians. But during the 1940s and 1950s, a large influx of New York Jews gave the city its first serious experience with ethnicity. Clustering in Miami Beach and south Miami, which became known as "New York's southernmost suburbs," tens of thousands of Jewish transplants made the Miami area a major center of Jewish culture. Indeed, by the 1980s, North Miami Beach, with more than 85,000 Jewish residents, had become the most densely populated Jewish community in the world. From the beginning, Miami's Jewish population has included a large number of elderly, eastern European–born Jews, thus accentuating the ethnic dimension of Jewish migration. Today, fueled by a reemergent migration from the Northeast, Palm Beach, Broward, and Dade Counties number a half million permanent Jewish residents. During the winter, however, over a million Jews can be found along the state's southeastern corridor.[41]

Jewish ethnicity remains a powerful force in the Miami area, but in recent decades it has been overmatched by an Hispanic tidal wave. As late as 1950, Miami's Spanish-speaking population was estimated to be less than 20,000. But that was before the Cuban Revolution of 1959. Following Fidel Castro's seizure of power, thousands of Cubans fled to Miami. During the first wave of migration, the so-called Golden Exile of 1959-1962, most of the Cuban emigrés were light skinned, relatively well educated, and solidly middle (or even upper) class. Aided by a federal government that was more than willing to expend money and resources to embarrass the Castro regime, these early Cuban emigrés generally found Miami to be a comfortable haven, even though they maintained the dream of returning to Cuba in triumph. Unlike the less-fortunate Puerto Ricans of New York or the Mexican Americans of the Southwest, the Cuban Hispanics of Miami frequently became prosperous, developing their own businesses and often moving into fashionable suburbs such as Coral Gables. The Cuban exodus was suspended for three years in the mid-1960s, but between 1965 and 1973 the "Air Bridge" brought thousands of additional Cubans to Miami. With this second wave of Cuban migration, large sections of greater Miami began to take on an Hispanic cast, complete with Spanish-language newspapers, Cuban restaurants, and *botanicas*. The "Little Havana" section of downtown Miami became a major tourist attraction, and hearing Spanish spoken on Miami streets ceased to be a novelty. Of course, of all the symbols of the new Miami, the most telling, and certainly the most ironic, was the proliferation of "English Spoken Here" signs. All of this made many native Miamians more than a little nervous. Thus, when the controversial Mariel boat lift of 1980 brought 123,000 new Cubans to the Miami area, very few natives rolled out the welcome mat. The Marielitos tended to be poorer and darker skinned than earlier Cuban migrants. And a number had criminal records, though the widely believed charge that Castro had emptied his jails represented a gross exaggeration.[42]

Racism and class prejudice undoubtedly made things worse, but even before the arrival of the Marielitos the sheer size of the local Hispanic community was enough to provoke a nativist backlash. By 1980, Hispanics (both native and foreign born) accounted for more than 40 percent of the population in the greater Miami area, and more than 60 percent in the city of Miami itself. In neighboring Hialeah, which was more than 73 percent Hispanic, 62 percent of the population was foreign born, the highest percentage of any community in the nation. The total Spanish-speaking population in Dade County was estimated to be 768,000 in 1985. Indeed, Hispanics passed non-Hispanic whites in numbers in the early 1980s. To appreciate this, one must realize that in 1950, non-Hispanic whites outnumbered Hispanics 747,748 to 50,000! But census figures have a very short shelf life in south Florida. Since 1980 the Hispanic presence in Miami has grown even larger with the addition of the Marielitos and sizable numbers of Salvadorans, Nicaraguans, Dominicans, Colombians, Venezuelans, and other South and Central Americans. The city has also attracted several thousand Haitian "boat people," who sadly have been all but shunned by their Miami hosts. To the dismay of embattled Anglos, some of whom have organized ambitious anti-immigration and "English language only" campaigns, Miami has become the unofficial capital of Latin America. In truth, the city has acquired the best and the worst of what Latin America has to offer—everything from Cuban cuisine and samba music to drug traffickers and gangland slayings. And all of it is caricatured weekly on prime-time television.[43]

Miami's ethnic cauldron is unique. But it is not an altogether inappropriate symbol of what has happened to Florida during the past century. Physically and culturally, the Miami of today bears little resemblance to the sleepy resort community of 1940, much less to the fishing village of the 1890s. And on a less spectacular level, the same kind of revolutionary change has visited much of the state. In the century since 1880, Florida has experienced massive urbanization and immigration, a series of transportation and communication revolutions, several booms and busts, the military intrusion of two world wars, the civil rights movement, and finally the mixed blessings of the Sunbelt. Granted, there are still Florida counties where the population is rural, native born, and relatively young; where the southern dialect reigns; and where tin-roofed cabins outnumber condominiums. But with each passing year the boundaries of "cracker" Florida recede, as the Sunbelt of superhighways and shopping malls advances. Somehow the state has managed to maintain its mystique as a land apart, differentiating itself from the general placelessness of the Sunbelt phenomenon. Despite congested roads, ugly strip malls, and brazen drug dealers, the Florida fantasy lives on for millions of Americans. How long this will continue depends on the vagaries of popular culture and the decisions of politicians. Can an ecologically fragile state with a longstanding commitment to development and a less than inspiring educational system marshal enough wisdom and restraint to reconcile progress and tradition? Can Florida maintain an expansive economy without destroying its natural environment? Can it strike a humane balance between heterogeneity and community? As the decade of the 1980s draws to a close, these questions remain perilously open.

NOTES

1. John Rothchild, "Florida: Sunset in the Sunshine State," *Rolling Stone* (October 1, 1981), 20.

2. See Table 9.1; *Tenth Census of the United States, 1880: The Statistics of the Population of the United States* (Washington, D.C., 1883); Charlton W. Tebeau, *A History of Florida* (Coral Gables, Fla., 1971), pp. 200-327; Jerrell H. Shofner, *Nor Is It Over Yet: Florida in the Era of Reconstruction, 1863-1877* (Gainesville, 1974).

3. See Tables 9.2 and 9.4; *Tenth Census of the United States, 1880*, Table IV, p. 7; Nelson M. Blake, *Land into Water—Water into Land: A History of Water Management in Florida* (Tallahassee, 1980), p. 25.

4. *Tenth Census of the United States, 1880*, Table 3, p. 180; Table 13; Table 21, pp. 570-71.

5. Ibid., Table 21; Works Projects Administration, *Florida: A Guide to the Southernmost State* (New York, 1939), pp. 61, 195-99, 240, 249, 285-86, 383-84. On St. Augustine, see Jean Parker Waterbury, ed., *The Oldest City: St. Augustine, Saga of Survival* (St. Augustine, 1983), Chapter 7.

6. *Tenth Census of the United States, 1880;* Works Projects Administration, *Florida: A Guide to the Southermost State, passim*; Gary R. Mormino, "Roadsides and Broadsides: A History of Florida Tourism," in *Essays in Florida History* (Tampa, 1987), pp. 14-19; Janet S. Mathews, *Edge of Wilderness* (Tulsa, 1983).

7. L. Glenn Westfall, *Key West: Cigar City, U.S.A.* (Key West, 1984); Gerald Poyo, "Cuban Revolutionaries and Monroe County Reconstruction Politics, 1868-1876," *Florida Historical Quarterly*, 40 (April 1977), 407-22; Gerald Poyo, "Key West and

the Cuban Ten Years War," *Florida Historical Quarterly* 57 (January 1979), 289-307; Works Projects Administration, *Florida: A Guide to the Southernmost State*, pp. 134, 196-99; *Tenth Census of the United States, 1880*, Table 14, p. 54.

8. See Tables 9.6 and 9.10; *Tenth Census of the United States, 1880*, Table X, p. 480, Tables XI and XII; Jerrell H. Shofner, "The Legacy of Racial Slavery: Free Enterprise and Forced Labor in Florida in the 1940s," *Journal of Southern History* 47 (August 1981), 411-26; Gloria Jahoda, *The Other Florida* (New York, 1967), pp. 225-45; Pete Daniel, *The Shadow of Slavery: Peonage in the South, 1901-1969* (New York, 1972); Roger Ransom and Richard Sutch, *One Kind of Freedom: The Economic Consequences of Emancipation* (New York, 1977).

9. See Tables 9.5 and 9.10; David R. Goldfield, *Cotton Fields and Skyscrapers: Southern City and Region, 1607-1980* (Baton Rouge, 1983), pp. 55-56; Randall M. Miller, "Immigrants in the Old South," *Immigration History Newsletter* 10 (November 1978), 8-14; George E. Pozzetta, "Foreigners in Florida: A Study of Immigration Promotion, 1865-1910," *Florida Historical Quarterly* 37 (October 1974), 164-80; Jason H. Silverman, "Writing Southern Ethnic History, An Historiographical Investigation," *Immigration History Newsletter* 19 (May 1987), 1-4.

10. *Tenth Census of the United States, 1880*, Table XXV; Earl F. Niehaus, *The Irish in New Orleans, 1800-1860* (Baton Rouge, 1965); Ira Berlin and Herbert Gutman, "Natives and Immigrants, Free Men and Slaves: Urban Workingmen in the Antebellum American South," *American Historical Review* 88 (December 1983), 1175-1200.

11. *Tenth Census of the United States, 1880*, Tables XIII, XXXIV, and XXXIX; Gary R. Mormino, *Tampa, The Treasure City* (Tulsa, 1983), pp. 87-139. On southern Jewry, see Stephen J. Whitfield, *Voices of Jacob, Hands of Essau: Jews in American Life and Thought* (Hamden, Conn., 1984), pp. 211-44; Nathan M. Kaganoff and Melvin I. Urofsky, eds., *Turn to the South: Essays on Southern Jewry* (Charlottesville, 1979); and Eli N. Evans, *The Provincials: A Personal History of Jews in the South* (New York, 1976).

12. See Table 9.10; Lucius and Linda Ellsworth, *Pensacola: The Deep Water City* (Tulsa, 1982), p. 60; Shofner, *Nor Is It Over Yet*, pp. 259-62.

13. See Tables 9.1, 9.2, and 9.4. On the boom and bust of the 1920s, see George Brown Tindall, "The Bubble in the Sun," in *The Ethnic Southerners* (Baton Rouge, 1976), pp. 185-208.

14. See Tables 9.1 and 9.9; U.S. Bureau of the Census, *Fifteenth Census of the United States: 1930, Population* (Washington, D.C., 1932), Table 44, p. 36.

15. See Tables 9.7 and 9.8. See also David Hackett Fischer, *Growing Old in America* (expanded ed., New York, 1978).

16. See Table 9.4; William C. Havard and Loren P. Beth, *The Politics of Misrepresentation: Rural-Urban Conflict in the Florida Legislature* (Baton Rouge, 1962), pp. 1-41; David Colburn and Richard K. Scher, *Florida's Gubernatorial Politics in the Twentieth Century* (Gainesville, 1980). See also Jahoda, *The Other Florida*.

17. See Table 9.6; Jerrell H. Shofner, "Florida and the Black Migration," *Florida Historical Quarterly* 57 (January 1979), 267-88; David Colburn, *Racial Change and Community Crisis: St. Augustine, 1877-1980* (New York, 1985); Raymond A. Mohl, "Black Immigrants: Bahamians in Early Twentieth-Century Miami," *Florida Historical Quarterly* 65 (January 1987), 271-97; Paul S. George, "Colored Town: Miami's Black Community, 1896-1930," *Florida Historical Quarterly* 56 (April 1978), 432-47; Jon L. Wilson, "Days of Fear: A Lynching in St. Petersburg," *Tampa Bay*

History 5 (Fall/Winter 1983), 4-26; Karl H. Grismer, *The Story of St. Petersburg* (St. Petersburg, 1948), 188-91; Samuel Davis, "The Same Deal: Blacks in St. Petersburg in the 1930s" (seminar paper, University of South Florida, 1986).

18. See Table 9.6; Robert E. Hemenway, *Zora Neale Hurston: A Literary Biography* (Urbana, 1977); Edward Akin, "When a Minority Becomes the Majority: Blacks in Jacksonville Politics, 1887-1907," *Florida Historical Quarterly* 52 (October 1974), 123-45; James Robertson Ward, *Old Hickory's Town: An Illustrated History of Jacksonville* (Jacksonville, 1982).

19. See Tables 9.2, 9.3, and 9.4; Paul S. George, "Brokers, Binders, and Builders: Greater Miami's Boom of the Mid-1920s," *Florida Historical Quarterly* 65 (July 1986), 27-51; David Nolan, *Fifty Feet in Paradise: The Booming of Florida* (San Diego, 1984); Donald W. Curl, *Mizner's Florida: American Resort Architecture* (Cambridge, Mass., 1984); Tindall, "Bubble in the Sun," 185-208; Mark Sullivan, *Our Times: United States, 1900-1925* (New York, 1984), p. 647.

20. Arva M. Parks, *Miami, The Magic City* (Tulsa, 1981); Helen Muir, *Miami, U.S.A.* (New York, 1953).

21. Ward, *Old Hickory's Town*; T. Frederick Davis, *A History of Jacksonville* (St. Augustine, 1925).

22. Gary R. Mormino and George E. Pozzetta, *The Immigrant World of Ybor City: Italians and Their Latin Neighbors in Tampa, 1885-1985* (Urbana, 1987); L. Glenn Westfall, "Don Vincente Martinez Ybor, The Man and His Empire" (Ph.D. dissertation, University of Florida, 1977); Susan D. Greenbaum, "Afro-Cubans in Exile: Tampa, Florida, 1886-1984," *Cuban Studies* 15 (Winter 1985), 59-72; *Key West Memories* (Key West, 1981).

23. See Tables 9.5 and 9.10.

24. See Tables 9.10; Work Projects Administration, *Florida: A Guide to the Southernmost State*, pp. 134-35, 462-63, 466; Robert Harney, "Canadian Ethnics in the Sun Belt," and William Copeland, "Finns in Florida: Contemporary Migration" (papers presented at the Institute on Migration and Ethnicity in Post-World War II America, University of Florida, Gainesville, April 27-28, 1984).

25. Ellsworth and Ellsworth, *Pensacola*, pp. 74, 79; Ted Carageorge, "The Greeks of Pensacola," in Jerrell Shofner and Linda V. Ellsworth, eds., *Ethnic Minorities in Gulf Coast Society* (Pensacola, 1979), pp. 56-86; Gordon Williams Lovejoy, "The Greeks of Tarpon Springs" (M.A. thesis, University of Florida, 1938); George T. Frantzis, *Strangers at Ithaca: The Story of the Spongers at Tarpon Springs* (St. Petersburg, 1962); Stetson Kennedy, *Palmetto Country* (New York, 1942); David Truman Seiber, "Historical Geography of Masaryktown" (M.A. thesis, University of Florida, 1957); George E. Pozzetta, "Foreign Colonies in South Florida, 1865-1910," *Tequesta* 34 (December 1974), 45-56; George E. Pozzetta, "A Padrone Looks at Florida: Labor Recruiting and the Florida East Coast Railway," *Florida Historical Quarterly* 54 (July 1975), 74-84; George E. Pozzetta and Harry A. Kersey, Jr., "Yamato Colony: A Japanese Presence in South Florida," *Tequesta* 36 (December 1976), 66-77; Wayne Flynt, *Cracker Messiah: Governor Sidney J. Catts of Florida* (Baton Rouge, 1977).

26. Mormino and Pozzetta, *The Immigrant World of Ybor City*; Durward Long, "An Immigrant Co-operative Medicine Program in the South, 1887-1963, "*Journal of Southern History* 31 (November 1965), 417-34.

27. Richard Bernard and Bradley Rice, eds., *Sunbelt Cities: Politics and Growth Since World War II* (Austin, 1983); Kirkpatrick Sale, *Power Shift: The Rise of the*

Southern Rim and Its Challenge to the Eastern Establishment (New York, 1975); Carl Abbott, *The New Urban America: Growth and Politics in Sunbelt Cities* (Chapel Hill, 1981); Raymond Arsenault, "The End of the Long Hot Summer: The Air Conditioner and Southern Culture," *Journal of Southern History* 50 (November 1984), 597-628; James R. Adams, "The Sunbelt," in John B. Boles, ed., *Dixie Dateline: A Journalistic Portrait of the Contemporary South* (Houston, 1983), pp. 141-57.

28. See Tables 9.1 and 9.2.

29. Ibid.; Tom Ankersen, "Coping with Growth: The Emergence of a Florida Environmental Policy" (M.A. thesis, University of South Florida, 1982); Nelson M. Blake, *Land into Water—Water into Land: A History of Water Management in Florida* (Tallahassee, 1980); Marjory Stoneman Douglas, *The Everglades: River of Grass* (New York, 1947); John D. MacDonald, *Condominium* (Philadelphia, 1977); *St. Petersburg Times* (April 10, 1987); *New York Times* (December 31, 1986).

30. John Rothchild, *Up for Grabs: A Trip Through Time and Space in the Sunshine State* (New York, 1985); Alex Shoumatoff, *Florida Ramble* (New York, 1974); Nolan, *Fifty Feet in Paradise.*

31. See Table 9.9.

32. Ibid.; *St. Petersburg Times* (November 7, 1982), 20b.

33. See Table 9.4; Havard and Beth, *The Politics of Misrepresentation*; Colburn and Scher, *Florida's Gubernatorial Politics*; Thomas R. Wagy, *Governor LeRoy Collins of Florida* (University, Alabama, 1985), pp. 18-35, 104-20; Peter D. Klingman, *Neither Dies nor Surrenders: A History of the Republican Party in Florida, 1867-1970* (Gainesville, 1984), pp. 155-95.

34. See Tables 9.7 and 9.8; *St. Petersburg Times* (November 7, 1982).

35. See Table 9.8; "Elderly Floridians: A Profile," *Miami Herald* (May 7, 1984); *St. Petersburg Times* (October 10, 1983, 38ff; January 9, 1984, 1b; September 20, 1982); "Florida and the Elderly: The Economic Romance May be Ending," *Florida Trend* 25 (August 1982), 54-59; Del Marth and Martha J. Marth, eds., *The Florida Almanac, 1986-87* (Gretna, La., 1985), p. 111; see also Maria D. Vesperi, *City of Green Benches: Growing Old in a New Downtown* (Ithaca, 1985).

36. See Tables 9.2 and 9.3; U.S. Bureau of the Census, *1980 Census of Population and Housing: Florida* (Washington, D.C., 1983); "The Fastest-Growing State," *Florida Trend* 24 (June 1981), 69-71.

37. Marth and Marth, eds., *The Florida Almanac, 1986-87*, pp. 103-10; U.S. Bureau of the Census, *State and Metropolitan Area Data Book 1986* (Washington, D.C., 1986).

38. See Table 9.6; Marth and Marth, eds., *The Florida Almanac 1986-87*, pp. 103-10; U.S. Bureau of the Census, *State and Metropolitan Area Data Book 1986*, Table A.

39. Works Projects Administration, *Florida: A Guide to the Southernmost State*, p. 457; Kennedy, *Palmetto Country*; Gary Moore, "Rosewood Massacre," *St. Petersburg Times* (July 25, 1982); Colburn, *Racial Change and Community Crisis: St. Augustine, 1877-1980*; James R. McGovern, *Anatomy of a Lynching: The Killing of Claude Neal* (Baton Rouge, 1982); Steven F. Lawson, David R. Colburn, and Darryl Paulson, "Groveland: Florida's Little Scottsboro," *Florida Historical Quarterly* 65 (July 1986), 1-26; Helen L. Jacobstein, *The Segregation Factor in the Florida Democratic Gubernatorial Primary of 1956* (Gainesville, 1972); Bruce Porter and Marvin Dunn, *The Miami Riot of 1980* (Lexington, Mass., 1984).

40. *New York Times* (January 7, 1987); Survey, National Italian American Foundation, 1987.

41. Muir, *Miami, U.S.A.,* pp. 191-300; Mohl, "Black Immigrants: Bahamians in Early Twentieth-Century Miami"; Ira M. Sheskin, "The Migration of Jews to Sunbelt Cities" (paper presented at "The Sunbelt: A Region and Regionalism in the Making?" Conference, Miami, Florida, November 3-6, 1985); *Miami Herald* (January 13, 1984), 6e; Sidney Goldstein, "Jews in the United States: Perspectives from Demography," in American Jewish Committee, *American Jewish Yearbook*, 1981 (Philadelphia, 1981), pp. 3-59; see also Deborah Dash Moore, "Jewish Migration to the Sunbelt," in this volume.

42. Thomas Boswell and James Curtis, *The Cuban-American Experience: Culture, Images, and Perspectives* (Totowa, N.J., 1984); Herbert Burkholz, "The Latinization of Miami," *New York Times Magazine* (September 21, 1980), 45-46, 84; Raymond A. Mohl, "Miami: The Ethnic Cauldron," in Bernard and Rice, eds., *Sunbelt Cities,* pp. 58-99; Raymond A. Mohl, "Miami's Metropolitan Government: Retrospect and Prospect," *Florida Historical Quarterly* 63 (July 1984), 24-50; Thomas B. Morgan, "The Latinization of America," *Esquire* (May 1983), 47-56; "Hispanics Make Their Move," *U.S. News and World Report* (August 24, 1981), 60-64. See also Hugh Thomas, *The Cuban Revolution* (rev. ed., New York, 1981).

43. Marth and Marth, eds., *The Florida Almanac, 1986-87,* pp. 106-10; Robert L. Bach, "The New Cuban Immigrants: Their Background and Prospects," *Monthly Labor Review* (October 1980), 39-46; Raymond A. Mohl, "Miami: New Immigrant City" (paper presented at "The Sunbelt: A Region and Regionalism in the Making?" Conference, Miami, Florida, November 3-6, 1985); "Non-Hispanic Whites Leave Dade Behind," *Miami Herald* (May 3, 1987), 2b; Joan Didion, "Miami," and "Miami: 'La Lucha,' " *New York Review of Books* 34, nos. 9, 10 (May 28, 1987), 43-48; (June 11, 1987), 15-18.

10

Migration to the Urban South: An Unfinished Agenda

George E. Pozzetta

Joe Delbova, an unemployed rubber worker, had not held a job for months as he contemplated leaving his hometown of Akron, Ohio, in 1981. The painful decision to move his family and leave his close-knit neighborhood weighed heavily upon him. Twenty years earlier, Carlos Arboleya of Havana, Cuba, had faced a similar dilemma as he pondered an uncertain future in Castro's postrevolutionary society. Ultimately, both decided to leave and head for the fresh opportunities beckoning in America's South, attracted in part by a host of enticing "Sunbelt" images of prosperity and expansion.[1] These arrivals—one an Italian American who had labored in a northern industrial center, the other a former Cuban bank worker—represented only two strands in a much more complicated pattern of migrations flowing to the fastest growing region of the United States. The social, cultural, and economic consequences of this movement of ethnic and foreign-born migrants—on the people themselves, the cities and neighborhoods that received them, the governments that provided them services, and the nation as a whole—are only imperfectly understood. The challenge to which this volume responds is to study these transformations in all their complexity, even if at this point in a preliminary and suggestive way.

This is not to suggest that the phenomenon of migration to the urban South has completely escaped scholarly attention. An impressive array of urban planners, growth management experts, political geographers, and public policy analysts have explored various facets of this broad topic.[2] Few, however, have addressed the ethnic dimension of migration to the South. This is a notable omission since many of the new residents entering the region have come from backgrounds in which ethnicity has played important roles in shaping both individual and group experiences.[3] Along with their household goods, newcomers have often arrived with ethnic identities that also require placement in new settings. To comprehend accurately the development of the urban South, and especially the "Sunbelt" South, one must take the results of this fact into account. This chapter will attempt to build upon the preliminary excursions presented to suggest fruitful directions for future research. It avowedly seeks to pose more questions than it answers in the hopes of continuing and guiding the discussion already under way.

At its heart ethnicity has always involved some sense of group identity based upon a conception of common culture and background. This quality is never static; rather, it responds to the shifting needs of individuals as they deal with varying life situations over time. Hence, ethnicity is a dynamic element in American life, one that changes as the nation's social and economic structures evolve and place people in new relationships with each other. As the essays of this volume make clear, changes in residence, socio-economic status, neighborhood development, societal attitudes, and demographic patterns—among many other things—have been significant in altering the contours of ethnic identity and behavior. They also reveal the power of ethnicity to shape lives beyond the first generation, even after Old World cultures have eroded and lost their original meanings. Even under changed circumstances ethnicity has retained the ability to mark off boundaries, both physical and mental, that can separate various subgroups in American society. Put differently, ethnicity still has the power to underpin the perpetuation of distinctive patterns of values and behavior.

Historically, these social forces have played a relatively minor role in the growth of the urban areas resting within the southern region. For these locations race has had a greater impact in determining the nature of city life. Black populations have been a long-term feature of most urban areas in the South, and residents still define much of their social relations in black-white terms. Although changes have taken place in race relations, the importance of color shows no sign of disappearing from the region's social landscape. As the chapters of this volume make clear, however, analyses of southern urbanism must now include an examination of ethnicity as well as of race.

Before exploring any research agenda, a few simple facts bear highlighting. A very diverse set of people has moved to the urban South. These individuals have included impoverished Haitian boat lifters, retirees from ethnic communities in the North, Cuban exiles, undocumented Mexican migrants, Vietnamese refugees, and unemployed third- and fourth-generation ethnic Americans from nearly every part of the nation, to name a few. Any effort to compact their collective experiences into useful generalizations faces formidable problems. Additionally, the very term *South* itself implies a regional homogeneity that in fact does not exist. Rather, there is much internal variety, both in terms of social and cultural patterns and economic activity.[4] Every conclusion drawn about southern migration, therefore, must be qualified by a recognition of these realities.

Although ambiguities persist, it is clear that a major factor contributing to the South's population gain has been a massive internal migration generated by the decision of thousands of Americans to move southward. In fact, this population exchange constitutes one of the most substantial human movements in American history. Internal migration, of course, has always existed in the United States as the nation's population has circulated in response to changing economic trends, perceived opportunities, and individual tastes.[5] Current migration, therefore, is but the latest link in a chain of movement that stretches back to the colonial period, and what is happening today fits comfortably into a solidly rooted national tradition. Yet there are unique features that give these movements a character and significance all their own.

Students of ethnic America have been struck by the large portion of this migration that is composed of second-, third-, and fourth-generation ethnic Americans.[6] Whether unemployed job seekers such as Joe Delbova or more affluent retirees, these people, for the most part, first crafted their ethnicity in the ethnocommunities that developed throughout the Northeast and Midwest in the previous century. Each of these entities possessed (and many still possess) particularistic traits resulting from peculiarly local characteristics. National identities such as Polish American and Italian American have struggled to define themselves on anything other than the local neighborhood or community level. We know little about how the shifting of physical place, with its potential for social and cultural change, influenced the continuing development of the specific ethnic identities people carry within themselves. More generally, how easily has a sense of ethnic community or neighborhood been transferred to new settings in the South? Have aspects of these images been jettisoned just like the worn-out appliances left behind as people confront new urban conditions? If so, we need to know what has continued and what has changed and how these choices have been made.

Deborah Dash Moore's essay examining Jewish migration suggests that those who leave do indeed come to hold different values from those who stay. "Where you live says a lot about who you are," she claims. For Jews, movement has not been a random process, either in the manner in which candidates for migration have been selected or in the new destinations chosen. Dash Moore shows how occupational background, point in life cycle, marital status, and attachment to ethnic values all played roles in determining the nature of the resulting resettlement. Have members of other ethnic groups manifested similar patterns in making their decisions? If the same criteria for selection have been used, have they led to similar social consequences in the end? For example, will the hypothesis that an important change in living preferences is signalled by Jewish movement from culturally pluralist communities to more homogeneous locations be equally true of Italian, Polish, or Greek Americans making the same kind of moves?

Migration is almost never unplanned, at least to the extent that it is voluntary; rather, it is the end product of a process of evaluation and judgment. As Robert Harney has keenly observed of Canadians, it also involves a variety of networks that facilitate movement, ranging from the highly personalized assistance of kin and family to the more business-oriented services supplied by travel and real estate agents. As we continue to examine the actual process of movement, more understanding will be gained about how these networks have exerted an influence on the clustering of settlement, the selection of who migrates and who does not, the permanence or transience of communities, and the nature of the cultural forms that arise in new locations. Such an investigation will also reveal information on the patterning of movement into the region.

There seems to be little doubt that individuals will work toward recreating at least selected aspects of their former environments as quickly as possible after their moves. To the extent that ethnicity can provide familiar mooring posts for identity and self-image, newcomers will not abandon these positive attributes. For Jews, the shift to less pluralist settings has apparently had the result of strengthening ethnic awareness and religious participation. In many new locations, it now takes more effort to possess a specific Jewish identity since there are fewer reinforcing institutions and environments. Will the nation experience more rather than less ethnic identity as a result of a movement that seems to auger greater homogenization? Perhaps the persistent clustering that typifies ethnic settlement, in both the nation and the southern Sunbelt, might allow ethnic identities to survive the larger homogenization process.

The mental worlds of people tend to undergo change from the mere fact of movement itself, but these alterations may affect groups in different fashions. Has the "new geographic perspective" on the United States that internal migration has created among Jews also occurred among groups that have manifested more widespread settlement patterns in their earlier history? Additionally, the function of migration as a solution to certain life problems remains as a potentially valuable insight for understanding the ethnic group experience in America. To use migration as a strategy for dealing with life-cycle situations appears to be a fixture in the Jewish experience, but is it as strongly rooted in other ethnic cultures?[7] To the extent that it is not, how have other ethnics learned to cope with the common problems of adjustment that come at certain ages?

Not the least of the new social forces the region has coped with has been the arrival of thousands of elderly ethnic migrants who have come to spend their retirement years in warmer climates. The size, complexity, and ethnic nature of many retirement communities that have sprung up in the South pose interesting new questions. For perhaps the first time in history, significant numbers of people have been moving in search of leisure. Has the presence of more free time served to make ethnic identities stronger or weaker? After interviewing scores of retirees in Florida, Vance Packard indicated that he was forced to change his early conceptions of what these settlements were like. "I learned in Florida," he explained, "that having a big solid house to retire into is not as important as being among people who respect you, who share your concerns, and who have a chance to know you well enough to become an authentic friend."[8] These very qualities have often been associated with ethnic groups. The search for these qualities may explain much about the nature of retirement settlement in the South. But are these outcomes observable only in those instances where moves to the Sunbelt South have resulted in group clustering? What has happened in the instances of individual migration and more scattered residence?

To the extent that retirement settlements can support some sort of communal life, the ways that retirees have chosen to organize their lives will tell us much about their outlooks and values. How have the institutions they have created been modified to reflect changed realities? Of what significance has the removal of a work experience (particularly in its institutional and social contexts) been to the perpetuation of ethnicity? Has the fact that roughly 40 percent of retirees move temporarily during the year perhaps served to perpetuate old ethnic ties as these people alternate summers and winters in former and new locations?[9] Can recreational activities serve the same purposes and support the same range of identities as did work and neighborhood rituals in the old locations?

The very fact of retirement itself poses questions as to the role of age and aging in the shaping of lives. Of what importance is it that the generational spread existing in retirement communities is so skewed toward the elderly? It is certainly possible that ethnic traditions and outlooks are actually reinforced in these settings since the leavening influence of younger—and perhaps more Americanized—family members is absent. But this hypothesis is empirically unverified. Differing outcomes are possible as well, and as the discipline of the old social order is disrupted, there may be a resulting loss of attachment to a sense of ethnic identity.

Ethnic clusters resulting from internal migration now dot the entire southern region. Whether they take the form of mobile home parks in the suburbs or heavily settled urban neighborhoods or the temporary vacation havens Harney observed among Canadians, each has evolved some means for defining ethnic identity. Yet the specific nature of these reconstitutions remains obscure. Is there a greater sense of rootlessness in these new creations, with a resulting change in values, behavior, and emotional well-being? Have the unofficial social controls that were at work in original communities continued to function or have they suffered dilution or abandonment? How have kinship and family ties been altered? How can one measure the psychic cost of the effort to rebuild social circles and community loyalties? Has mental illness, divorce, or crime increased? Has religiousness decreased?

The introduction of ethnic cultures into areas of the nation not traditionally possessing such elements has caused changes. Physically, many southern urban areas now sport pockets of import stores, ethnic clubs, and specialized recreational areas that are clear indications of a new presence.[10] Bocce courts and jai alai fontons, for example, have proliferated throughout Florida and they speak as eloquently of the new population as any census statistic. By determining where these creations are and who they serve, the student of migration can begin to chart out the geographic spread of ethnic settlement. One can also start to measure the impact of this movement on local economies by examining the range of jobs and opportunities generated by these specialized tastes. These transformations, however, have sponsored even more fundamental alterations in the social forms of the region. What needs to be explored are the new combinations of social interactions between new and old residents that have taken place. How have these changes influenced the ways in which people think of themselves and their neighbors? How will ethnic stereotypes, for example, alter as people are placed in new relationships with each other?

We are told that even the simplest resettlement has the ability to modify expectations, lifestyles, and perceptions.[11] How have these elements sorted themselves out within groups that have sent not only elderly retirees but also job-seeking second- and third-generation ethnic Americans? Has the fact of southern residence altered generational relations within groups and, if so, how? It appears, as in the case of the Jews, that different clusters of individuals from the same ethnic group are creating distinctive new settlements in the nation. This suggests that ethnicity will take on a different character in both old and new locations as communities are increasingly segmented by movement.

How have ethnic institutions survived the moves? We know that migration has often spawned a network of institutions to meet the needs of individuals and to support some notion of the group. How effectively have ethnic clubs reconstituted themselves in new locations?[12] What have been the processes of reestablishment and what ends have been served by the recreation? What of "national" organizations such as the Sons of Italy and the various Jewish umbrella groups? Do they perform new functions in the changed settings, perhaps affording different opportunities for ethnic expression and continuity?[13] How have churches and synagogues been affected? For many areas of the South, predominantly Protestant communities are confronting a heavy influx of Catholics and Jews for the first time. What has been the nature of the resulting tensions and how have they been dealt with on both sides of the equation? Has suspicion or hostility on the part of receiving areas encouraged a greater consciousness of kind among ethnic migrants and stimulated an increase in religious participation and fervor? How effectively has the Catholic church hierarchy reacted to these sorts of conditions?

Social boundaries have undoubtedly been redrawn as clusters of ethnic Americans have come into being, living alongside and amidst new kinds of people. Have these shifts underwritten new conceptions of community among these people? That is, as Little Italies and Little Russias have re-formed themselves in southern locations, how has the collective understanding of the social and cultural freight attached to these terms in the minds of the people involved changed? Do new definitions of community support more or less intermingling in new locations? Are ethnic lines fading because of mobility? Precisely how have ethnic boundaries been redrawn in this process of change?

As Gary McDonogh suggestively points out, the mental worlds of people allow for many interpretations of a shared history. Ethnic and racial groups have different perspectives of their common experiences and, importantly, these distinctive pasts have important consequences for the creation of social relations. They shape the ways in which people interact, plan for their own futures, and view the urban community they cohabit. McDonogh also identifies ways in which ethnicity can be used to assist in integrating groups into urban societies. An understanding of how these divergent tracks have been constructed and how they continue to influence people's lives can lead to more clear-sighted policymaking and ultimately the building of more workable and humane urban societies. Each major urban center in the South can benefit from this sort of scrutiny but especially those that historically have had heterogeneous populations.

More needs to be known of the impact that these movements have had on the receiving areas themselves. Migration and immigration continue to mold the economic contours of the region. Ranging from migrant field workers servicing agriculture to skilled industrial workers seeking employment to retired professionals interested in part-time work, newcomers have been important elements in shaping the nature of the South's labor force and the economic possibilities flowing from this base. The specific relationships between migration and economic development require more scrutiny, including an examination of the macro consequences emanating from large-scale in-migration and the effects on the micro level as well. For example, do members of ethnic groups own and operate small businesses and are these subsidized by local financial institutions? Are these businesses frequented by longer-established community residents? Have consumer needs changed because of new populations? Are ethnic districts sources of tourist interest and, if so, how important has been the economic activity generated?

Ethnic and racial identities clearly possess the ability to influence the political landscape, and conditions in the urban South seem constructed to ensure that economic and political issues will continue to generate appeals to these labels. In short, as long as rewards in society can be sought and potentially won on the basis of group identity, ethnicity will continue to have a saliency and importance. Even when cultural practices and symbols have faded into the past, such interest group activities can survive. In this sense, ethnicity is *emergent*, to use the social science term, and will appear whenever certain structural conditions are present to give it meaning.[14]

Ronald Bayor's chapter reveals that the urban political arenas have been extremely sensitive to the migration phenomenon. New groups have arrived and attempted to stake out areas of turf and power in their new locations. They have also brought with them different perspectives on how the process of political participation and debate should be conducted. Ironically, the images of stability and untroubled progress that have served to attract so many people to southern cities are threatened by the very successes that the images have generated. A pluralistic political system, with multiple competing groups, appears to be the ascending model, at least in the principal cities of the region. The political strife characteristic of Miami and the neighborhood confrontations taking place in Memphis, Atlanta, and Richmond are indications that the tensions surrounding growth and in-migration are not amenable to easy solution. As migration continues to underpin the creation of new coalitions, the chances for increased fragmentation and conflict intensify. Such polarization would almost surely be centered on neighborhood alliances and racial/ethnic combinations, factors that will be unusually responsive to the influence of continued in-migration.

Urban growth, whether by internal migration, immigration, or natural increase, always imposes costs. The need to provide services and urban amenities in locations swelled by population increases has been critically felt by many southern communities. A significant part of the future political agenda of these cities and states will necessarily focus on the means of providing services, while simultaneously responding to desires for fiscal moderation, controlled growth, and environmental planning. Such competing goals can often put ethnic newcomers in competition with each other, as seen in Florida where ethnic retirees resist spending for education while their younger compatriots who have moved with families support greater funding for public schools.

The dispute over school funding is only one manifestation of the growing class and demographic differentiations between the generations that are coming to characterize America's older ethnic groups. As the migration trends already described continue, such splits will undoubtedly increase. Ethnic institutions will find it necessary to alter their images and services to account for diverse clienteles. Chapters of the Sons of Italy, for example, often target their programs to reach specific elements within the Italian-American community. Some southern chapters have refocused their programs to meet the needs of elderly retirees (with newsletters containing tips on nutrition for senior citizens), while others have aimed at upwardly mobile, middle-class memberships (with opportunities for access to country clubs and expensive overseas tours).[15] Even the move to suburbia has apparently not dealt a death blow to ethnicity, as ethnic institutions have sprouted in this supposedly unfertile soil as well. All of this suggests the resiliency and adaptability of ethnicity as a force in people's lives.

Urban renewal has placed its own distinctive stamp on the character of intergroup relations in southern cities. As elsewhere in the nation, many urban residents believed that the renewal projects of the 1960s would mean a civic renaissance for struggling cities. The vast sums supplied by urban programs, coupled with those made available by the Interstate Highway Act, more often meant the permanent leveling of large sections of older cities. Those areas most affected have frequently been black, poor, and politically powerless, but this has not always been the case, as certain southern cities such as Tampa and New Orleans have seen old ethnic quarters fall to the wrecking ball. The legacies of distrust and estrangement left over from these failed experiments have vitally affected the texture of urban politics. In some instances, black and ethnic neighborhoods have organized themselves for the first time to fight for their preservation and to secure their proper share of city services. The long-term result has often been a more polarized political landscape, pitting group against group. Whether this will ultimately result in more effectively governed cities remains to be seen.

The issue of race lays heavily on the past of southern cities and, as nearly every contributor to this volume has pointed out, has often served to obscure facets of ethnicity. Pre-World War II southern society largely defined social relations in black-white terms and these distinctions are still extremely influential. Much more needs to be known of the role played by ethnics and immigrants in the continuing process of defining the place and the position of blacks in southern society. Do ethnic residents intermingle more or less with blacks after having made the transition to the South? Do they act as buffers between new immigrant groups and blacks? Between longer-settled whites and blacks? What sort of racial attitudes and interests have newcomers brought with them and how have they interacted with local attitudes and interests? To the extent that some migrants are competing with blacks at the lower end of the economic scale, how has this redrawn the map of social relations in the South? We know that physical proximity and even shared class position do not guarantee intergroup solidarity. Indeed, the historical record suggests the strong possibility of just the opposite outcome. Which route appears likely in the present situation?

In terms of the inner lives of cities themselves, the tensions that have marked the entry of immigrant and ethnic groups have flashed most brightly when these movements have involved encounters with blacks. At a time when the civil rights movement began to result in progress for southern blacks, many of their economic gains appeared threatened by migration into the region. The competition of Latin American immigrants for jobs—especially the low-wage positions underpinning growth in the service and industrial sectors—has further fractured community relations in many locations. As one social analyst observed, "there is the threat that the ranks of a permanent underclass will be swollen by economic and political refugees who will compete in an atmosphere of racial animosity with blacks. . . . "[16] Efforts to build bridges between groups are complicated by linguistic and cultural differences, by an economy that is slowing in its growth rate, and by the confusions generated by rapid social change. The chances are that these dislocating tendencies will intensify during periods of economic slowdown when the ability of cities to provide services and accommodations to residents will decline.

The complex dynamics of city life and the nature of the ethnic-immigrant/black contact that has increasingly come to typify them have not been restricted to economic competition. As Raymond Mohl reveals, Miami presents the clearest example of the range of responses, in that blacks and newer arrivals have competed not only for jobs but also social services, residential space, and political power. In this exchange, blacks have most often lost out in the competition, in part because new groups have not sought them out for coalition building or have actively tried to exclude them. Although the particulars have differed elsewhere, the results have generally been the same. With urban renewal, neighborhood planning, and suburban development reshaping the texture of urban life in fundamental ways, the chances for black losses appear on the increase. Do these events foretell even more fragmentation of the South's urban areas along racial, class, and ethnic lines?

As more Latin American, Asian, Middle Eastern, and African immigrants look toward the United States as a new home, the South will likely remain a focal point for issues centered on foreign immigration. National questions of how many immigrants should be allowed to enter and from where have assumed a new intensity in the region. This is true partially because answers to these queries have been and remain vitally important to the region's development, particularly for its cities, which have shouldered an unequal share of the costs of receiving newcomers.[17] The heightened public attention, however, owes much of its sharpness to the racial dimensions of immigration in the South. The debates generated over basic policy issues, therefore, are likely to be pursued with special emotion and with particular potential for conflict and competition.

One unmistakable outcome resulting from heightened immigration has been an upsurge in nativist activity. Historically, the South has most often resonated to the ebb and flow of national attitudes toward immigrants; seldom has it been a center of nativist sentiment. Recently, however, the region has assumed something of a leadership role in these matters. Large Asian and Latin American immigrations have often placed longer-settled residents in new and disturbing relationships with newcomers.[18] Working-class southerners, for example, have resented the job competition generated by Latin American immigrants in farm work and unskilled labor, while middle-class individuals have felt pressure from upwardly mobile Cuban exiles. These economic concerns have been supplemented by a host of other considerations ranging from the health fears generated by AIDS disease among Haitians and migrant workers to local struggles over bilingualism, school policy, and political control. Some of the animosity no doubt stems from a legacy of Old South views toward foreigners and strangers generally. The city of Miami has managed to combine nearly all of these elements, made more sharply felt since many residents believe that present problems result from decisions made by a distant federal government that forced the city to accept and provide for unwanted aliens. Similar though less sharply drawn reactions have surfaced in smaller southern communities which have received Vietnamese and Hmong refugees.[19]

Nativism in the South has translated into support for more restrictive immigration legislation, increased acceptance of hate groups such as the Ku Klux Klan, and campaigns in support of English-only laws. As the future promises that immigration will play a greater rather than lesser role in the region, there exists a critical need for reducing these tensions. Failing this, the hostilities that have marked Miami's political and cultural environment may become the dominant pattern for southern cities as they continue to receive immigration. If the explosive potential of increasing diversity is to be defused, or at least managed to the lowest possible level, the dynamics that produce nativist outbursts require more understanding.

In some ways the potential for disillusionment in southern locations is higher than other areas since the region has emerged as the nation's newest frontier. Accordingly, all of our national myths and images surrounding the frontier—involving opportunity, openness, and unlimited advancement— have attached themselves to the region, especially in its "Sunbelt" guise. Situations of economic recession or social tension and hostility will place these expectations in jeopardy, and the blunted hopes of both planners and migrants alike will be factors of political importance. How the burdens of economic hardship will be allocated and adjusted await inquiry, but surely this process will result in a restructuring of alliances and relationships currently in existence.

Julia Blackwelder has drawn a complex portrait of women's social and economic adjustments as they have confronted southern cities, but more needs to be known about how they have reacted to the demands of migration. Sociologist Robert Gutman has suggested that women experience a different range of problems from men when moving. In particular, "women who tend to be very expressive emotionally," he explains, "especially from ethnic cultures such as the Italians and Polish, have problems relating to a new settlement."[20] Have such women migrants to the South behaved in this way? If so, how has the distinctive character of the South affected these gender-specific problems and what makes the move significantly different from earlier migrations? Blackwelder's view that "elite or middle-class families coped more easily with new environments" suggests that class position can override what are essentially ethnic approaches to life situations. More generally, how have women viewed the migration process and how has this differed from the perceptions held by men? It is conceivable that women have used ethnicity differently from men, but precisely what roles has ethnicity played in their lives and how may this help explain dissimilar adjustment patterns as men and women seek new roots in the South?

What has been the outcome of the processes that have been discussed in this volume? Clearly, we see a region in the process of defining its own image and character as it is buffeted by the forces of migration, immigration, urbanization, and industrialization. Elements of an older, more traditional culture remain, even though they are being increasingly overtaken by a host of competing influences. The result is a dynamic process of social change and transformation, the exact nature of which is still imperfectly understood.

Not only will scholars have to ask the proper questions of this phenomenon, but they also will have to devise effective methodologies and research techniques to explore the relevant questions. Life histories, family histories, oral testimony, and documentary analysis will all play a role in charting out the essential details. Properly used, they can yield the insights needed to shed light on the complex adjustments taking place. What is certain at this point is that the social forces examined in this book—ethnic identity, pluralistic politics, neighborhood development, urban transformation, internal migration, ethnic adaptation, and immigration—will continue to play decisive roles in the future of the South. Whatever its exact contours, the development of an ethnic, urban South is a matter of immediate public importance. On this basis, therefore, the subject begs for further inquiry and investigation.

NOTES

1. "Escape to the Sun Belt," *Newsweek* (April 27, 1981), 67; "Flight from Cuba: Castro's Loss is U.S. Gain," *U.S. News and World Report* (May 31, 1971), 74; "It's Your Turn in the Sun," *Time* (October 16, 1978), 48. Arboleya settled in Miami, becoming president of Fidelity National Bank and later of the area's Barnett Banks. Delbova's destination is unclear from the report describing his plight, but the article mentions several locations in the South that were attracting such people. See Carl Abbott, *The New Urban America: Growth and Politics in Sunbelt Cities* (Chapel Hill, 1981), for a discussion of the regional growth pattern.

2. There is already a huge literature in existence. A sampling can be seen in the following: David Perry and Alfred Watkins, ed., *The Rise of Sunbelt Cities, Urban Affairs Annual Reviews*, vol. 14 (Beverly Hills, 1977), pp. 277-305; Steven C. Ballard and Thomas James, eds., *The Future of the Sunbelt* (New York, 1983); Jeanne C. Biggs, "The Sunning of America," *Population Bulletin* 34 (March 1979), 1-42; Bernard L. Weinstein, *Regional Growth in the U.S.: The Rise of the Sunbelt and Decline of the Northeast* (New York, 1978); Steve Barsby, *Interstate Migration of the Elderly: An Economic Analysis* (Lexington, Mass., 1975); Michael Gronwood, "Research on Internal Migration in the U.S.: A Survey," *Journal of Economic Quarterly* 49 (December 1978), 553-61; Eugene Litwak, "Geographic Mobility and Extended Family Cohesion," *American Sociological Review* 25 (June 1960), 385-94; Julie DaVanzo, "Does Unemployment Affect Migration?—Evidence from Microdata," *The Review of Economics and Statistics* 60 (1978), 504-14; Fred M. Shelley and Curtis C. Roseman, "Migration Patterns Leading to Population Change in the

Nonmetropolitan South," *Growth and Change* 9 (April 1978), 14-22; David Mathews, "The Future of the Sunbelt," *Society* 19 (July/August 1982), 63-65; Thomas Bender, "A Nation of Immigrants to the Sunbelt," *The Nation* (March 28, 1981), 359-61.

3. An exception would be Franklin James, *Minorities in the Sunbelt* (Piscataway, N.J., 1984), but the volume is much narrower than the title would imply, only dealing with Mexicans and blacks.

4. See Richard Bernard and Bradley R. Rice, eds., *Sunbelt Cities: Politics and Growth Since World War II* (Austin, 1983), for one effort to define this slippery term.

5. See Donald Parkerson, "Internal Migration: Research Themes and New Directions," *OAH Newsletter* 11 (August 1983), 17-20, for a discussion of these issues.

6. Morton D. Winsberg, "Relative Growth and Distribution of Florida's European Born" (mimeographed paper, 6 pp., in possession of author). Geographer Winsberg found that the number of European-born residents of the state of Florida rose from 75,123 in 1950 to 309,362 in 1980. He determined that the majority of these individuals did not come directly to the state from their homelands, but rather had first resided in northern states or Canada. See also his "Changing Distribution of the Black Population: Florida Cities, 1970-1980," *Urban Affairs Quarterly* 18 (March 1983), 361-70.

7. See Barbara Myerhoff's evocative *Number Our Days* (New York, 1978) for a statement on East European Jews who have retired in Venice, California.

8. Vance Packard, *A Nation of Strangers* (New York, 1972), p. 103.

9. Ibid., p. 97.

10. A reading of city directories, phone books, and other social or business listings covering southern urban areas will reveal the diversity of such entities already in existence. The east coast of Florida, from Palm Beach to Miami, has scores of clubs, stores, and groups.

11. George W. Pierson, *The Moving American* (New York, 1973), p.203.

12. The town of Inverness, Florida, has received large numbers of Italian-American retirees from the Northeast. There are already three different clubs in existence, the result of splits from the original organization formed in the 1970s. Interview with a club official by the author.

13. See *Miami Herald* (September 19, 1982) for a listing of some forty-five ethnic clubs active in the Ft. Lauderdale area. These groups include the Peruvian Club, Sons of Norway, Estonian National Association, Alliance Francaise, Polish-American Club, and Irish Emerald Society. See also the Ft. Lauderdale *Carpatho-Russian Echoes* (September 1986), as an example of an ethnic newspaper currently being published.

14. William Yancey, Eugene Erickson, and Richard Juliani, "Emergent Ethnicity: A Review and Reformulation," *American Sociological Review* 41 (June 1976), 391-403.

15. Gary R. Mormino and George E. Pozzetta, *The Immigrant World of Ybor City: Italians and Their Latin Neighbors in Tampa, 1885-1985* (Urbana, 1987), p. 309, for examples of developments in Tampa, Florida.

16. William Taylor, "Access to Economic Opportunity: Lessons since *Brown*," in Leslie Dunbar, ed., *Minority Report: What Has Happened to Blacks, Hispanics, American Indians, and Other Minorities in the Eighties* (New York, 1984), p. 51.

17. *Gainesville Sun* (September 21, 1981). At a time when the federal government was contemplating cutting refugee aid by $100 million, the state of Florida had already spent $30 million assisting Cuban and Haitian refugees. Also see Morton D.

Winsberg, "Ethnic Competition for Residential Space in Miami, Florida, 1970-80," *The American Journal of Economics and Sociology* 42 (July 1983), 305-14.

18. *Gainesville Sun* (January 18, 1981). Perhaps the most celebrated incident involved clashes with Texas shrimpers and Vietnamese fishermen in 1979. Before calm returned, the confrontations resulted in one death, several burnings, a fire bombing, and multiple arrests.

19. "The New Immigrants," *Newsweek* (July 7, 1980). Many Asian newcomers to the region see themselves as temporary exiles. Their hope of return has influenced the way in which they have adapted to America.

20. Quoted in Packard, *A Nation of Strangers*, p. 143.

Bibliographic Essay

As recently as twenty years ago the literature on southern urban development was sparse, and assessments of the post-World War II era almost nonexistent. Indeed, William Thorp in his survey of "Southern Literature and Southern Society," in Edgar Thompson, ed., *Perspectives on the South: Agenda for Research* (Durham, 1967), lamented the paucity of historical research on southern cities. In many ways, Thorp echoed the concern of Dewey Grantham, Jr., who two years earlier had called upon scholars to discover the modern South generally as a field of inquiry: Grantham, "The Twentieth-Century South," in Arthur S. Link and Rembert W. Patrick, eds., *Writing Southern History: Essays in Historiography in Honor of Fletcher M. Green* (Baton Rouge, 1965). Within the past two decades, however, an abundant foliage of studies on southern urban culture and growth has appeared. Much of the work has been done by social scientists rather than by historians, who have been somewhat tardy in tilling the field of the new urban South, and many of the most accessible works have been written by journalists fascinated by the latest new South *qua* Sunbelt. Despite the flowering of interest in the urban South, much of the literature remains narrowly conceived and preoccupied with particular localities. And the spread of interest is uneven. Atlanta commands considerable attention from scholars, journalists, and others—so much so that it seems that exclusive of Florida, Atlanta has become the metaphor for the new urban Sunbelt South in the public mind. Other places have received less study, even though in many ways they are probably more representative of the emerging urban Sunbelt South than is the large city of Atlanta. Only recently have synthetic works appeared to bring together the diverse, and sometimes contradictory, literature on urbanization and urban culture in the post-World War II South.

Adding to the confusion in tracking trends in the study of southern urban development is the elusive definition of the Sunbelt. To some scholars, the post-World War II urban South and the Sunbelt are discrete terms and experiences; to others, they are almost synonymous. For those who separate the terms, the continued poverty, racism, and lassitude in southern cities stand out; for those who conflate the terms, the population growth, prosperity, and new construction in southern cities are the salient points. Different scholars see southern (and Sunbelt) cities in different ways.

It is not possible to survey all the significant literature on southern/Sunbelt urban history and growth in so short a compass as this brief essay. The notes to the various chapters in *Shades of the Sunbelt* provide references to key works in the various subcategories of urbanization and migration represented in this volume. Rather than offer a comprehensive bibliography of works on the urban South/Sunbelt, this bibliography will suggest a few selected works that provide an introduction to the issues discussed in this volume.

For fuller bibliographical surveys on recent southern urban history, the reader should consult James C. Cobb, "Urbanization and the Changing South: A Review of the Literature," *South Atlantic Urban Studies* 1 (1977), 253-66; Don H. Doyle, "The Urbanization of Dixie," *Journal of Urban History* 7 (1980), 83-91; and Charles P. Roland, "Sun Belt Prosperity and Urban Growth," in John B. Boles and Evelyn Thomas Nolen, eds., *Interpreting Southern History: Historiographical Essays in Honor of Sanford W. Higginbotham* (Baton Rouge, 1987), pp. 434-53.

Among the overviews of southern urban development, the work of David Goldfield provides the most provocative and important approaches. Goldfield emphasizes the persistence of regional values in an urban setting. Key works include "The Urban South: A Regional Framework," *American Historical Review* 86 (1981), 1009-34, and *Cotton Fields and Skyscrapers: Southern City and Region, 1607-1980* (Baton Rouge, 1982), which has a fine bibliographical essay. Goldfield sets the post-World War II city and the Sunbelt phenomenon in historical context in his *Promised Land: The South Since 1945* (Arlington Heights, 1987). Goldfield's book is valuable because it devotes so much attention to urban issues. Less successful in that regard are such otherwise excellent surveys of recent southern history as Charles P. Roland, *The Improbable Era: The South Since World War II* (Lexington, 1975); Pete Daniel, *Standing at the Crossroads: Southern Life in the Twentieth Century* (New York, 1986); and Jack Temple Kirby, *Rural Worlds Lost: The American South, 1920-1960* (New York, 1987). Of the many anthologies on the recent South, readers will want to examine the perceptive essays in John B. Boles, ed., *Dixie Dateline: A Journalistic Portrait of the Contemporary South* (Houston, 1983), especially Neal R. Peirce's "The Southern City Today," William K. Stevens's "A New Culture Emerges in the Oil Patch," and James R. Adams's "The Sunbelt." Useful in gaining a longitudinal perspective on southern cities is Blaine Brownell and David Goldfield, eds., *The City in Southern History: The Growth of Urban Civilization in the South* (Port Washington, N.Y., 1977), with the excellent essays by Blaine Brownell and Edward Haas (despite Haas's overreliance on New Orleans as a model) being the most relevant for readers of *Shades of the Sunbelt*. Brownell and Goldfield collaborated again, writing a textbook, *Urban America: From Downtown to No Town* (Boston, 1979), that devotes considerable space to the new southern city and distinguishes modern southern cities from northern ones by suggesting that the former offer more congenial living environments. A seminal brief survey of southern urban growth and southern urbanization is Blaine Brownell, *The Urban South in the Twentieth Century* (St. Charles, Mo., 1974). In February 1976 the *Journal of Urban History*, vol. 2, published a special issue on the urban South that suggested a research agenda for applying urban themes to southern history. An inventive essay that locates and measures subregions of southern urban and metropolitan development is Carl Abbott, "The End of the Southern City," in *Perspectives on the American South* 4 (1986), 187-218. Michael Conzen provides a comparative geographical perspective in "American Cities in Profound Transition: The New City Geography of the 1980s," *Journal of Geography* 82 (1983), 94-101. Of the earlier works recognizing the importance of the urban South, the best is George Tindall, *The Emergence of the New South, 1913-1945* (Baton Rouge, 1967), which includes a fine short treatment of southern cities during World War II, among other relevant topics. Readers can glean useful statistical information on southern urbanization in the first half of the twentieth century from T. Lynn Smith, "The Emergence of Cities," in Rupert P. Vance and Nicholas J. Demerath, eds., *The Urban South* (Chapel Hill, 1954), a collection reflecting a Regionalist perspective.

Discussions of southern urbanization and the Sunbelt phenomenon often occur within the larger context of the persistence of regional identity. Leonard Reissman, "Urbanization in the South," in John C. McKinney and Edgar T. Thompson, eds., *The South in Continuity and Change* (Durham, 1965), along with several other essays in that anthology, views the developing urban South with misgivings. Likewise, Pat Watters, in the intensely personal *The South and the Nation* (New York, 1969), approaches southern urbanization with ambivalence. Contributors to H. Brandt Ayers and Thomas H. Naylor, eds., *You Can't Eat Magnolias* (New York, 1972), admitted to many problems nagging the region but held out the South as a redemptive force in America. Especially relevant is Joel L. Fleishman's essay on "The Southern City: Northern Mistakes in Southern Settings," which remarked on the advantages southern cities had in their small size, low density, and newness. In *The Americanization of Dixie: The Southernization of America* (New York, 1974), journalist John Egerton was less optimistic, as revealed in his warning that the South was adopting the worst features of northern society and perpetuating and extending its own ugly traits. For a more balanced view, see Ernest M. Lander and Richard J. Calhoun, eds., *Two Decades of Change: The South Since the Supreme Court Desegregation Decision* (Columbia, S.C., 1975). Especially insistent on the continuing viability of a distinctive southern culture amid social, population, and political change are Fifteen Southerners, *Why the South Will Survive* (Athens, 1981); and William C. Havard and Walter Sullivan, eds., *A Band of Prophets: The Vanderbilt Agrarians After Fifty Years* (Baton Rouge, 1982). Sociologist John Shelton Reed has tracked persistent southernism most relentlessly, and although he observes ethnic diversity and modern urban values rising in the Sunbelt-like sections of the new South, he finds evidence of southern values in religion, language, family, and community resisting absorption into an amorphous national culture. See Reed, *The Enduring South: Subcultural Persistence in Mass Society* (Lexington, Mass., 1971); *One South: An Ethnic Approach to Regional Culture* (Baton Rouge, 1982); and *Southerns: The Social Psychology of Sectionalism* (Chapel Hill, 1983).

The Sunbelt side of southern cities is assayed in several influential works. David C. Perry and Alfred J. Watkins, eds., *The Rise of the Sunbelt Cities* (Beverly Hills, 1977), includes essays on boosterism, media images, urban services, education, welfare, annexation, and other topics relevant to *Shades of the Sunbelt*. Also valuable are the uniformly good essays in Richard M. Bernard and Bradley R. Rice, eds., *Sunbelt Cities: Politics and Growth Since World War II* (Austin, 1983), especially the editors' introduction and the chapters by Rice (on Atlanta), by Raymond A. Mohl (on Miami), by Arnold R. Hirsch (on New Orleans), by Gary R. Mormino (on Tampa), by Martin

V. Melosi (on Dallas–Fort Worth), by Barry J. Kaplan (on Houston), and by David R. Johnson (on San Antonio). Perhaps more than anyone else, Carl Abbott has grappled with defining the urban Sunbelt. His influential *The New Urban America: Growth and Politics in Sunbelt Cities* (Chapel Hill, 1981, rev. ed., 1987) offers a broad definition of Sunbelt based on economic indicators of growth, a strategy that excludes many deep southern cities and includes ones above the Mason-Dixon line. See also Abbott, "The American Sunbelt: Idea and Region," *Journal of the West* 18 (July 1979), 5-18, and *Urban America in the Modern Age: 1920 to the Present* (Arlington Heights, 1987), which pays considerable attention to the Sunbelt.

Cutting through the boosterism of much recent writing about the Sunbelt South is the work of the Southern Growth Policies Board. The best summary of the Board's assessments for the region's future economic and social urban development, with pessimistic forecasts regarding the problems of strained race relations, inadequate public services, and urban blight, is Pat Watters, ed., *The Future of the South* (Research Triangle Park, N.C., 1981). The best scholarly assessments of the political, social, and economic factors directing the growth of the new South/Sunbelt are James C. Cobb's two books, *The Selling of the South: The Southern Crusade for Industrial Development, 1936-1980* (Baton Rouge, 1982), and *Industrialization & Southern Society, 1877-1984* (Lexington, Ky., 1984). The economic transformation of the South is searchingly analyzed in Gavin Wright, *Old South, New South: Revolutions in the Southern Economy Since the Civil War* (New York, 1986). A good comparative treatment of job structures is Thomas M. Stanback, Jr., and Thierry J. Noyelle, *Cities in Transition: Changing Job Structures in Atlanta, Denver, Buffalo, Phoenix, Columbus (Ohio), Nashville, and Charlotte* (Totowa, N.J., 1982). The literature on the shift to the Sunbelt is large, but applications to southern metropolitan areas less so. A good collection relevant to readers of *Shades of the Sunbelt* is Larry Sawers and William K. Tabb, eds., *Sunbelt/Snowbelt: Urban Development and Regional Restructuring* (New York, 1984).

The shape and urban-suburban dynamics of metropolitan areas are subjects needful of study for southern/Sunbelt cities. On suburbanization, the standard work is Kenneth T. Jackson, *Crabgrass Frontier: The Suburbanization of the United States* (New York, 1985), which is surprisingly thin on southern/Sunbelt developments. Fragmentation between city and suburb is the subject of Jon C. Teaford's important *City and Suburb: The Political Fragmentation of Metropolitan America, 1850-1970* (Baltimore, 1979), and it receives additional attention in his *The Twentieth-Century American City: Problems, Promises, and Reality* (Baltimore, 1986), though in neither book does Teaford assay southern/Sunbelt cities in depth. Within cities, efforts at planning were important. But here, too, southern/Sunbelt experiences remain understudied. The model book on the connections between race, politics, business, and culture in affecting planning policies is Christopher Silver, *Twentieth-Century Richmond: Planning, Politics, and Race* (Knoxville, 1984). Though it only covers the period from 1900 to 1940, the collection edited by Catherine Bishir and Lawrence S. Earley, titled *Early Twentieth-Century Suburbs in North Carolina: Essays in History, Architecture, and Planning* (Raleigh, 1985), shows that housing segregation developed early on as a normal part of the city building process. Also instructive on zoning and segregation are Robin Flowerdew, "Spatial Patterns of Residential Segregation in a Southern City," *Journal of American Studies* 13 (1979), 435-47; and Barry J. Kaplan, "Race, Income, and Ethnicity: Residential Change in a Houston Community, 1920-1970," *Houston Review* 3 (1981), 178-202.

Examination of individual cities is one way to observe social and political changes in detail. Good recent studies include Don H. Doyle, *Nashville Since the 1920s* (Knoxville, 1985); T. D. Allman, *Miami: City of the Future* (Boston, 1987); David G. McComb, *Houston: A History* (Austin, rev. ed., 1981); and the essays in Bernard and Rice, eds., *Sunbelt Cities*. Important for its use of the "total community" concept of studying ethnic groups in a particular setting is Gary R. Mormino and George E. Pozzetta, *The Immigrant World of Ybor City: Italians and Their Latin Neighbors in Tampa, 1885-1985* (Urbana, 1987). Atlanta has been well served by historians. Dana F. White and Timothy J. Crimmins have been especially active in recovering the city's recent past, with an eye to informing its future development. See their contributions regarding the city's spatial development in "Urban Structure, Atlanta," *Journal of Urban History* 2 (1976), 231-52, and the special issue on the same theme in the *Atlanta Historical Journal* 26 (Summer-Fall). For Atlanta, see also the January-February 1978 special issue of *Atlanta Economic Review*, vol. 28, which focuses on Atlanta's past and future development. Bradley Rice uses the Atlanta model to suggest a broader pattern of modern metropolitan growth in "Urbanization, 'Atlantaization,' and Suburbanization: Three Themes for the Urban History of Twentieth-Century Georgia," *Georgia Historical Quarterly* 68 (1984), 40-59. See also his chapter on Atlanta in Bernard and Rice, eds., *Sunbelt Cities*.

Key urban political leaders await their biographers. Two good studies of such leaders suggest the possibilities for observing particular urban environments through the political styles, agendas, and constituencies of strong mayors. They are: Edward F. Haas, *DeLesseps S. Morrison and the Image of Reform: New Orleans, 1946-1961* (Baton Rouge, 1974); and Harold H. Martin, *William Berry Hartsfield: Mayor of Atlanta* (Athens, 1978). On the limited role of civic reformers in addressing problems of blacks and public services, see, for example, David M. Tucker, *Memphis Since Crump: Bossism, Blacks, and Civil Reformers, 1948-1969* (Knoxville, 1980). The role of ethnicity and race receives treatment in essays on Atlanta, Miami, New Orleans, Tampa, and San Antonio in Bernard and Rice, eds., *Sunbelt Cities*. A good collection focusing on one city's experiences, with attention to ethnic and racial factors in politics, is David R. Johnson, John A. Booth, and Richard J. Harris, eds., *The Politics of San Antonio* (Lincoln, Neb., 1983). The effects of civil rights activity on southern politics have generated a huge literature. Of interest for readers of *Shades of the Sunbelt* will be Chandler Davidson, *Biracial Politics: Conflict and Coalition in the Metropolitan South* (Baton Rouge, 1972), which, with its overly optimistic forecast of black-white political convergence based on a Houston sample, should be compared to Virginia H. Hein, "The Image of a 'City Too Busy to Hate': Atlanta in the 1960s," *Phylon* 30 (1972), 205-21. Also useful is Peter K. Eisinger, *The Politics of Displacement: Racial and Ethnic Transition in Three American Cities* (New York, 1980); and, for Atlanta, Floyd Hunter, *Community Power Succession: Atlanta's Policy Makers* (Chapel Hill, 1980), and Clarence N. Stone, *Economic Growth and Neighborhood Discontent: System Bias in the Urban Renewal Program in Atlanta* (Chapel Hill, 1976). On the election of Maynard Jackson, see F. Glenn Abney and John D. Hutchinson, Jr., "Race, Representation, and Trust: Changes in Attitudes After the Election of a Black Mayor," *Public Opinion Quarterly* 45 (1981), 91-101.

Alexander D. Lamis, *The Two-Party South* (New York, 1984), is a good recent overview of the vagaries of post–World War II southern politics, which in the tradition of V. O. Key provides state-by-state analysis; unfortunately, Lamis ignores metropolitan concerns in defining local-state politics.

Race looms large in any discussion of the South, but its urban dimensions are not fully explored. Good overviews of the changing racial politics are Manning Marable, *Race, Reform, and Rebellion: The Second Reconstruction in Black America, 1945-1982* (Jackson, 1984); and Harvard Sitkoff, *The Struggle for Black Equality, 1954-1980* (New York, 1981). Also useful for understanding the larger southern context are: Catherine A. Barnes, *Journey from Jim Crow: The Desegregation of Southern Transit* (New York, 1983); Numan V. Bartley, *The Rise of Massive Resistance: Race and Politics in the South in the 1960s* (Baton Rouge, 1969); Jack Bass and Walter DeVries, *The Transformation of Southern Politics: Social Change and Political Consequence since 1945* (New York, 1976); Steven F. Lawson, *Black Ballots: Voting Rights in the South, 1944-1969* (New York, 1976); Lawson, *In Pursuit of Power: Southern Blacks and Electoral Politics, 1965-1982* (New York, 1985); Morton Sosna, *In Search of the Silent South: Southern Liberals and the Race Issue* (New York, 1977); Joel Williamson, *The Crucible of Race: Black-White Relations in the American South Since Emancipation* (New York, 1984); and Raymond Wolters, *The Burden of Brown: Thirty Years of School Desegregation* (Knoxville, 1984). Of special interest for urban concerns are the chapters in Elizabeth Jacoway and David R. Colburn, eds., *Southern Businessmen and Desegregation* (Baton Rouge, 1982).

The historical literature dealing with ethnicity in the Sunbelt South is very thin, reflecting the state of the wider scholarship in ethnic and immigrant history. Few volumes examining the major immigrant groups of the late nineteenth and early twentieth centuries, for example, treat anything but the first generation and fewer still extend to the post–World War II period. A handful of concluding chapters and epilogues, such as those found in the already cited Mormino and Pozzetta, *The Immigrant World of Ybor City*, and Lucy M. Cohen, *Chinese in the Post Civil War South: A People Without a History* (Baton Rouge, 1984), provide insights, but their truncated treatments permit only preliminary conclusions. Some more sociologically oriented studies have included contemporary developments, yet their focus has tended to be national and their coverage brief. Richard Alba, *Italian Americans: Into the Twilight of Ethnicity* (Englewood Cliffs, N.J., 1985), is an example.

Insights into the nature of ethnic group experiences in the southern region have often come as a side benefit from studies concerned with a variety of public policy issues not directly related to ethnicity. Many of the current policy issues are discussed in a series of essays contained in Ronald Takaki, ed., *From Different Shores: Perspectives on Race and Ethnicity in America* (New York, 1987). Vance Packard, *A Nation of Strangers* (New York, 1972), offers sharply drawn viewpoints on the importance of internal migration to the nation, particularly those movements involving the elderly. George Pierson, *The Moving American* (New York, 1973), speculates on the role played by migration—including movement to the Sunbelt region—in shaping American society.

Perspectives on the new immigrants coming to the nation can be gleaned from David Reimers's *Still the Golden Door: The Third World Comes to America* (New York, 1985). The words of the immigrants themselves are contained in Thomas Kessner and Betty Boyd Caroli, *Today's Immigrants, Their Stories: A New Look at the*

Newest Americans (New York, 1981), while Nathan Glazer, ed., *Clamor at the Gates: The New American Immigration* (San Francisco, 1985), offers a series of interpretive essays on the newest arrivals to America's shores. The problems of inserting refugees are examined in Bruce Grant, *The Boat People* (New York, 1980), and Barry Wain, *The Refused* (New York, 1981).

A useful overview of one major element of the new immigration is contained in Robert Lindsey, "The New Asian Immigrants," *New York Times Magazine* (May 9, 1982), 22-28. Other studies examining specific groups that have come to the Sunbelt South include Alejandro Portes and Robert L. Bach, *Latin Journey: Cuban and Mexican Immigrants to the United States* (Berkeley, 1985); Franklin James, *Minorities in the Sunbelt* (Piscataway, N.J., 1984); Thomas Boswell and James R. Curtis, *The Cuban-American Experience: Culture, Images, and Perspectives* (Totowa, N.J., 1984); and A. J. Jaffe et al., *The Changing Demography of Spanish Americans* (New York, 1980). Raymond Mohl's many writings on Miami reveal the diversity of that important city's immigrant population. See in particular his "An Ethnic 'Boiling Pot': Cubans and Haitians in Miami," *Journal of Ethnic Studies* 13 (Summer 1985), 51-74, and "The New Caribbean Immigration," *Journal of American Ethnic History* 5 (Spring 1986), 64-71. For Chicanos consult Rodolfo Acuna, *Occupied America: A History of Chicanos* (New York, 1981), which includes discussion of the relations of Chicanos and Mexicans. Thomas Sowell's *The Economics and Politics of Race* (New York, 1983), contains information on Asian immigrants as well as provocative insights into a variety of other groups.

The national and regional tensions resulting from illegal immigration are covered in John Crewdson, *The Tarnished Door: The New Immigrants and the Transformation of America* (New York, 1983). An eclectic excursion through the varieties of questions and issues resulting from contemporary immigration and ethnicity—including discussions of affirmative action, American pluralism, and black relations with ethnic groups—can be found in Nathan Glazer, *Ethnic Dilemmas, 1964-1982* (Cambridge, 1983).

There is a growing literature detailing the clashes of immigrants and blacks in society, most of it in article form. Useful introductions are found in Ivan Light, "Immigrant and Ethnic Enterprise in North America," *Ethnic and Racial Studies* 7 (1984), 198-210, and Robin Ward and Richard Jenkins, eds., *Ethnic Communities in Business* (Cambridge, 1984). Not to be overlooked is Stanley Lieberson's, *A Piece of the Pie: Blacks and Immigrants Since 1880* (Berkeley, 1980), which is particularly useful for the prewar period.

Migration and demographic change are discussed in Dudley L. Poston, Jr., and Robert H. Weller, eds.,*The Population of the South: Structure and Change in Social Demographic Context* (Austin, 1981); Joseph J. Spengler, "Demographic and Economic Change in the South, 1940-1960," in Allan P. Sindler, ed., *Change in the Contemporary South* (Durham, 1963), pp. 26-63; and John D. Reid, "Black Urbanization of the South," *Phylon* 35 (1974), 259-67. Donald B. Dodd and Wynell S. Dodd, comps., *Historical Statistics of the South, 1920-1970* (University, Ala, 1973), provides convenient access to data on internal migration. The U.S. census tables and published reports remain essential for charting inter-regional migration, immigration, and metropolitan in-migration.

Index

Action Program Advisory Committee, 121

Advertising, tourism and, 31

Affirmative Action, 132

Agriculture, mechanization of, 3, 184

Air Canada, 30

Airplane: as carrier for tourists, 24, 26, 30–31; promotional practices of, 30

Alabama, 5, 162, 164, 172, 177, 179. *See also names of specific cities*

Alabama Dry Dock and Shipbuilding Company, 5

Albuquerque, N.M., Jews in, 45

Aliens, illegal, 148

All Citizens Registration Committee (Atlanta), 129

Allen, Ivan, 129

American G.I. Forum, 134, 136

American Jewish Committee, 131, 133

Anglo-Canadians, 22, 178. *See also* English Canadians

Annexation: failure of, 8, 13–14; politics and, 130, 135, 137, 138. *See also names of specific cities*

A. P. Hill Civic Club (Memphis), 115

Arizona, 174. *See also names of specific cities*

Arkansas, 173, 177. *See also names of specific cities*

Asian Americans, 110; employment patterns of, in South, 85–86; family organizations of, in South, 88; and politics, 130, 131, 132. *See also names of specific groups*

Asian immigrants, 110; employment patterns of, in South, 87. *See also names of specific groups*

Askew, Reubin, 181

Atlanta, Ga.: annexation by, 8, 13; Asians in, 130, 131, 132; and automobile, 8; blacks in, 11, 117, 128, 129, 131; city planning in, 117, 120; civil rights movement and, 129–30; density of, 8; downtown development of, 8, 11; employment patterns in, 8, 86; federal aid to, 6; highway construction and, 7; Hispanics in, 130–31; housing in, 117; Jews in, 44, 45, 132–33; office space in, 8; politics in, 11, 120, 127–32; population of, 8; racial discrimination in, 10; residential segregation in, 10, 117; urban renewal in, 8, 120; worker cooperatives in, 83; World War II and, 4; zoning in, 10

Atlanta Board of Education, 129

Atlanta Community Relations Commission, 131

215

specific cities
Southeast Asian immigrants, 83, 110.
See also names of specific groups
Southwest Voter Registration Education
Project, 134, 135
Soviet immigrants, 78; earnings of, in
South, 82
Spanish immigrants, 131, 135, 152,
153, 180
Spanish American League Against Dis-
crimination, 152
Stern, Steven, 98
Stuttgart, Germany, 23
Suarez, Xavier, 133, 149, 155
Suburbs: and annexation, 13–14;
development of, 122, 202; federal
policies and, 7, 8; Jews in, 48; jobs
in, 8, 13; migration to, 1, 8, 138; and
politics, 13; southern historical symbols and, 68. *See also* Metropolitan
planning; *and names of specific communities*
Sun City, Fla., 182
Sunbelt: concept of, 43; consumerism
in, 7; definition of, 1, 15, 43;
economy of, 3, 13; growth in, 9; environmental damage in, 14, 183; and
ethnicity, 21; federal government
programs and, 6–7; image of, 179;
migration to, 1, 6, 21–36, 41–50,
180; military expenditures in, 6;
population of, 1; political alignments
in, 13; and race, 6
Sunshine Project (Richmond), 113
Swedish immigrants, 177, 178
Sweetwater, Fla., 145, 147

Tallahassee, Fla., 147, 165, 175; bus
boycott in, 184
Tampa, Fla., 170, 177, 184; Cubans in,
170, 178, 184; federal expenditures
in, 6; Italians in, 177, 184; politics
in, 12, 177, 184; World War II and, 4
Tarpon Springs, Fla., 178, 184
Tenerife, 26
Tennessee, 177. *See also names of
specific cities*
Texas: annexaton laws in, 13; migrant

workers in, 3; racial discrimination
in, 84–85; urbanization in, 76. *See
also names of specific cities*
Texas Monthly, 43, 136
Thomas, Richard, 95
Thompson, A. L., 115
Tindall, George, 68
Toledo, Ohio, Jews in, 45–46
tontons macoutes, 147
Torrijos, Omar, 148
Tourism, 9, 23, 168, 179
Tourists, 9, 23, 168, 174, 181
Travel agents, 27
Tucson, Ariz., Jews in, 44, 45, 46
Tulsa, Okla., 4
Turkish guest workers, 22
Turks and Caicos Islands, 26

United San Antonio, 136
U.S. census, 24, 106, 116, 120, 144,
153, 173, 183
U.S. Department of Justice, 135, 137
U.S. English, 152
U.S. Supreme Court, 105, 129, 181
Urbanizaton, 1–15; and agriculture, 3–
4; crime and, 5; geography of, 1, 13–
14; in Florida, 176–77, 182–83; and
Great Depression, 3; highway construction and, 7, 109–11; industrialization and, 76–77; military
expenditures and, 4, 5, 6; neighborhood identities and, 109–11; racial
segregation and, 109–10; rate of, in
South, 1–3, 67, 76, 122, 194, 200;
and World War II, 4–6
Urban redevelopment, 7–8, 10–12, 114,
120
Urban renewal: federal policies and, 7–
8, 9–10; politics and, 10–12; and
residential segregation, 10, 200–201;
in Memphis, 111–12; in Richmond,
113–14, 120; in Savannah, 73 n.19.
See also Housing

Venezuelan immigrants, 148, 186
Vietnamese immigrants, 58, 67, 130,
194, 203
Virginia Municipal Review, 105

About the Editors and Contributors

RAYMOND ARSENAULT is an Associate Professor of History at the University of South Florida, St. Petersburg. A graduate of Princeton University (B.A., 1969) and Brandeis University (Ph.D., 1981), he also has taught at the University of Minnesota and at the Université d'Angers, in France, where he was a Fulbright lecturer in American Studies in 1984-1985. A specialist in the social history of the American South, he is the author of *The Wild Ass of the Ozarks: Jeff Davis and the Social Bases of Southern Politics* (1984), and "The End of the Long Hot Summer: The Air Conditioner and Southern Culture," *Journal of Southern History* (1984), which was awarded the 1986 Fletcher Green–Charles Ramsdell Prize by the Southern Historical Association.

RONALD H. BAYOR is Professor of History at Georgia Institute of Technology and editor of the *Journal of American Ethnic History*. His publications include *Neighbors in Conflict: The Irish, Germans, Jews, and Italians of New York City, 1929-1941*, which recently has been republished in a new edition by the University of Illinois Press; "Klans, Coughlinites and Aryan Nations: Patterns of American Anti-Semitism in the Twentieth Century," *American Jewish History*; and "Roads to Racial Segregation: Atlanta in the Twentieth Century," forthcoming in the *Journal of Urban History*. He is presently working on a study of race and urban development in Atlanta.

JULIA KIRK BLACKWELDER is Associate Professor of History at the University of North Carolina at Charlotte. She received the A.B. degree from the University of Pennsylvania and the M.A. and Ph.D. degrees from Emory University. She is the author of articles on women in southern cities and of a book, *Women of the Depression: Caste and Culture in San Antonio, 1929-1939* (1984).

ROBERT F. HARNEY is Professor of History at the University of Toronto and academic director of the Multicultural History Society of Ontario. He has written extensively on Italian immigration, particularly to North America, and has authored *Dalla Frontiera alle Little Italies: Gli Italiani in Canada, 1800-1945* (1984), and most recently, "Italophobia: An English-speaking Malady?" *Studi Emigrazione* 77 (1985), 6-43.

GARY W. McDONOGH is Associate Professor of Anthropology at New College of the University of South Florida. He is the author of *Good Families of Barcelona: A Social History of Power in the Industrial Era* and is currently completing field work on Roman Catholicism among southern blacks.

RANDALL M. MILLER is Professor of History at Saint Joseph's University in Philadelphia. He is the author or editor of ten books on aspects of southern, immigrant/ethnic, and religious history. He recently has published articles on immigrants in the urban South in *Southern Studies, Perspectives on the American South*, and elsewhere. He is currently writing a book on immigrants in the South.

RAYMOND A. MOHL is Professor of History and Chairman of the Department at Florida Atlantic University. He is the author of *Poverty in New York, 1783-1825* (1971) and *The New City: Urban America in the Industrial Age, 1860-1920* (1985), and coauthor of *The Paradox of Progressive Education: The Gary Plan and Urban Schooling* (1979) and *Steel City: Urban and Ethnic Patterns in Gary, Indiana, 1906-1950* (1986). His most recent book is *The Making of Urban America* (1988). He is an associate editor of the *Journal of Urban History*, has held research fellowships from the National Endowment for the Humanities and the American Council of Learned Societies, and has served as a Fulbright lecturer in Israel, Australia, and West Germany. He is currently completing a book on the history of race and ethnicity in the Miami metropolitan area.

GARY R. MORMINO is Professor of History at the University of South Florida. He has served as executive director of the Florida Historical Society. He has recently written *Immigrants on the Hill: Italian-Americans in St. Louis* (1986) and *The Immigrant World of Ybor City: Italians and Their Latin Neighbors in Tampa, 1885-1985* (with George Pozzetta, 1987).

DEBORAH DASH MOORE teaches Jewish Studies and American Culture at Vassar College where she is an Associate Professor of Religion. She is the author of *At Home in America: Second Generation New York Jews* (1981) and *B'nai B'rith and the Challenge of Ethnic Leadership* (1981). Her chapter in this book represents the first fruits in a larger study of postwar Jewish migration to five Sunbelt cities.

GEORGE E. POZZETTA is Professor of History at the University of Florida, Gainesville. His research interests include the themes of immigration and ethnicity in American society. He has written, with Gary Mormino, *The Immigrant World of Ybor City: Italians and Their Latin Neighbors in Tampa, 1885-1985* (1987) and edited *Pane e Lavoro: the Italian American Working Class* (1980). He is presently working on a study of race and ethnicity in post–World War II America.

CHRISTOPHER SILVER is Associate Professor of Urban Studies and Planning at Virginia Commonwealth University, Richmond, Virginia. He received a Ph.D. from the University of North Carolina and teaches courses in urban history and the history of planning. His publications include *Twentieth-Century Richmond: Planning, Politics, and Race* (1984) and articles on planning history in the *Journal of the American Planning Association*, the *Journal of Urban History*, and *Planning History Bulletin*. He is currently at work on a history of planning in the urban South since 1900.